Praises for

Welcome To My World

What a great book! As a reminder of our childhood days of long ago and of growing up in a small town of 950 people. Traces the career of a small town boy who leads a great life. As a believer in Christ and as a basketball coach but especially of a Christian man. Those who think that because they come from a small town and don't have much of a chance in the world are able to see that they can affect a lot of people by the kind of life they live. This book is a great read.

– Harl C.

* * *

In writing this book, Jack has not only compiled an excellent memoir for his grandchildren, but also an account for guys like me to recall and enjoy the great memories we shared in our time together. I'm glad our paths crossed and I was part of the journey through his world!

– Greg G.

* * *

As I read the final words of "Welcome To My World" the memories of yesteryear came flooding back and I thank God I was a small part of the world of Jack Sutter. Some who read this book will call it another "Boy from small town makes good", book, I on the other hand call it a book of transition. We see the transition of a boy from a small town with a passion for the sport he loves, basketball, into an example one from every walk of life can look up to.

As Jack said "Maybe there will be an addendum to this story, I am "only" 75 years old as I write this, but we are not promised tomorrow. In the mean time, Welcome To My World. My prayer is that those who read this book will forever remember that great things can be accomplished, and lives changed, even by someone from a small town in a far away place that nobody knows about.

– Peck B.

* * *

Really fun reading "Welcome To My World", a real world life story that starts with a young boys life and his big dreams and a love for basketball. Just as in all our lives I could see the twist and turns in Jack's life and when you stick to what you love the end result is exciting to see as a full and complete life. "A very enjoyable book".

– Tom R.

* * *

When I began reading this book I did not want to put it down! I thoroughly enjoyed reading about the influence basketball had on the life of Jack and his family.

– Sue W.

* * *

If you like the movie Hoosiers, you will like this book. A simpler time, a basketball journey, an interesting, likable character, and a realization of what really matters in life. Jack's story will resonate with a lot of different types of people.

– Bill H.

* * *

Reading "Welcome To My World" was like traveling back in time. I love this book because I learned about faith, basketball and my Grandpa's wild and adventurous childhood.

– Caroline Sutter | Author's granddaughter | 9 years old

* * *

Jack does a great job capturing what it was like growing up in a small Illinois town, as well as recounting his experiences coaching basketball at the high school and college levels. I hope his kids and grandkids appreciate the gift he has given them by writing this book ... I certainly do!

– Steve M.

* * *

"Welcome To My World" is a memoir/book written by my friend Jack Sutter. It is well edited, easy to read, written in the first person with humor and wit and follows Jack's career and life in chronological order. Jack was a teacher and a basketball coach for over 30 years. More importantly, he was a leader of young men. He set the example for young impressionable high school and college basketball players. In this role, Jack was under constant evaluation by academic administrators, fellow teachers and coaches and athletes who want to learn and excel at their chosen sport.

In this book Jack tells his story from growing up to successfully playing and coaching at the high school and collegiate levels. He tells about his ups and downs, his accomplishments and failures, his hopes and dreams, and some regrets as a player and a coach. Throughout his book Jack interweaves his all-encompassing religious affiliation and his belief in a higher power that influences his daily life. Jack also has put family interests above his own. There is lots of respect shown in the book for his grandparents, parents and siblings and lots of love expressed for his own family.

Jack's ability to recall names of friends, teachers, fellow coaches, teammates and players throughout the different phases of his life is absolutely remarkable. He details some basketball games period by period with scores and locations. He discusses tournaments and points ahead or behind with good and bad outcomes.

He frankly discusses his expectations with the resultant successes and disappointments.

Jacks narrative is exciting and I found myself turning the page quickly to see if his team won or lost.

My friend Jack has an engaging personality and he has made friends all over the world. He is certainly not a braggart. Some of his stories are self-deprecating. His modest and unassuming story telling becomes fun to read and hard to put down. The one most enjoyable issue brought out in Jack's story is how it relates to myself and others who grew up in the 1950s. Jack's narrative allowed me to recall how my friends and I got into and out of trouble pretty much the same way Jack and his buddies did. I guess all kids back then at least the well-adjusted ones experienced the same things. I never wrecked my Grandpas car like Jack did but I did try to smoke cigarettes; we used to play outside all day and only stop when it got dark; we rode our bikes everywhere and went swimming where we wanted; like Jack I ogled older girls and fell in unrequited love with a beautiful teacher. Another issue that Jack mentioned that I experienced was the cockiness that an athlete has which sometimes leads to being brought down to reality by a better athlete. Another experience that Jack talked about was taking his eldest child to college the first time. I guess we all react the same way Jack and his wife did. I can vividly recall saying goodbye to our oldest son at his college. It was a sad time looking in the mirror and seeing him standing there all alone. The drive home was quiet and tears were flowing. Taking the other kids to their colleges the first time didn't have the same emotional impact.

Jack's story, detailed in his book, is all our stories in reality but he tells it in a fun and easy to read and recall format. "Welcome To My World" makes me want to write my own memoir but I would certainly need help.

— Dave & Karen S.

* * *

"Welcome to My World" is a wonderful local book. It was a great read about life in Saline county, Illinois. Our patrons enjoyed both the interesting local history and the sports reflections.

– Galatia Public Librarian

* * *

Coach, your family history is inspirational and reflects the faith, hard work and love put forth by your grandma, grandpa, mom, dad, aunts, uncles, cousins and the community of Galatia to help lay the foundation of your early childhood journey. It's remarkable that you experienced nicknames like "Hardrock" in Galatia, which is also a common nickname in Scottsboro, Alabama.

There was something special about Oral Roberts University that attracted not only coach Ken Trickey, Jack Sutter, Art Polk and Dwayne 'Moose" Roe, but also, a multitude of young men seeking to enhance their basketball skill set, and also, to be part of a new exciting brand of basketball at ORU. At night, ORU campus lights lit up the sky like Disneyland. Jack, your faith, love, and hard work contributed to a successful brand of basketball that became a major attraction across the country. It was indeed an honor to be a part of that success, and I am proud of the opportunity to work with the outstanding coaches at ORU. Congratulations Jack Sutter on your successful memoir, and for capturing some remarkable memories of your ORU journey.

– Sam M.

* * *

WELCOME
To My World

Welcome to My World

Copyright © 2020 by Jack L. Sutter

This book is a memoir. It reflects the author's present recollections of experiences over time. Some names and characteristics have been changed, some events have been compressed, and some dialogue has been recreated.

First Edition Published in 2020

ISBN-13: 978-0-578-23733-6

Library of Congress Cataloging-in-Publication Data

Category: Memoir, Autobiography, Sports, Basketball, Christian

Written by: Jack L. Sutter | jackomaxo1@gmail.com

Edited by: Amy Crosby & Ashlee Predmore

Cover Design by: Eli Blyden Sr. | www.EliTheBookGuy.com

Printed in the USA by: A&A Printing & Publishing | www.PrintShopCentral.com

Cover Picture. Choosing up sides in the backyard, with my three best friends. My back to the camera, and I'm holding the basketball. Harl Cockrum is on the left barely in the picture. Lenny Duane is under the basket with his head visible above the ball. Fred Mitchell is in the center behind me in the striped shirt. Also in the picture is my neighbor Kenny Pemberton.

It is my joy to dedicate this book to:
my eight grandchildren.

Welcome to My World

Acknowledgments

I'd like to thank my fantastic daughters, Amy and Ashlee, for their input and editing. I'd also like to thank my son, Andrew, for writing such an insightful foreword.

Last but certainly not least to my wife, Diane, for encouraging me to share my story and supporting me through it all.

Welcome to My World

Table of Contents

Foreword

By: Andrew Sutter

"Yay!" It was one of the first words I ever remember hearing my dad say. Before caller ID, in our little house in El Dorado, Kansas, the phone would ring and my dad would answer. In his booming voice, he would call out, "Yay! Moose." It was Jack Sutter's combination of "yes" and "hey," or something of the sort. It was his own personal greeting.

But, "yay" is more than a greeting. It can be used to describe a lot the facets of Jack Sutter's life. It is a word that captures triumph and excitement yet is also simple and straightforward. It's the perfect word for an inspiring player and coach. It's the perfect word for a devoted husband and father. It's the perfect word for a caring friend. It's the perfect word for Jack.

Welcome to My World has plenty to cheer about. Jack's recollection and recognition of the loves, the thrills, and the struggles in his life will captivate you. From humble beginnings in Southern Illinois, to a stand out basketball player at both the high school and collegiate levels, Jack overcame considerable odds to achieve some of the highest athletic accolades and honors. From one of the youngest coaches in Division I college basketball to dedicated father of three, he modeled teamwork, self-sacrifice, attention to detail, and humility - traits that helped him lead on the court and at home. From his loyal, enduring friendships to his providential marriage to Diane, an amazing wife and mother, Jack has always had the ability to see the best in others and help them see it too. Sometimes with a spirit of love and encouragement. And other times with a very vocal, face-to-face encounter. His face red. Your face white. Jack didn't demand perfection, only perfect effort, which is a fine line few people can balance. He did. Perhaps, it is because you knew Jack was investing more than words. He was investing himself in your success.

I was 6 or 7 years old in this photo, circa 1950.

In some respects, Jack's excellence is a testament to self-lessness. Not only his own tireless sacrifices, but also how the selflessness of others impacted his successes. A trait that traces back some 80 years before Jack was born. In fact, if it were not for the selfless act of a stranger, a Union soldier 700 miles from home, fighting a civil war in the Deep South, Jack's family would not be here. It is safe to say, if it were not for this 20 year old, Corporal R. C. Flannigan, Jack would not be here. Indeed, without his intercession, I would not be here.

Corporal Flannigan's story intersects with Jack's family tree in a way only Providence could orchestrate. As the Civil War raged in the early 1860s, men began to take loyalties to each side. Solomon Shirah, a Georgia-born Southerner, joined the Confederate Army's 3rd Regiment Alabama Infantry in April of 1861. Such misplaced ambition might be expected of a man with family roots planted in South Carolina and forged by its military role in the Revolutionary War. At 33 years old, Solomon left behind his wife, Temperance Ann; his 3-year-old son, William; two infant children; and two teenage children from a previous marriage. By early 1864, Solomon's fighting campaigns had taken him to the Shenandoah Valley to fight in some of the Civil War's bloodiest battles. One such battle occurred on October 19, 1864, the Battle of Cedar Creek, in Northern Virginia. During the fighting, Solomon suffered a serious leg injury and spent months recovering in the North.

Meanwhile, the Union Army was advancing well into the South and had taken control of much of Alabama. Specifically, the 6th Illinois Calvary Regiment had decimated the Confederate fighting force under famed General John Bell Hood at the Battle of Nashville in Tennessee on December 15-16, 1864. Hood lost his command and the Confederate Army in Tennessee was never able to fight again. Part of the 6th Illinois Calvary fighting force was 20-year-old Corporal Richard Cantrell Flannigan.

Corporal Flannigan rode south to Montgomery, Alabama, near where Solomon's family lived as the Civil War began to wind down in the spring of 1865. The agonies of war were, however, still very present. In June of 1865, Solomon's wife, Temperance and his two infant children died of starvation. His two, teenage children were taken away by a family member. Why Solomon's middle son, young William Shirah, was left alone in the care of a war refugee and neighbor, Mrs. Sorrell, we do not know.

William, short on food and clothing, roamed freely among the Union Army camps near Montgomery. When he wandered into the camp of the 6th Illinois Calvary, Corporal Flannigan, moved by compassion, took a liking to the young boy. Flannigan took him in, kept him for some days, and at the pressing of Mrs. Sorrell, sent him to his home in Flannigan Township in Illinois. William lived with Corporal Flannigan's parents and his wife, Eliza, until he was able to rejoin them at the end of his deployment in November of 1865. Over the years to come, R. C. and Eliza Flannigan raised William and were known to have cherished him as their own son, so much so, that William was known by the name William Flannigan, until he was old enough to decide for himself how to embrace his previous life as a "Shirah."

Even as an adult, the flame of his past must have continued to burn, however, because William openly searched for his father for years. Publishing requests for information in the newspaper and with the help of R.C. Flannigan, William was able to find Solomon some years later and reunite with him shortly in Alabama. But William was not able to bridge the divide of many years of separation and the two vastly different worlds he and Solomon inhabited. To William, not only did Alabama not seem like home, but Solomon did not seem like his father, so he returned to Illinois.

Having found his true home in Southern Illinois, William went on to make a life of his own there. He married Delcenia Davis, worked as a farmer, and raised seven children, including a son named Richard and two daughters named Eliza and Louvenia. Jack would come to know Louvenia "Lou" Minor as "Grandma."

Jack's story, *Welcome to My World,* like the story of his great grandfather William Shirah, is one of searching and finding, loving and losing, hoping and succeeding. But, most of all, it is a story of faith. A Christian faith that shapes Jack Sutter's life. A faith found in his family history. A faith that illuminates the victories, sustains the hopes, and elevates the blessings. A faith that gives evermore meaning to Jack's word, "Yay!"

WELCOME
To My World

A Memoir by

Jack L. Sutter

CHAPTER 1

The Early Childhood Days
(1944-58)

I only have a few memories of my first four years in Peoria, Illinois where I was born on December 21, 1944. I'm going to assume, since my mom did not tell me otherwise, that she was not in labor long while having me. It was the day of winter solstice, the shortest day of the year, so there wasn't much time! I was named after my dad's best friend. We moved from Peoria to a little town in Southern Illinois in 1948. My dad's family, which included his dad, his sister (his only sibling), an uncle and aunt lived in Peoria all their life. We lived in a very modest, middle-class neighborhood in a small two bedroom house. The house had an enclosed front porch; I don't know why I remember that, I just do. We had a small front yard, but there was a vacant lot next to our house that we played in all the time. It was on one of those days that we were playing in that lot that I remember my cousin, Mikey, stepped on a nail, and then going to the doctor to get a tetanus shot. I also remember running into my dad with my new little red wagon and leaving a permanent scar on his shin. I'm sure I got into trouble over that shin shenanigan.

Dad's Family L/R: Mary Lou (niece), Grandpa Sutter, Grace (sister), Mom, Dad
In Front: Mike (Mary Lou's Husband) and Cherri (my sister). Circa 1953

My Grandpa Sutter, was a quiet, tough, no-nonsense man. He came and lived with us for several years when I was in high school. He would sit on our front porch in the swing and smoke his pipe and read. I remember at the dinner table, if he thought there was too much talking, he would say, "eat, eat, eat." My sisters and I would remember that and laugh about it when we got older. He never had too much to say.

Grandpa Sutter had always worked hard and had little or no formal education. He was tough on my dad. He kicked him out of the house at the age of 12, and told him he needed to get a job to help support the family. My grandpa's family had originally come from Germany/Austria before settling in Pennsylvania. The Sutter's, our ancestors, were cobblers and shoemakers, but my Grandpa Sutter made a living driving a truck. My dad's sister, Grace, was a few years younger than my dad. Grace married a guy named Mike, who my dad did not care for much. Dad always said that he was a "freeloader," meaning his wife did all the work and supported the family. I never knew my dad's mom; she passed away when he was twenty-one, several years before I was born.

My dad, Henry Albert Charles Sutter, went by the name of Butch. I don't know how true it is, but people that knew my dad and how hardheaded he could be would always say that was the Dutch in him. My dad only went to school as far as the sixth grade. He still was a pretty smart man, very good with his hands, and good about figuring out how things worked. He could be very gruff, quick-tempered, but he was a hard worker who loved his family. He could also be very personable. Before we moved to Galatia, he worked his way up to being a foreman at a plant that made washing machines.

My hometown— Galatia, Illinois, Population 1000. Fay's Café, in the middle of town, is where everyone hung out. "The Rock of Knowledge" can be seen near the front door, next to the sidewalk.

My mom, Ruby Leilah Minor, was known as Lee. She was very quiet, sensitive, independent, and a private person. She was about 5' 5" tall, like her mom, she came up to my chin. I loved hugging her and kissing her on the forehead. The Minors were Irish-English. Their ancestors had settled in the Midwest, maybe Indiana. Mom had grown up on a farm not far from Galatia, with her parents and four brothers. She had worked hard all her life, helping the family make ends meet on that farm. She also worked for some friends in a general store out in the country, not far from Galatia. Mom always wanted to teach school, she had the disposition and the intelligence to have been a good

schoolteacher. Her mom and dad made her drop out of school in the 10th grade to help them on the farm. She always regretted that she never had the opportunity to teach.

Mom and dad soon after they married in 1941. They lived in Peoria, Il. This was the first picture that I ever saw of them.

After mom met my dad and they had my older sister, Judy and me, they decided that they wanted to get back closer to her family. Dad was tired of taking orders from other people and wanted to own his own business. My younger sister, Cherri, was born in 1948, the year we moved to Galatia. They bought a feed store and grocery store in this little farming and coal mining town of 1000 people. I always thought it was interesting that dad would leave his home, in a midsize city, making a respectable living and buy a business that he knew very little about. Mom, actually had some background in farming and working in a general store. Dad, on the other hand, knew nothing about farming or running a feed store. Dad was a quick study and took some classes that were offered by the Pillsbury Company on running a livestock feed business. I am not surprised that he and mom ran a successful business for over 30 years. They were in the store six days a week, 9 to 10 hours a day. They were never away for more than a couple of days at a time except for the few trips we made back to visit dad's family in Peoria. We never had a vacation when I was a kid growing up. Ironically, after I became the basketball coach at Butler County Community College in El Dorado, Kansas in 1979, I went back to Peoria several times to recruit players. On one of those trips, I went back to our old neighborhood to look for the house that I was born in, but it had been torn down.

I remember one family trip that we took back to Peoria a year or two after we had moved to Galatia. The only mode of transportation that we had, at that time, was a pickup truck that dad used in the feed store. He put some straw down in the bed and mom covered the straw with blankets for us to lay on. Dad put a tarp over the side boards and across the top, so we had a modern day van except the back was open. Judy, who was about eight years old at the time, had a problem of sleepwalking. So being the next oldest at five years old, it was my "job" to make sure that Judy did not walk out the back of the truck. Can you imagine an eight-year-old walking out the back of a pickup truck going 60 miles an hour down the road? I did my job well, we all made it safely to Peoria and back. We had too much fun to sleep. Cherri, my youngest sister was only two years old at the time, so she rode up front with mom and dad. Judy and I loved riding back there. The 200 mile trip that took us five hours seemed a lot shorter.

We moved to Galatia in 1948 and bought the feed store and grocery store in the middle of town. They also bought a big, old house that was up on a hill behind the stores. At the time my parents bought the house, it didn't even have an indoor bathroom. The house was over 100 years old. My parents lived in that house for 35 years. I had my own bedroom in the back of the house that was originally the garage. There was no insulation in the attic over my room or in the walls. In the winter, I would lay in bed covered with three or four blankets. It was so cold in my room I could see my breath. I hated sleeping with all those heavy covers on. I don't like having to sleep in under covers even today. The kitchen was small and had a step down from the living room. Dad would always sit on that step at the end of the day and take off his shoes and socks before getting ready for supper. At Thanksgiving, when my aunts, uncles and cousins would come down from Michigan and everyone would be at our house for dinner, there was barely enough room to turn around. The property that the house set on included about 5 acres of land. Dad built a really nice barn, complete with a concrete floor. He began to raise pigs and cattle right in the middle of town. At the time, there were no restrictions or ordinances against having farm animals inside the city limits. At times, the smell from the barn and barnyard would be a little hard to deal with. If we complained, dad would remind us that the pigs and cattle were making us money, even when we were asleep. We had a big backyard where dad put up a nice basketball goal for me when I started playing basketball in the third grade.

Galatia had five grocery stores, a barber shop, two beauty salons, two dry cleaners, six gas stations, two hardware stores, a drug store, two lumber yards, two restaurants, a pool hall, a theater (which closed when I was in the fifth grade), a post office, four churches, a funeral home that you could call by dialing 86R2, and no signal lights. It certainly wasn't even close to a midsize city, like Peoria, but it was a great place to grow up. I lived there for 14 years until I graduated from Galatia High School in 1962. Next to my parents, that little town, with 1000 friendly townspeople, instilled in me the qualities I so admire and respect in people, to this day. People worked hard, cared for one another, trusted one another, believed in God, and loved this country. It seemed like everyone in town had a nickname. There was a Jellyroll, Frosty, Ninety-eight, Fawnskin, Hardrock, and Frog just to name a few.

When we moved into the house in 1948 it did not have a bathroom.
My dog Skizeeks is on the porch.

My sisters and I worked in the stores from the ages of nine until we left home. Our parents instilled a work ethic in each one of us that has served us well. I really never minded working. I enjoyed the satisfaction that I got from doing a good job and finishing a task. I was never too good at just "hanging out." My parents knew practically everyone in town and everyone knew them. That could be a mixed blessing for an eight or nine-year-old boy out with his buddies having a good time. Mom and dad allowed customers to get groceries and feed for their livestock "on the credit." They wrote out a small "statement" on a pad of paper to keep a record until the customer came back and paid them. They never asked them to sign anything; they just took the people at their word. Several of their customers worked in the coal mines and would only get paid twice a month, so my parents let them buy things on the credit until payday. In the 30+ years they were in business, there were very few times when their customers failed to come back and pay off their bill. It certainly was a different time; you couldn't run a business like that today.

Lenny Duane and me with our dogs: Boots and Skizeeks.

My grade school had about 300 students in First through Eighth grades. The school had been built in the late 1800's but looked like it was just built when I started there in 1950. I took Diane, my wife, on a tour of the school in 2010. She was amazed at how good it looked and how well it had been maintained, even then. I was proud of my grade school. We were the Galatia Hornets. I made a lot of memories in the 8 years I spent walking the halls in that school. My two best friends in grade school were Harl Cockrum and Lenny Duane. Harl was a year younger than me. Harl's dad had a grocery store in Galatia too. My other buddy Lenny was in the same grade, we went all through grade school together. The fourth member of our gang moved to Galatia in the fourth grade: Freddie Mitchell. The four of us were inseparable.

Harl Cockrum and me (age 10 or 11) with my Huffy bicycle I bought from mowing yards. We are in the driveway between the stores. Our house is in the background. Circa 1955.

We all liked sports, liked to swim, fish, and be outside. Harl had a dog named Peatie that went everywhere with us, even if it was 5 or 6 miles out in the country, Peatie ran alongside of us on our bikes. Lenny's dog, Boots, went with us most of the time. My dog, Skizeeks, had to stay in the yard. She was small and couldn't keep up with us. Besides my buddies, there were two other students that I really cared about those grade school days: Sharon Lewis and Janet Wickham. Sharon was my first girlfriend. She was a year older than me and a pretty blonde. We "went together" for a couple years until she graduated and went to the high school. She got too old for me. Anyway, she started dating a boy much older. At 17 and a junior, she had to get married and had a little boy. She did come back to high school a year later and graduated the same year that I did. Several years later after I graduated from college, I started dating Sharon again when I came home from Detroit. I really liked Sharon and her parents. She told me on several occasions that she should never have "quit" me. My only other "serious" girlfriend when I was growing up in Galatia was Janet Wickham. Janet was a tomboy, athletic, and was the only girl that we allowed to hang out with our "gang". She fit right in, no matter whether we were playing ball, swimming, or just hanging out. Janet lived about a mile out in the country and had a really nice pond on her farm that we could fish and swim in. We were out at her house two or three days a week in the summer and just about every weekend during school. She also had a tractor that we drove out all over her property. Most of the time Harl or Fred would drive the tractor; Janet and I would ride in a trailer behind the tractor, kind of like a chauffeured driven limousine, only this was an Allis

Chalmer tractor. Besides Diane, my wife, Janet is the best kisser I have ever dated. Janet's mother was an English teacher at the high school and was really a "cool" lady.

I played trumpet in the orchestra at Galatia Grade School. Mr. Adkins, our music teacher, is playing the piano in this picture taken in 1955 or 1956.

I got involved in a lot of things in grade school. I played the trumpet in the band, was in a major play, and was on the tumbling team, but my first love was basketball. Our orchestra was an award-winning grade school band led by a great teacher and unusual man by the name of Mr. Adkins. Mr. Adkins would actually write out the music for any of us who could not read music. He was a taskmaster and a no-nonsense music teacher. On many occasions I saw him get so mad he would get red-faced and pop a student on the head with his baton or worse tell the student to just get out of the room. Mr. Adkins died of a heart attack when I was in the eighth grade. We all really respected him and probably half of the school's 300 students attended his funeral. He was the one who convinced me I should play the lead character in the play "Johnny Get Your Gun" when I was in the seventh grade. I really wasn't that good of an actor, but I could sing like my mom. Once I agreed to be in the play, several other boys also signed on to participate in the production.

I had the lead role in grade school production of "Johnny Get Your Gun". I was a lot more nervous being in this play than I was playing basketball.

I wanted to make good grades so I studied when I needed to, and made the honor roll every year. My favorite subjects were history, English and a class we had to take in seventh grade: phonics. My sisters and I were rewarded a quarter for every A and B we got on our report card. Anything below a B was not acceptable. I remember Judy trying to change a D to a B and dad caught it. She was grounded for a couple weeks.

Me working on my Jump shot in the back yard. I spent a lot of hours on this dirt court. My grandparents house is in the background left over the barnyard gates.

I began to play basketball in the fourth grade and was fortunate enough to have a good coach who understood and taught sound fundamentals. Mr. Hawkins, a sixth-grade teacher, was a very strong disciplinarian. He was a big man who had played basketball in high school; he was a hard worker who hated to lose. He was also a little biased. If he liked you, he gave you a lot of playing time. My buddy Lenny was not a really a good basketball player, but his older brothers played so he played, too. His dad was a sports guy so Lenny tried. He was kind of a clown always getting people to laugh and trying to be funny. One day during practice, Mr. Hawkins blew his whistle and called us all in to talk to us. Everyone was quiet and listening except Lenny. Mr. Hawkins was holding a basketball under his arm, and while he was talking right in the middle of a sentence he took the basketball and threw it hitting Lenny right in the nose. Blood started pouring out of his nose, and we were all stunned. Mr. Hawkins told Lenny to go to the bathroom and just kept right on talking.

My love for basketball began to explode in the fifth grade. I was always playing basketball; I even quit smoking because I knew I couldn't play my best if I wasn't in the best physical condition. How many people you know who say they quit smoking when they were in the fifth grade? But some of my teammates, actually, didn't quit. As a sixth grader, I got moved up to play on the JV team, which was made up mostly of seventh graders. I didn't get to play in many games, but I didn't care. I got a uniform and I got to travel on the bus to all of the away games. I also got to hang out with some of the eighth graders who made up the varsity team. One of those players was a guy named

Valar Beers, who had flunked a couple of grades; he was probably 16 years old and still in the eighth grade. Valar was 6' 3" and weighed about 200 pounds. He was like our version of Shaquille O'Neal. Valar and my sister, Judy, were in the same grade and good friends. Valar was big in stature, but was really a big 'ole' teddy bear. He rode a big Harley-Davidson motorcycle to school, or drove his dad's truck and parked it in the teacher parking lot. He was always taking some of us on a ride on his Harley. He was so much bigger than most other grade school players that he would just dominate some games. Later on in high school when the other boys caught up to his size, he actually stopped playing basketball and quit school.

Me in the front of the grocery store in 1957. The bench in front of the store is where my grandpa and other older gentleman in town would come to whittle and tell stories.

The next year, my seventh grade year, I was starting on the JV team and subbing a lot on the varsity team. Before we were halfway through the season, I got moved up to the varsity, and as a seventh grader I was playing a lot on the varsity. It was during this seventh grade year that I faced one of my toughest losses in my young 12 year life. In the seventh and eighth grade, we had two teachers: one taught math and science, and one taught history, English and the arts. Both of these men were terrific, dedicated teachers that a little town like Galatia was fortunate to have teaching in their school. Mr. Ryan, the math and science teacher, was always a chaperon on the bus to away basketball games. He loved sports particularly the Galatia Hornets. He was stern but fun, and all of us liked being on his bus. It was a lot better than being on the bus with Mr. Hawkins, our coach. He wanted it quiet and serious. We were playing a little town named Muddy. Yes, that is a real name of a town. Sometime during the varsity game, Mr. Ryan got sick and had to be rushed to the hospital. We found out later that he had a heart attack and died on the way to the hospital. The bus ride home was sober; all of us cried the entire way home. Mr. Ryan and Mr. Gunn had taught at Galatia together for over 20 years. They were like an institution; no one could imagine one without the other. Needless to say, the last three months of the school year were very tough and long for all of us seventh and eighth graders. As I look back on those school days reflecting as a retired teacher myself, I realize how blessed I was to have so many outstanding teachers at Galatia. I remember every teacher's name I had my entire

12 years in Galatia. They were all very special to me and prepared me for college and life.

Despite the loss of Mr. Ryan, I was looking forward to my eighth grade year and being the "big man" on campus, even if I had lost my first girlfriend who dropped me when she move onto high school. I was still only 5′ 8″ and 135 lbs., so I really wasn't all that "big." I loved basketball and played every day during the summer. I played 2 or 3 hours practically every day, I even slept with my basketball some nights. My favorite nights were the nights we had a full moon, so I could shoot hoops in my backyard at 10 or 11 at night when it was cool. If it rained or snowed, I would get some straw out of the barn and put it on my court to soak up the moisture and keep it from getting too muddy.

I am accepting the conference tournament championship trophy in 1958. Mr. Gullic, who was the principal at Galatia for over 20 years, presenting the trophy.

My eighth grade team was pretty good. We won 15 of the 20 games we played including our conference tournament. We had a couple hundred people come to most of our games. The craziest thing that happened to me during that season happened in practice or I should say after practice. Mr. Hawkins had left the gym to do something and a bunch of us were "horsing around," shooting trick shots and acting crazy like middle school boys do. One of my trick shots was to shoot the ball from behind the backboard, up over the top of the board and make the basket. I had done this a hundred times so it wasn't that big of a deal, but this time I hit a metal backboard support and knocked it loose. I just stood there, stunned, and at the last minute I ducked my head but not before the metal bar hit me right on top of the head. It didn't knock me out, but blood gushed out of the top of my head everywhere. Mr. Hawkins got the bleeding stopped and took me home. My parents took me to the hospital to get me stitched up. Actually, they put clips in my head after they shaved the spot. I told Mr. Hawkins how it happened and what we were doing. He didn't really say much, I guess he thought I had already suffered enough. Besides, I was kind of his favorite.

My favorite player in the 50s was an NBA player who played for the St. Louis Hawks by the name of Bob Pettit. He was a great shooter who had an unusual one-handed jump shot. Harl, Lenny, Fred, and I would play basketball for hours. They didn't like it is much as I did, but they knew I wasn't going anywhere or going to do anything with them if they didn't play basketball with me. Fred was the smallest in our gang and I was the best, so it was always Fred and me against Lenny and Harl. We would give ourselves a different name; I was always Pettit. We kept score and played to win, and Fred and I usually did. I was always playing basketball in my backyard.

My two sisters and me in 1958. Cherri on the left and Judy on right.

If my buddies weren't around, my sisters or sometimes even my mom would rebound for me so I didn't have to chase after the basketball. Judy would often volunteer because she saw how much I really loved to play and she had to be the big "sister." There were days that I must have taken over 200 shots; I would be outside on that dirt court for hours. I also liked to go up to Joe Upchurch's outdoor court and watch the high school boys like Sammy Duane, "Trigger" Higgins, Buddy Peyton and Joe play. Sometimes they would need an extra player to make the sides even so I would get to play. All of these guys are considered some of the best players to ever play at Galatia High School. I loved getting to play with them on that "special" outdoor court at Joe's house. My senior year I broke "Trigger" Higgins record of most points in a single game.

Our gang was always trying to find things to keep us busy. The four of us would go out on our bicycles looking for "adventures." We had a clubhouse in our friend Melvin Fowler's barn. We would stay all night together in that barn talking, eating, playing cards, and sometimes just doing dumb stuff. Everybody in town knew us and who are parents were. The four of us were inseparable, but we "allowed" other boys to hang out with us like Larry Bell and Jerry Malone. Larry moved to Galatia as an eighth grader and played basketball with me all four years in high school. Jerry was in my grade and went to school with me until he quit school as a junior. Jerry had a tough home life; his older brother stabbed his dad several times with a kitchen knife. For a few weeks they thought he might die. Jerry's dad was an alcoholic and abused his wife and sons. Fortunately, his dad stopped drinking and stopped being abusive after that incident. One of the strangest families in town was the Riddles. Makes sense doesn't it? Robert Riddle was one of about eight kids in the Riddle family. Robert actually had an older brother named Bobby. Robert's dad was a "hot head" and always wanted to pick a fight with someone. He sucker punched Mr. Hawkins on the sidewalk one morning as he was walking to school because Coach Hawkins had spanked one of his kids. The standing joke around Galatia was if you got into it with one of the Riddles, you would have to fight and whip them all, including dad. Robert was not part of our gang, even our extended gang, because he was quick tempered like his dad. We never knew when he would get mad at one of us and want to fight. He was little, but he was tough. We loved to get him to "rattle" off the names of all his siblings in about 5 seconds; it was funny. I got along with him most of the time because he respected me. However, there was one time when we were in the fifth or sixth grade and I said or did something to him during recess at school. He told me after school he was going to kick my butt, and I knew he meant it. As soon as the bell rang for dismissal, I ran out of school, got on my bike and started home. Robert also ran out of class and ran me down about a block from the school. He grabbed my bike, pushed me around, and begged me to fight him. After about 15 minutes of pushing me around, he let me go. I rode my bike home crying and told my mom what had happened. My dad came into the store and told me to get right back on my bike, go back there, and stand up for myself. He said if his older brother or anyone else in the family, including his dad, got involved, he would have my "back." By the time I got back, Robert had gone home, and I was glad he had. I wasn't about to go to his house looking for a fight. I really appreciated my dad standing up for me. I had never heard him talk like that before. I knew my dad was not a fighter, in that sense, but I knew he was tough and strong and would do whatever was necessary if any of the other Riddle family members got involved. I regretted later that I had not stood up to Robert that day even if he would have kicked my butt. After that, Robert really didn't mess with me again; he was always picking on Lenny or someone else at school.

There was a group of about six boys that were tough, crazy, and several years older than us; all of them had a motorcycle. My friend, Melvin, was one of the younger brothers of one of these boys. Terry Joe had a motorcycle and lived just up the street from us. We always asked them to take us for rides and always wanted to hang out with them when they were around. The two craziest boys were the Walker Brothers: Charlie and Dale. One day we were hanging out with them at the Walker house, just listening to them and watching them work on their bikes. One of them, I don't remember whether it was Dale or Charlie, caught a snake and asked us if we had any money. We never had any money! He told us that if we gave him $.50, he would bite the head off of the snake. I think we had about $.25 between the four of us, so he took the $.25, bit the head of the snake off, and spit it at our feet. Nobody, not even the Riddles, messed with the Walker Brothers. They were Galatia's version of Hell's Angels.

Galatia had two restaurants, but everyone hung out at Fay's, which was right in the middle of town. After basketball games and most any Friday or Saturday nights it was standing room only at "The Rock" outside the restaurant. You had to get up town early to get a seat on the "Rock of Knowledge." I don't know how much knowledge or wisdom was shared from that rock, but there sure were a lot of stories told around that rock; some were even true. The rock was a very large slab of concrete that had been put over the mouth of a well. Before Galatia had city water, the townspeople came to that well to draw water. Fay and her sister owned the café. Both were single, and even though they were in their 40s, they lived at home with their parents. They were nice, but they could be tough, especially when things got a little rowdy in the restaurant. We used to tease them and antagonize them just to get them upset. We would put the pinball machine legs up on ashtrays so the balls would go slower and we could win more free games. If they caught us they would make us stop playing and make us get out of the restaurant. I don't know why they even cared. They marked all of their nickels, which is what it cost to play, with red fingernail polish and got them all back anyway. We would also order a "wiener" knowing that we were not going to get one unless we called it a "hot dog." Fay hated it when we called them wieners. Fay, who had the body of Dolly Parton only a little bigger in some places, would get so annoyed with us that she would order us out of the café and tell us to never come back. Fortunately for us, she had a short memory. Many years later, both Fay and her sister got married, thus ending the rumors that started around the rock about whether or not they liked men.

It was at Fay's, around the rock, that a lot of crazy things got planned, particularly around Halloween. Halloween in Galatia was like Mardi Gras in New Orleans. A lot of weird things happened at Halloween. It was very common to have "outhouses" which are known today as Porta-potties turned over all around town. A yearly Halloween "tradition" was to put one of the outhouses on the roof of the high school. Many of Galatia's town folk came out of their houses on Halloween night to someone screaming "fire" so they would stomp out a bag filled with cow manure that was set on fire at their doorstep. In Galatia, even if there was a treat, there would be a trick. My gang was too young to get into the "outhouse" caper, so we just soaped everyone's windows. Halloween was a major holiday in Galatia. Christmas was also a big deal to us. It usually snowed sometime during the Christmas school break. We would always build a huge snowman and put it in the middle of the street. We would also hide and throw snowballs at cars that drove down the one highway that went through our town. Occasionally, someone would stop and act like they were going to chase us, but they never did. We were so bundled up that no one ever really knew who we were, so we would be pretty bold. Another one of our pet things to do was climb around and hang out at an old mill that had been abandoned. In the summer, the mill and the mill pond were our favorite places to hang out. We would fish and swim at the old dam, and have rock wars inside the mill. Yes, we would actually throw rocks at each other as we hid and climbed around in that two-story abandoned building. It was also a great place to just hang out and smoke.

At the dam I witnessed one of the most amazing feats I have ever seen in my lifetime. A wild and fearless young man in his early 20s named Dion got on top of the shed over the dam, which was probably 20 or 25 feet above the water, and dove head first into the water. What's so daring about that? The tiny pond at the dam that Dion dove into (where we swam) was about twelve feet wide, twenty feet long and only 5 feet deep. There was a concrete wall that we dove off of, or more often jumped off of, next to the water. Dion not only dove 20 or 25 feet off the shed, but out about 10 feet over the concrete wall and into the water. We had never seen anyone even jump off the top of the shed. I realized many years later when I went back there that we could have witnessed a person kill himself if he would have hit that wall.

Later, when we were all in high school, Mr. Russell, a local businessman, bought the old mill. He tore it down, thus, ending one of our favorite activities: the rock wars. Ironically, Mr. Russell's oldest son, Leon, ended up buying my mom and dad's stores and house; he tore them down also to expand his service station and oil business. When we had rock wars, Fred would always be the first one picked on a team because he was small and could hide in little areas. He was also extremely accurate at throwing those pieces of mortar that we used as our weapons. Mr. Russell, after he tore the building down, paid us a penny a brick to break the mortar off the bricks and clean them so he could sell them, probably for $.10 a brick. That was hard work and could be hazardous to your hands. I only did that a couple of days. I decided to stick with my yard mowing business, a whole lot safer and better pay. I would continue to mow yards, as many as 10 or 12 a week, until I was a junior in high school. On occasion, I would help a man named Mr. Murphy mow cemeteries. It was much harder than my regular yards. I was out in the blazing sun mowing around all of those tombstones with a mower that was not self-propelled. Mr. Murphy was an old man that was all bent over, probably from mowing so many yards and cemeteries. We laughed at him because when he was driving his car you could barely see him over the dash. He always wore a "Jungle Jim" hat. So if you saw him coming down the road, all you could see was that hat and the steering wheel of his car. He had to be 60 years old at the time that I worked with him and even though I was 13 or 14 years old, I couldn't keep up with him. He was a hard worker who might not say five words all day.

My parents worked hard, but we struggled to make ends meet. All of the money that I made mowing the yards was money that I could spend on myself to buy school clothes and for spending money. By the time we got in the fifth grade, Freddie's family had moved from the country into town, which meant Fred was always around. Fred's family was really poor. When they moved to Galatia, they moved into the old bank building. I remember this so well because Fred's sister, Peggy, had a bedroom inside the vault, an unusual place to have a bedroom. We always thought it would be terrible if someone got locked in that vault. Peggy was my sister Judy's age; they were good friends and hung out a lot together. That was okay with me because I always thought Peggy was cute, so I didn't mind her being over at our house. One of the funniest things about Fred was that, because of his home life, which wasn't very good, he always wanted to hang out at my house. If it got to be late in the afternoon and he was still at our house he would say, "I will stay and eat dinner with you, if you want me to," and of course, mom always invited him to stay.

I suppose everyone looks back on a particular period of time or times in their lives and wishes they could go back and have a "do over." I could say that about three or four periods of my life now that I'm 75 years old and looking back through the rear view mirror. But really there isn't anything "major" in my life that I truly regret. I have been so blessed and thank God every day for all my blessings. However, I do have a small minor regret from my grade school days. Back in 1955 when I was in the sixth grade and 11 years old, I discovered a new hobby, collecting and playing with baseball cards. While I loved basketball, my favorite thing to watch, or in those days, listen to, was St. Louis Cardinal baseball. St. Louis had a super station named KMOX that broadcast their games over about six states. I listened to them about every night, often times falling asleep. Harl was a Dodger fan; Lenny liked the Cincinnati Reds. Fred didn't really care too much. We spent about every nickel that we had on baseball cards that came in a pack with a stick of bubblegum. At that time, the gum was just as important as the cards. In the early 50s and into the 60s, baseball cards were in their heyday. We opened pack after pack and traded them to each other for our favorite player or team. The cards nobody wanted went into our bicycle spokes to make a motorcycle sound when we rode them. Nobody had any idea that those cards would be so valuable today. I am certainly not alone when I say we probably threw away or destroyed a million dollars worth of baseball cards in today's market. None of us liked the Yankees, so no one kept the Mickey Mantles, Whitey Fords and Yogi Berras. We probably had 25 or 30 Mantles that would be worth $10,000 each today. I did keep a few Yankees, but like a lot of my favorite players from the Cardinals, they ended up on my bedroom wall with a pin sticking through them. Even at that, I was more fortunate than most of the kids who collected those cards. My mom was a very neat person who did not throw away my stuff. Many of my cards ended up in a shoe box with a rubber band around them. I still have some of those cards today; a few are worth $500 or more a piece. Not a bad investment for the nickel that I spent to get a pack of five cards with that gum. Andrew, our son, and I would get back into collecting in a big way, 30 years later.

I had an awesome early childhood, never boring, a lot of companionship, a lot of love, and enough success along the way to build a pretty healthy self-esteem. But the best of all my experiences and the greatest life-changing event happened to me during a Vacation Bible School assembly when I was 10 or 11 years old. My buddies and I signed on for a week of Vacation Bible School at First Baptist, where we attended. Our whole gang attended Sunday school on a regular basis during our fourth and fifth grade years, mostly because we had a teacher by the name of Mr. Powell. Mr. Powell was in his 30s, a farmer who I remember as having a Charlie Atlas like build. He was a really good Sunday school teacher and spent a lot of time with us boys, taking us fishing and camping. My dad did not go to church at this time, so my mother was the spiritual leader in our home. My mom was also the choir director at the church for several years and taught a Sunday school class. She was a godly woman who loved Jesus, the church, and her family. Even though my dad did not go to church, he supported her and wanted us kids to go. Mr. Powell encouraged us to go to Vacation Bible School, we knew that they played games, had treats, and did some fun things there. On the last day, our pastor talked at an assembly of all of the kids and presented the gospel. He talked about believing in Jesus and having Him in your heart and that was the only way to Heaven. Harl was the first one in the assembly to go forward during the invitation. As he left the pew I was right behind him. A few minutes later, Lenny and Fred also came to the front. That was pretty cool. We did everything else together so why not give our hearts to Jesus and go to heaven together?

Me being baptized by Pastor Merle McDonnough in 1955.
I accepted Jesus as my Lord and Savior at Vacation Bible School.

We all four were baptized the following Sunday along with a half dozen other boys and girls. The only person happier to hear about my life changing decision than Mr. Powell was my mom. Harl would become a full time minister about 15 years later and is still preaching at a little church in southern Illinois today. There are church members that still remember my mom from when she worked in that general store, near McLeansboro, so many years ago.

I would like to say that from that summer on I led an exemplary Christian lifestyle, but nothing could be further from the truth. God has taken me on a most unique and interesting journey. I can personally attest to that Scripture in the Bible that says "train a child up in the ways of the Lord and even when he is old he will not depart from it." Years later, after spending four years at Oral Roberts University as an assistant basketball coach and after moving to Florida, I rededicated my life to Christ and was baptized a second time but this VBS experience was my first encounter with Jesus.

When our kids were young, I would share stories with them about what happened to me and about some of my experiences back in Galatia. Sometimes I would take liberty to embellish some of those stories, but for the most part everything I told them was accurate to the "best of my recollection." It is funny that while our kids were not totally convinced that all of these things happened, they still liked to hear the stories. One of their favorite stories and mine, as well, happened when I was about 13 or 14 years old during the county fair in

Harrisburg. Harrisburg was a town of about 8000 people located 10 or 12 miles from Galatia. My buddies and I would hitchhike to Harrisburg every day of the fair. The fair went on for seven days and we went every day! We never had much money to spend on rides and stuff, but went anyway and just hung out all day. We found a hole in the fence of the fairgrounds by the livestock barns that we crawled through and would sneak into the fair without paying the one dollar admission fee. We had a plan and it always worked, we never got caught. One of the days that we sneaked in, we were leaving the fairgrounds about five in the afternoon when someone pointed out a big sign at the entrance that stated it was "Free Admission Day." We had walked a half a mile through weeds and bushes to crawl through the hole in the fence when we could have just walked in the front gate! That made a lasting memory, and our kids got a big laugh out of that dumb experience of mine.

Another memorable event was our all night camping trip at Harrisburg Lake. We went to the lake almost every day in the summer to swim. There was a concrete pump station out in the lake about 200 feet that we would swim out to and dive off of. The water was about 10 feet deep there, clean and cold. We decided that we should stay all night and the highway bridge (which was about a quarter mile from the lake) would be a good place to camp out. It was after midnight when cars quit passing over the bridge; they sounded like a train every time they passed over. We slept about four hours that night.

We stayed until daylight and decided to go home to get something to eat. Later that day we went back to get a couple things we had left and discovered a nest of snakes about 30 feet from where we had been sleeping.

We were adventurous, naïve, 10-11 year-old boys pretty much willing to explore anything. We were always riding our bikes out in the country to fish or swim, sometimes we would ride out 10 or more miles. I must've put 10,000 miles on my Huffy bicycle that I bought with my earnings from mowing all those yards. Sometimes Fred's bike was broke, so we would take turns "toting" him. We also liked to walk the railroad tracks to see what we could find. On one of those adventures, we ran across a hobo village about 2 miles out of town alongside the tracks. We decided that we should just hang out there for a few hours and see if any hobos showed up. No one showed up, so we decided to come back a couple days later and stay all night. We had fun for a while until we began telling each other scary stories and decided at about 4 in the morning that we should go home. We all four had a nice home and great parents, but you wouldn't know it because we were never there. Our parents never worried about us, most of the time they didn't even know where we were. They trusted us and knew we were not going to do anything "real" stupid. You couldn't do what we did in this day and time. Every day we were looking for a new adventure having fun just being together. One of our other "great adventures" happened when we were riding our bikes out in the country one day and noticed a small cemetery in a field close to the road. We decided to investigate. One of us came up with the idea that it could be an Indian burial site. We had found some arrowheads in a spring and woods not far from there, so it was possible, we thought. We decided to go home, get some shovels and start digging. We hauled the shovels and rakes out on our bikes to the graveyard. Because the cemetery was close to the road, we had to be careful to not let anyone see us. After 2 days of digging, we didn't find any Indian relics, so we decided we should put the bones and everything back like we found them. We were so disappointed that we did not find a spear or arrowheads.

There were a lot of farm ponds and small lakes around Galatia, and we knew where to find every one of them. We would either fish or swim in one of them about every day in the summer time. The ones that always seemed to have the most fish in them were the ones that were posted signs stating "Keep Out" or "No Fishing." Those were also the ones that were the most fun because we had to figure out a way to sneak in. We were like outlaws planning our next big heist. We would "case" the ponds, farmlands, and the farmer to try to figure out the best way to get into the pond or lake without being caught or in some cases, the best way to get out. One day we were swimming in this pond when a farmer rode out on his tractor after us. Since we almost always swam nude, we had to grab our clothes and make a mad dash for the nearest fence row. Once over the fence and on the property of someone else we were in the clear. We never got caught, but we had several close calls. I'm not sure the farmers really cared and really wanted to catch us. I think they were just trying to scare us, and some of them really did. We were just always looking to have a good time. Occasionally, we would get bored, like the day we thought it would be fun to ride my dad's pigs. It was a hot day, in the middle of summer. Pigs can easily get too hot and even die from being overheated. Riding them in the middle of a hot day is not a good idea. Fortunately for us, none of them died, but my dad busted my butt for that adventure.

My childhood wasn't all fun and games. Growing up, I was the only one of the gang that had to work and had daily chores around the house. My mom and dad worked hard six days a week as did my sisters, so I had to pitch in and do my part. I was helping my dad in the feed store when I was 11 or 12 years old. I would even make deliveries out in the country, by myself, driving the truck long before I had my driver's license. Harl, Lenny, and Fred would often come to my house and help me with some of my chores, so I could finish faster and go play with them. By the time I was 10 or 11, I bought my own lawnmower and was mowing 12 or 13 yards a week. The boys would often help me do my yards too, so I could go with them. Sometimes I would even pay them. I have always done a lot of physical work, which served me well later on when I began playing sports. Lifting 50 and 80 pound bags of feed and fertilizer, shoveling corn, and mowing yards are good ways to develop strength and stamina. Later on when I began playing basketball in high school my coach, JW Pulliam, came to the feed store one Saturday when I was working. We had a basketball game that night and Coach Pulliam was concerned about how much energy I would have for the game. He asked my dad if I could get off work by noon so I could rest and be ready to play the game that night. I don't think my dad had ever thought about that and the effect that it might have on me for the basketball game. After that visit from my coach, I only worked a half day on the days we had a game. I loved getting off at noon so I could watch the Big Ten basketball game of the week that was on Saturday afternoon. I worked harder than any of my friends. My sisters and I grew up having to work to help keep the businesses running.

We really never did any destructive or harmful things to anyone other than to ourselves; for instance, like when one of us decided it would be cool to smoke. In the 50s, everyone smoked. I even remember seeing men stand out in front of the church on Sunday morning between services smoking. Interestingly, my dad was the only parent in our gang of four who smoked. Since my mom and Harl's dad both owned a grocery store that sold cigarettes. We decided that we could sneak them out by the pack and not get caught. Harl was really good at sneaking cigarettes from his dad's store. He could practically steal a pack while his dad was standing on top of him. I was pretty good too, but I was not as bold as Harl. Between Harl and me we always had a good supply of smokes. In the summer time when school was out, we would smoke every day, all day. We had all of these so-called hideouts that we would ride our bike to so we could smoke. One of these hideouts was an old abandoned barn across the street from my house, which made it pretty convenient. I have often wondered what people thought as they passed by that barn and saw all that smoke coming out from the four of us in their puffing away. I'm surprised no one ever called the fire department. Of course we thought smoking made us more grown-up, but it was just a terrible bad habit. One time our boldness about smoking actually got us into big trouble. We decided that we should play a game of Monopoly at my house and smoke while we were playing; this was not one of our smartest decisions. My mom was working in the store, which was only down the hill less than 100 yards from our house. We began to play Monopoly around our kitchen table. We were all smoking and of course the entire house was filled with smoke. My mom came up to the house for something and walked in to see us all playing Monopoly in a smoke filled room. We were all "dead meat." She sent Harl, Lenny, and Fred home and told my dad what had happened. To this day, I don't think she ever told my buddies' parents that she had caught us smoking. But for me, my punishment was not anything like I imagined it would be: a serious butt beating. My punishment was to go to the store and pick out a cigar or two or three, and set out by the feed store in the sun and smoke. I was going to have to smoke however many it took to get sick enough to not do that again. It upset my mom and my dad's customers that saw me sitting out there having to smoke those cigars. They felt sorry for me, but it didn't matter too much to my dad. I didn't even get through the first cigar until I was feeling pretty lightheaded and began to turn a little green. Dad finally let me go to the house and lay down. I have since heard of this kind of punishment for smoking; it never works.

Another dumb stunt of mine was when I poured turpentine on a black cat that hung out around the feed store. My dad didn't really like cats, but this cat caught a lot of mice around the feed store and my dad did not want anyone to harm him. I don't know why I did that. The cat survived, but I got grounded for a week over that.

Harl and Lenny were the smart ones in our gang. They liked to read comic books and play board games. We would start a game of Monopoly and finish it two or three days later. Fred and I would rather be playing sports and be outside. The only time I wanted to go to Harl's dad's store and read comic books was when Donna Eubanks was working. Donna was the prettiest girl in Galatia. She won the Ms. Saline County beauty contest when she was a senior in high school. She was 6 or 7 years older than us and worked for Max (Harl's dad) all through high school. I would "pretend" I was reading, but I was mostly just watching her with googly-eyes, and so were my buddies.

Galatia, at the time I was growing up there, had a Teen Town that was open on Friday and Saturday evening. We would hang out there almost every weekend. None of us liked to dance, so we mostly just played ping pong or pool, and had snacks. One of the greatest weekends ever in Galatia was the Saturday evening that the owner of the town theater invited Hopalong Cassidy to make an appearance. He even brought his horse, Topper. Practically the whole town turned out to see William Boyd, who played Cassidy in the Western movies. My buddies and I got an autographed picture, but I don't know what happened to it. I think ole Hopalong had been drinking that night. We all thought we could smell alcohol and he did act a little strange. The theater closed down a few years later. From then on, we would have to go to Harrisburg to go to the movies. Almost every weekend one of our parents would drive us over and drop us off so we could see a show. We only needed $.25 for admission, popcorn, candy, and a soda. I loved going to the movies, especially if it was a western or action movie.

CHAPTER 2

A Galatia Bearcat
(1958-62)

I had a great early childhood and a lot of fun during my grade school years, but I really was excited about going on to high school. Before I even got to high school, the high school coach, Millard Davis, came to our home and talked to my parents and me about coming down to the high school. He wanted me to come by after my school (I was still in grade school) let out and play basketball with the high school players. That was a pretty big deal, and I couldn't help but think that I was "hot stuff." Of course, some of the high school players didn't exactly look at it the same way I did. They had a new "rookie" to pick on. It took a couple weeks for me to show them I belonged, and gain their respect. I survived the towel popping in the shower and all the other childish locker room games that they played. I won them over when they saw that I was a pretty good basketball player. I was better than some of them that were two or three years older. That proved to be an advantage that I enjoyed when I started high school a few months later. They already knew who I was, and I knew my way around. Nevertheless, that did not keep me from going through ninth grade initiation week.

Look closely at the girls in this photo taken during freshman initiation at Galatia High School. Initiation went on for a week with different "activities". On this day boys had to dress up like girls: L/R Fred Mitchell, Me, Larry Bell, Robert Riddle, and Dwight Mildren.

At Galatia High School in the 60s there was a week when the upperclassmen were "allowed" to harass the incoming ninth graders. Everyone participated, including the teachers. They let the seniors pretty much do whatever they wanted to the freshman short of physically hurting them. We had to dress up as girls one day. We had to wear our clothes inside out and backward on another day, which made it tough to go to the bathroom on that day. We had to carry the seniors' books to class, shine their shoes, get their lunch for them, and generally be their servant for the week. What we had to do then would be called harassment or even abuse and grounds for dismissal from school today. The high school initiation did not just take place at school, but there were two other major events in town that the freshman boys were "invited" to participate in. The freshman boys were expected to show up at Fay's on a particular night during initiation week to participate in the "sport" of pushing a penny down the street with your nose, while wearing only your underwear. After you successfully completed that event, usually with a bloody nose from the concrete street, you would have to climb the flagpole that had been lubricated with grease, also while wearing your skivvies. This was not only tolerated by the school personnel, who knew all about it, but a lot of the townspeople would actually turn out to cheer on the poor freshmen. If a freshman boy did not show up for the night activities the seniors would make that freshman miserable throughout the next day of school. It was pretty easy to spot the freshman boys that had showed up. They were the ones with the red noses and scabs on the tip of their nose. My high school days seemed to fly by so it wasn't too long until I was the one on the other side doing the harassing. The leaders at the high school were the varsity basketball players so they were the ones who came up with all the "activities" for the freshman. I was a little fish in a big pond, but I was a bigger fish than most of my freshman classmates. The two best players on the varsity, Larry Jones and

Gary Hill, came up with a nickname for me. They called me "cream jeans" because I always wore cream colored pants to school. I was never "into" the jeans thing so I usually wore slack pants that were off white. I certainly received my share of harassment. It probably helped me that my older sister, Judy, was an 11th grader and was very popular in school. She had always thought of herself as my big sister, and no one better mess with her little brother. I was always her "little brother" even when we were both in our 70s.

As a typical 14-year-old boy I was always trying to get my due respect and act like "Mr. Cool." I contributed my share of gray hairs to many of my high school teachers. We had a Spanish teacher, who was a very smart lady and really knew her Spanish, but had no classroom management skills or discipline. As immature ninth graders, we would harass her and give her a hard time in class almost every day, nearly bringing her to tears. Sadly, my buddies and I were more concerned about getting attention than learning Spanish, which, not surprisingly, I learned very little of. Mr. Gibson was our math teacher. He taught algebra and geometry. He was a very smart man but could not teach. He had a hard time explaining concepts so that those of us who were not proficient in math could understand. He would stand up at the board for minutes on end, the chalk just flying, trying to explain a concept that half of the class had no idea what he was saying. To this day, as a retired teacher, I have a lot of empathy for students who sit in class and feel lost. Mr. Gibson liked me and gave me some extra tutoring that enabled me to get through both Algebra 1 and 2, as well as Geometry so I could fulfill my pre-college requirements. Then there was Miss. Williams who possessed all the characteristics a high school boy might look for in a teacher: young, attractive, single, and very big busted. She taught typing and business courses, both elective courses that were usually full. I have to confess there were a few times I raised my hand in class to get her to come to my desk for a quick peek at her rather large chest. She was way ahead of us though and "on to" our schemes; she rarely wore a loose or revealing top. I did learn to type sixty words a minute with the minimum of three errors and got an A in her typing class. Miss. Williams became a Mrs. my senior year and broke a lot of young boys' hearts when she showed up with that ring on her finger. My favorite teacher was Mr. Pulliam, who taught Driver Education and Industrial Arts. He became the basketball coach my sophomore year and would become, not only my favorite teacher, but one of my dearest friends. JW Pulliam was an icon in Galatia. He had grown up in Galatia and taught at Galatia High School for 35 years. They named the baseball field after him. He helped build the school, literally. He told me he remembered helping put the beams up in the gymnasium in the mid-50s. He was a very good teacher, but a much better human being. He was a strong disciplinarian who believed that you should work for everything you get. He was a good Christian man that I never heard use profanity, and rarely did he ever really get mad and yell at anyone. Coach

Pulliam played a major role in the success I had as a high school basketball player and as a young man. He and his wife, Barbara, remain pillars of the community even today. One of my other favorite teachers was Lester Gill, our science teacher. He taught there many years, and later become the principal. Mr. Gill was always coming up with interesting experiments for us, but I remember him most for his unusual sayings and antics in the classroom. He would often whistle like a bird in class and look around the room with a blank, silly expression then ask the class, "Did anyone hear that?" He would come up with corny expressions or jokes and then laugh at himself more than the students did. Another one of my favorite teachers was Mrs. Wickham, who was the mother of Janet, my grade school "heartthrob". Perhaps the best and most interesting teacher I had was Mrs. Throgmorton, my social science teacher. I loved history and geography, and she made both of them very exciting and interesting.

My freshman year, I was a pretty typical student. I was more concerned about having fun and being cool than I was interested in my grades. I made okay grades, mostly B's. But as a sophomore, I began to mature and understand what was at stake and that I needed good grades to go to college, no matter how well I played basketball. I had some good skills, but I still had not hit a growth spurt. I was about 5'8" and 130 pounds as a freshman. Things changed dramatically between my 9th and 10th grade year. I grew a couple of inches and put on 20 pounds. During my freshman year I got moved up to play on the JV team with sophomores and juniors. I knew what I wanted, but more importantly I knew what was going to get me to my ultimate goal: hard work. It really wasn't a big surprise to my buddies Lenny, Harl, or Fred when I began to spend less time with them and more time playing basketball. We continued to be good friends, just going in different directions. Both Fred and Lenny moved away from Galatia while we were in high school. Harl, was our basketball manager all through high school so I still hung out with him quite a bit.

Millard Davis, who had brought me up to play with the high school kids when I was in eighth grade, decided he was going to move on and no longer wanted to coach at Galatia. Coach Davis had helped me to believe in myself and had been a big encouragement to me. Coach Pulliam, who became the coach, helped me develop my game even more. Between my freshman and sophomore year, I practically lived in the gym. My sophomore year, I was moved up to the varsity and played quite a bit. I would still play about half of the JV game and maybe half of the varsity game, so I was getting some great game experience. It was a tough year for all of us getting used to a new coach and a new system. We won 6 games, but one game in particular stood out that season. We played McLeansboro High School, near the end of that season in our gym. The Foxes, as they were called, had only lost two games that entire season. They were ranked in the top 10 in the state and had a great player by the name of Jerry Sloan. Besides

Sloan, they had another 6' 5" player named Reed, the Burns twins, who were both 6' 6," and an outstanding guard, David Lee. They were well coached, big, and very talented. We had absolutely no chance against them, but that didn't stop our fans and a lot of fans from McLeansboro from packing out our gym. Our gym would seat about 200 people with extra chairs on the stage. Considering we only had 150 students and there were only 1000 people in the entire town that was pretty remarkable. There were people standing at one end of the court three or four deep. It was the biggest crowd I had ever seen in our gym. To say I was a little nervous before the game would be an understatement. Sloan was 6' 6", muscular, hard-nosed, and one of the top two or three players in the entire state. He would end up being a two time All-State player and a high school All-American. He signed a scholarship to play at the University of Illinois. He transferred after a year and finished up his college career at Evansville University where he was a small college All-American and was drafted by the Chicago Bulls to play in the NBA. He ended up being an NBA All-Defensive Team player. He played 11 seasons in the NBA, and became an outstanding coach of the Utah Jazz. We played the game on a Saturday night, so I had all day to think about playing Sloan and the Foxes. We were behind by 20 points at halftime, and Sloan had scored about that many points himself. He ended up scoring 35 points and never even played in the last quarter. He was unbelievably good. I scored 10 points, and two of those points came when he was guarding me. I couldn't help but smile as I was running back down the court. That game made an indelible impression on me, as to what I wanted to be and what I wanted to achieve. After the game at the local hangout, Fay's Cafe, I overheard a businessman in town say "in a couple of years, we might have a player as great as Sloan in the Sutter boy." As if I needed any more motivation that certainly didn't hurt. Jerry Sloan motivated me that entire summer as I practiced just about every day, two or three hours each day. To this day, I have a picture of Sloan from that game in my scrapbook. He was the best high school player I ever played against.

Although my sophomore season was not as successful as I had hoped it would be, I had gained a lot of experience playing on the varsity and all of us had adapted to Coach Pulliam's way of doing things. He was a much different personality and coach than Coach Davis. We only had a couple of seniors who graduated from the 1959-60 team, so we were all pretty excited to get the 1960-61 season started. One of the players returning was one of the best athletes to ever play at Galatia High School: Robert Boyette. We all called him "Peck." He was not only a good basketball player but an outstanding baseball pitcher. Peck could throw a baseball close to 90 miles per hour as a freshman. As a sophomore, when he developed other pitches, there were major league scouts coming to watch him play. Unfortunately, he hurt his arm his junior year, and that pretty much ended his chances to ever play professional baseball. I think Peck was so good at such a young age that he threw his arm away before he actually matured and developed. Peck, who was a senior, had started on the basketball team as a freshman. He was 6' 0" but probably weighed close to 200 pounds and was a very good offensive player. Because of his experience, he was also a very smart player. One of us, or both, scored 20 points every game. We had a good supporting cast with Larry Bell at 6' 3," Gaylord Paris at 6' 3," Terry Bond at 6' 2," and a good jumper in Richard Nevious, who was 6' 2". For a small school we had good size, and we played well together.

There are four high schools in Saline County, and Galatia is the smallest. Every year in January, we had the Saline County basketball tournament. The tournament was a big deal for basketball fans in the county. To handle the big crowds, the tournament was always played in Harrisburg or Eldorado on a Friday and Saturday night. Harrisburg's gym held about 3,000 and Eldorado's nice, new gym held over 4,000. The other school in the county, Carrier Mills, had about 300 students and a rich basketball tradition. They had a player in the mid-fifties named Oliver Rollins, who played with the Harlem Globetrotters right after graduating from high school. The Wildcats, from Carrier Mills had African-American players in the early 50's, long before integration in most communities. They were loaded with very talented players like Gary Taborn and Marshall Stewart in the 60s. Carrier Mills was coached by an outstanding coach by the name of KO Willis. Coach Willis went on to coach at a college in Alabama. Almost every year either Harrisburg or Carrier Mills would win the championship. Harrisburg, who had 800 or more students, played in the very tough South Seven Conference and were very competitive every year. They had two outstanding players named Roberson and Shelton and a player I would end up playing with at Middle Tennessee State University, Ed Cannon. The format for the tournament was very unique. All four of the county school's coaches would meet at 6 o'clock on the Friday night of the first round and draw the names of the schools out of a hat to see who they were going to play. No one knew who the opponent was until the first night about an hour before the tip off of the first game. There might be 500 people already in the gym when the coaches drew for their opponents. As usual, Harrisburg and Carrier Mills had several really good players my junior year, and most of the county figured they would see them play in the finals on a Saturday night. However, they drew each other on Friday, which meant we played Eldorado, who also had a very good team. The tournament was played in their gym, and most fans thought it would be Eldorado playing in the finals. I loved playing in this tournament because of the excitement it generated around the county and because the fans really turned out. Eldorado's gym was only a few years old and unlike most gyms, it was sunk in the ground and had seats all around the floor. They had a state of the art scoreboard with the player's names, fouls, and points displayed much like the scoreboards in college arenas. Since they were the host school, we played them after the Harrisburg versus Carrier Mills game. Carrier Mills won the game by two or three points. It was a great game that went right down to the wire. We came into the tournament with a 10-4 record and second place finish in our conference tournament right before Christmas. In the Greater Egyptian Conference (GEC) tournament we upset Cave-In-Rock in the semifinals and were beaten by an outstanding and ranked Shawneetown team in the finals. I was the leading scorer in the tournament, scoring 85 points in our three games, including 35 points in the finals. We had a good team and were playing with a lot of confidence. Unfortunately, the week before the county tournament, I hurt my back and was having back spasms. I had not practiced for several days, and I really didn't know if I could play or how effective I could be if I played. I got an ultrasound treatment from the trainer at Eldorado in the afternoon on Friday just before our game. That treatment really helped, but it still hurt me to even bend over and tie my shoes. We played very well and beat Eldorado by two points on a shot at the buzzer by Peck. He had an outstanding game and scored 20 points. I managed to play about three fourths of the game and score 15 points, seven below my average. After the game, my back hurt so bad I could hardly get around. I was just hoping with another treatment and a day of rest, maybe I could play. I certainly was going to try. We would have been underdogs to the Carrier Mills Wildcats even if I would've been healthy. Most of the talk on the radio and in the newspaper on Saturday was that the real championship game had been played on Friday night between Harrisburg and Carrier Mills. No one, except our most die hard fans and our team, thought we could beat Carrier Mills. Honestly, with my back the way it was, I wasn't too sure myself. We got to the gym early so that I could get another treatment like the one the day before. After the treatment I felt good enough to at least give it a go, but I really didn't know if I could make it through a game. It was such a big game that I wasn't about to miss it. The adrenaline must have taken over after the jump ball to start the game because I barely noticed the pain. Coach Pulliam came up with a great game plan to neutralize the size and talent of the Wildcats. We were going to spread the floor on offense and use as much of the clock as we could before each shot. Carrier Mills would have to expend a lot of energy on defense and not have the ball as much on offense.

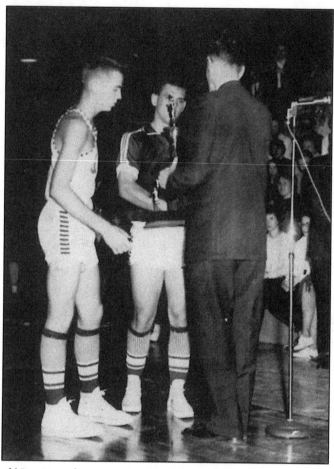

'Peck' Boyette and me accepting the championship trophy for winning the Saline County Tournament in 1961. We beat Carrier Mills. Only time in history that Galatia won the tournament.

We controlled the tempo of the game, and the strategy really frustrated their players. The game plan worked perfectly, and to most everyone's surprise, we won the game by six points. We had three players who scored in double figures, led by Peck's and my 15 points each. In over 10 years of playing in the Saline County tournament, that was the one and only championship Galatia ever won. My only regret was that I felt so bad after the game that I went straight home and didn't get in on all of the celebrating at Fay's. Peck and I both made the All Tournament Team.

Homecoming in 1961, I escorted my grade school "heartthrob" Janet Wickham.

The 1960-61 team was the best team I played on in my three years on the varsity at Galatia. We won 16 games, which was double the wins we had the year before. We ended up finishing second in our conference. It was truly a "break out" year for me. I had averaged nine points a game as a sophomore. I finished this season averaging 22 points a game as a junior. We finished the year, as we always did, playing in the West Frankfort Regional tournament against schools seven or eight times bigger than us. This was the year we believed we could win the tournament. Galatia had only won the Regional three times in their history. We played the Benton Rangers in the first round, and even though they had great tradition and a Hall Of Fame coach, Rich Herrin, we thought we had a chance. They played in the best basketball conference in Southern Illinois, the South Seven, made up of the largest high schools in Southern Illinois. They were a good team, but going into the tournament they actually had a losing record. Coach Herrin would go on to win over 500 high school games and coach at Southern Illinois University. I didn't know it at the time, but a couple years after our game, I became teammates with two of their players: Terry Thomas and Tom Whittington. All three of us ended up at Middle Tennessee State University (MTSU) on basketball scholarships. Tom and I roomed together our last two years at MTSU. We all three remain good friends to this day. When we matched up with Benton in the regional back in 1961, all we knew was that each of us wanted to beat the other and play for the regional championship. Tom was a very good 6' 5" center, and Terry was a hard-nosed very good defensive guard. Terry later told me that he had heard I was a good scorer and how it made even more determined to stop me. Terry was also a good football player, and a lot of that football mentality carried over to the basketball court. He played me very physical and tough, but I still managed to score 16 points. Years later, Terry and I had a little different perspective about that game. Benton beat us and started a six game winning streak that carried them all the way to the State tournament. In hindsight, even though they came into the Regional tournament with a losing record, they were really pretty good and "jelled" at the right time. That game ended our season, but it was an enjoyable season played with some really great guys. I had made several All-Star teams and had begun receiving inquiries from several colleges. I had a long way to go to be as good as my idol, Jerry Sloan, but I was trying and getting closer.

In the summer before my senior year, I went to Kalamazoo, Michigan to work. I stayed with my cousin George and lived with my Uncle Ewell and Aunt Agg. They lived in a really small two-bedroom bungalow just outside of Kalamazoo. All of my aunts and uncles had left the farm and gone to work in a state mental hospital in Kalamazoo. George had a younger brother named Lester, who was also living at home. When I moved in, it really became quite cozy, but we managed. I really had a lot of fun that summer. George's older brother, Clyde, had lived with my mom and dad his senior year in high school after his mom and dad decided to leave the farm and move to Kalamazoo. I wanted to get away from home for a while; Kalamazoo offered a good opportunity for me to get a job and make a few dollars. I stayed with them for about 8 weeks and worked at a Phillips 66 service station. I had never worked at anything like that before, but I had worked in dad's feed store so I was use to dealing with customers. I made a good and quick impression on the owner.

1962 my senior year. I made several all star teams including MVP of our conference. All-Southern Illinois, and Champaign News-Gazette All-State.

After about three weeks, I was the night foreman and often ran the station by myself. Most weeks, I worked six days, as much as 10 hours a day. I didn't mind working all those hours because I was trying to save all the money I could to enjoy my senior year in high school. By the end of the 8 weeks, I was beginning to miss home and was ready to get back to Galatia. Even though George and I played basketball often, it wasn't anything like what I had played in previous summers. It was a good summer, and I got to spend more time with my cousins and relatives on my mom's side than I ever had before.

My senior year, 1961-62, was a blur. So much happened so fast; it seemed like I barely had time to enjoy the experience. Several players on the 1960-61 team had graduated, including Peck. Larry Bell, Bobby Oglesby, and Frank Knight were about the only players coming back that had played much. It would be hard for me to improve my points per game average from my junior year, because I became the main focus of other team's defense. I did not let that deter me. I had worked hard and was really looking forward to the season. I was determined to improve on what I had done as a junior. My focus was on getting a college scholarship. I loved playing this game and didn't want it to end. I went by Coach Pulliam's house every Sunday afternoon to get the keys to the gym; no one was going to work harder than me. I loved practicing inside that cold gym on a Sunday, making up "mind games" and playing different game scenarios. I always made the winning basket! Our first game of the season was against a good, well coached Cave-In-Rock team that had finished third in our conference the year before. Their best player, Jerry Douglas, had graduated the year before, but they were always good. We won that first game; I scored 27 points, a harbinger of things to come for me. I would end up the season averaging over 25 points a game, three points a game more than I had the year before. I was the second tallest player on the team at 6' 1" which meant on most teams I would have played forward. Coach Pulliam understood that my future in basketball was as a point guard; he allowed me to play point guard and run the team. I made that decision easier for him since I knew what he wanted done on the court and was good enough to do it. Coach Pulliam recognized that we did not have the talent that we had the previous year and began the season playing more of a slow down and deliberate style of basketball. However, after about six or seven games, he decided to open up our offense and play a little quicker, which really benefited me. He pretty much turned the team over to me and gave me the "green light." I would not have made all of the All-Star teams I did, or received the recognition I had received if we continued to play that slow down style. There was one stretch during the season of about eight games where I scored over 30 points every game, including a school record 44 points. I got "fired up" and played my best games against the best teams. I loved playing in front of big crowds in big gyms. There was at least one college coach at almost all of our games the last month of the season. I began to get more and more recognition. By the end of the year, I had received about 25 scholarship offers from schools like Memphis State, Mississippi State, Dayton, Southern Illinois, Western Kentucky, Murray State, Vanderbilt, and Virginia

Tech. I kept scoring points, and my favorite reporter and class-mate, Robert Bockiewicz, kept putting out stories about my achievements.

I was chosen on the All Southern Illinois team, the MVP of our conference, special mention on the Chicago Daily News All-State team, All-Star on the Evansville Courier-Journal newspaper, and picked as one of the top 15 players in the state by the Champaign News- Gazette newspaper. It had been a dream season for me, even though our team had struggled and won only 8 games. We played a lot of teams close but just did not have the size or the talent to win. A microcosm of our season was our two games in the Saline County tournament, my favorite tournament. We played a good Eldorado team, led by two good players: Kingery and Kotner. Joe Kingery and I got to be good friends. He told me that when they played us, which was twice a year, their coach would constantly remind them that they had to extend their defense because I was looking for a shot as soon as I crossed the center line. In the Friday night game against Eldorado, we lost by four points. Harrisburg beat Carrier Mills in the other game on Friday so we played an outstanding Carrier Mills team on Saturday night. But unlike the year before when we beat them in the finals, we lost by eight points. This year the tournament was played in Harrisburg. I loved playing in their big gym in front of all those fans. I led all scorers with 53 points for the two nights and was again picked on the All Saline County team.

During my 12th grade year a rather unusual friendship developed in my life. A man by the name of Gail Lawrence, a rehabilitated drug addict who lived in Galatia with his mother and invalid sister began hanging out with us at Fay's. Gail was in his late 30s and had been a heroin addict many years before I met him. Gail loved basketball and never missed a home game at Galatia or many of our away games. He also attended First Baptist Church of Galatia the same church that I attended. Gail was just a really nice man who wanted to get involved in my basketball career. He had a car, some money, and a lot of time that we would spend going around Southern Illinois watching high school basketball games. Gail had poor eyesight and did not drive after dark, so I ended up driving his car around to all of the games. On the nights that we did not have a game, he could always find a good high school game for us to go to if I was up to it. I really loved basketball and enjoyed watching other teams and players. I was always trying to learn as much as I could, so I was usually willing to go. We certainly looked like the odd couple, me at 17 and Gail in his 30s, but we both loved basketball and enjoyed each other's company. I know I filled a void in his life and gave him something to look forward to.

There were a several games that stick out in my memory about my senior year. We lost an overtime game to our conference rival, Ridgway High School, in our gym the night I scored 44 points. Ironically, I scored 22 points in each half and did not score in the OT. We played an outstanding and ranked

McLeansboro team to a stand-off for three quarters before losing to them in their gym by 10 points. I scored 28 points and their 6' 6" All-State forward, Jim Burns scored 25 points. Shawneetown won our conference both my junior and senior years. They were very good and very big with a starting lineup of 6' 6", 6' 5", 6' 5", and 6' 3". In our games with them I scored 25 points in one game and 39 in the other. The most memorable game was our game with West Frankfort in the first round of the Regional tournament. This would be my last game as a high school player. In those days, Illinois only had one basketball class for all schools. West Frankfort had an enrollment of over 1000 students. West Frankfort was 7 times bigger than we were, and we were playing them in their gym. They had three really good players. Their best player was a 6' 4" All-State player by the name of Bobby Brown. Brown was a great athlete, who was also the quarterback on their football team. He was being recruited by over 50 colleges and universities. He ended up signing to play at the University of Illinois. By the end of the season I had also created a following, both in the media and among college scouts. However, because I was from this little school, some in the media were not convinced that I could play with Brown and the "big boys". The night before this much anticipated game, Gail came to the house to wish me well and to offer some encouragement. He knew how big a game this would be for me and wanted me to know that he had confidence in my ability to play against anyone. He also wanted us to pray about the game. We had hung out together for the past year and outside of praying over a meal, he had never asked to pray for me before. I appreciated that, and it has stuck with me all these years. On our knees, we asked God to bless the game and to give me a good game. There was going to be several college coaches at the game to see Brown but there were a few coming like Dayton, Memphis State, Mississippi State and Southern Illinois University coming to see me. West Frankfort had been picked to win the Regional, and a lot of people thought they had a chance to advance through the Sectional and maybe on to state. They not only had Brown but they had another 6' 3" really strong, football-type player by the name of Dave Pike. They had an outstanding team that was well coached. They had won 20 games during the season in the tough South Seven conference. This was truly a David versus Goliath game. We had played several schools much larger than us, and our conference, Greater Egyptian, had a couple of really good teams that year so we were not intimidated. The West Frankfort gym was full, over 2000 fans, many I'm sure to see how bad they were going to beat us. Some were there to see if this "hot shot" from this little school even belonged on the court with Bobby Brown. We got off to a great start. Our whole team played a good first half. I seemed to be playing in slow motion, in a zone, running our offense and pretty much controlling the game. West Frankfort and Brown were playing well, also, but it was not the blowout many expected to see. At halftime they were ahead of us by four points. Brown had scored 18 points and I had scored 22. A side note to this game was that I needed to score 14 points to set a new school record for the most points in a season by a player. The old record, which stood for several years, was 546 points. I finished the season with 560 points and 1320 points in my career. Both school records, at the time. My former teammate, Peck Boyette, said I might have set scoring records that would still be standing today if the 3-point line existed back then. Peck also said "Jack had such great range I think he could have scored from Borden's Feed Store, a block away, if you would have left the gym door open." After the game, several of our fans told me that all the talk in the lobby and in the stands at halftime was about how good a player I was. One of the announcers on the radio station said that all of the publicity that I had received was deserved. The second half was not nearly as good, unfortunately. I scored four points in the first couple minutes of the third quarter but Frankfort, to their credit, changed defenses and went from man to man to a 1-3-1 zone. The zone really took away my space with the basketball and allowed two men to guard me all the time. That allowed my teammates to be more open but they were just not able to hit their shots. Brown played well, and Pike was just too big and strong for us inside. To add to our woes, I picked up my fourth foul in the third quarter and finished the quarter on the bench. We started the fourth quarter down by 13 points, but in the first three minutes I was called for a charging foul, my fifth foul. Any chances that we had of an upset flew out the window when I went to the bench. Ironically, I had only fouled out of a couple games all year and none via a charging foul. I went to the bench, threw a towel over my head, and sat there the rest of the game with tears in my eyes. After hundreds of hours of practice and over 70 games, it all ended with me sitting on the bench that last five minutes of my final game. I finished the game with 28 points, Brown had 35 and we lost by 25. After the game, I was disappointed, thinking of what could've been, and realizing my high school career was over. Many of the West Frankfort fans who had come to see a blowout realized that "little" Galatia for over half of the game had played their Red Birds "toe to toe." After the game there were three or four college coaches waiting to talk to me, including the University of Illinois. IU had only shown token interest in me, even though I had let it be known, I wanted to go there. Obviously, I had made an impression that night even on the University of Illinois. God does answer prayers.

Another memorable experience that I had with Gail Lawrence was when he took me to Champaign, IL to meet and talk with the coach at Champaign High School, Leo Cabutti. Coach Cabutti was a Hall of Fame coach who grew up Herrin, a town in Southern Illinois. He was a classmate of Gail's. Coach Cabutti was also on the selection committee for the Illinois high school All-State basketball team. He was very influential around the state, and Gail thought I should meet him. He thought it would give me a better chance of making the Chicago Daily News All-State team that was voted on by the high school coaches in the state. There were never many players selected from small high schools, and only 20 players were selected from the whole state. I was a little apprehensive about meeting with Coach Cabutti and "politicking" for this selection. Gail didn't look at it that way. He thought that I was deserving and putting my name out there couldn't hurt. Coach Cabutti was very kind and said he was aware of what I had accomplished during my senior year, but did not make any promises. I knew there were a lot of deserving players who also had great seasons, so I understood. I did not make the team, but I was chosen along with 9 other players in the state in a category called the "just missed". Ironically, I did make the Champaign News-Gazette All-State team which selected only 15 players and was the most prestigious of all of the all-state teams selected in the state. I was the first and only Galatia player to ever be picked on that all-state team. Twenty years later, when I was coaching at Salem High School, we would meet again when we played Champaign in the Centralia Christmas tournament. We won.

There were several people besides my family that played a role in my success in high school. There were four who played a special role, and I owe a deep sense of gratitude to each one: Gail Lawrence, JW Pulliam, Robert Boczikewicz (my classmate), and a friend named Jesse James. Robert was a brilliant student and an extraordinary writer. He was such a good writer that as a high school student, he would submit stories to newspapers, and they would print the article exactly as he had

written it, often without editing. Robert would go on to graduate from the outstanding University of Missouri journalism
school with honors. He was the Missouri State capital reporter
for the St. Louis Post-Dispatch newspaper for several years. He
got me so much more recognition around the state than any
athlete in a school of 150 students could ever expect to receive.
He was always submitting some kind of article on my behalf. I
think he liked to write the news more than I liked to make the
news. He would submit articles about me to the Evansville
Courier-Journal, Chicago Daily News, the Paducah Sun-
Democrat, and St. Louis Post-Dispatch, in addition to our local
paper in Harrisburg. I still have several articles about me written by Robert. Jesse James, not the outlaw, owned a dry cleaner
across the street from our store and was an outstanding high
school basketball referee. I hung out over at his cleaners all the
time. I even worked for him one summer, not an easy place to
work in the summer. Jesse had been an outstanding baseball
and basketball player in Galatia back in the early 50's. He refereed for about 20 years, and had seen a lot of great players
throughout Southern Illinois during his days. I loved to hear
him talk about some of the "ole timers". He was a mentor and
a man that I listened to when it came to how the game of basketball should be played. If I wasn't playing I would often go
with him to the game he was refereeing.

Galatia's rich basketball tradition went back to the 1940s
and included some outstanding coaches that started their ca-
reers at Galatia HS as either a coach or a player. George Iubelt

[pronounced You-belt], Sammy Mirandi, and Sammy Duane went on from Galatia to coach at Division I schools. Iubelt was an assistant coach at Southern Illinois University for a former NBA great Harry Gallatin. Mirandi went on to have a very successful high school coaching career before joining Ted Owen's staff at Kansas University. Duane, who like me only played at Galatia, became a Hall of Fame high school coach in Arizona and became an assistant coach at Northern Arizona University. Several years later I would coach against Mirandi when our Oral Roberts University team played Kansas in the final of the Midwest Regional college basketball tournament. It is truly remarkable that a town with a population of only 1000 and a high school with 150 students could have produced four Division-I coaches!

I had many great experiences throughout my high school career and was blessed to have some great support from several people. After the season, I begin the process of choosing a college to attend. I had received over 25 scholarship offers; it was exciting yet challenging to choose which college would be the best fit for me. I was the first person in my family to ever go to college. Neither one of my parents really knew enough about colleges to offer much advice. Coach Pulliam gave me some direction, but ultimately it was going to be my decision.

Grandma and Grandpa Minor in my high school years 1958-62. I would go to their house every school day morning for homemade breakfast. Grandma always had her apron on whether in the kitchen or not.

There were many remarkable and unforgettable moments in my life before that last high school basketball game in West Frankfort. I have always believed that "one should enjoy the journey, not just the destination." I want to go back a few years and pick up the story. A good place to begin would be with the two people besides my parents that had a profound influence on my life, my grandma and grandpa. They moved into town after they sold their farm when I was about 14 or 15 years old. I had a unique relationship with my mom's parents, Ellis and Lou Minor. As a kid growing up, I would spend a lot of week-ends and summer days out on their farm. They lived about 5 miles outside of Galatia on a 50 acre farm. I loved riding out to that farm in the "rumble seat" of my grandpa's Mode T Ford automobile. I worked hard with my grandpa, feeding the stock, and working in the fields. He was a hard worker up until the day he died at the age of 91. I loved being with them out on the farm. It certainly wasn't for the plush amenities of their home. I remember when they didn't have electricity. I remember sleeping in a feather bed, and I certainly remember having to go outside to their outhouse to go to the bathroom. Grandpa had a couple horses, one named May.

May was a paint quarter horse that I loved to ride. May and I got to be good buddies. We spent a lot of time together going all over the country side. The only time I ever got thrown from a horse was while riding May, but it wasn't her fault. My cousin Charlie and I were riding her at the same time, when my grandpa thought that she was "acting out" and decided to change her bridle to make her behave a little easier. We were both about 12 years old at the time. Grandpa thought that we could just stay on her while he changed the bridle. She was a very gentle horse and easy to ride, but after you rode her and took the bridle off she would always spin and take off for the pasture. Grandpa knew that but this particular time, he wasn't thinking. Right on cue, the minute he took the bridle off she yanked her head, spun, and took off for the pasture without her two passengers. I landed on top of Charlie, unscathed, but he was totally knocked out. I had knocked the wind out of him and fractured a rib when I landed on top of him. Grandpa really felt bad for Charlie, but he knew that it was he who had messed up, not May.

Me riding May, my favorite horse. Grandpa is leading us through the gate. I loved hanging out with my grandpa on the farm.

There were a lot of days on that farm that I would just sit, talk, and listen to my grandma and grandpa. That's about all there was to do if you weren't working. Grandpa was use to physical labor, so there were a lot of days he would come over and help my dad in the feed store even when he was in his 80s. One of his most important jobs was helping my dad and me castrate pigs. Grandpa was "the surgeon." About three times a year, we would have 20 or 25 piglets that had to be castrated. My job was to hold the back legs while dad held the front legs and made sure they didn't bite while grandpa would cut and remove the testicles. I have certainly seen my share of what is called "mountain oysters," but to this day I have never eaten one. Grandpa would always remind me to keep my mouth shut while he was performing his "surgery."

I loved being around my grandpa and while he was not an emotional man, I knew that he loved me. My grandma was a small, petite woman who wore an apron all the time even when she wasn't in the kitchen cooking. I loved to hug her because she was so tiny, she didn't even reach my chin. She would act like I was annoying, but I know she liked the attention. My grandma, Louvenia (Lou), might have been a petite woman but she was tough as nails. Her dad, William Shirah, had survived being orphaned during the Civil War. (His story is written in the foreward.) I was always cleaning my grandpa's car, mowing his lawn, helping in the garden, painting, or doing whatever else that needed to be done around their house. One of the dumbest things I ever did involved my grandpa's car. My grandpa and grandma rarely left Galatia, but on this one occasion they went to Michigan for a week to visit their boys and their families. The day before they were to return, I thought I would wash the car for them. I got a couple of my buddies to help, and we got his old black car shining. Well, I thought it would be a shame to just clean that car and put it right back in the garage, so my buddies and I decided to take it out for a spin. I didn't bother to ask my parents for permission, besides they would never know if I got back in 20 or 30 minutes. We were out in the country, on a gravel road, in a clean car, when I decided to show out and give my buddies a thrill. I went around a curve, shoved the gear shift up into second gear, and "gunned it" so I could make the car "fish tail" around the curve. The car began to spin in the gravel and I lost control. I ran off the road straight into a ditch. The front end was banged up pretty good. Fortunately, none of us got hurt. Right away I began to think of what my dad was going to do to me, and for the only time in my life, I seriously considered running away from home. I was also heartbroken over what I had done to my grandpa's car. The car would still run, so we pushed it out of the ditch and began the long, long ride home. I thought of 100 stories to tell my dad but none of them made any sense, even to me. I decided the only thing I could do was tell the truth and just get my butt beat, and be put on restrictions for about five years. When we got back to my grandpas, I went home to tell my dad what had happened. He looked at the car for about 10 minutes, which seemed like 10 hours to me, before he said, "It looks like about $200 worth of damage. You will have to mow a lot of yards to pay for this joyride." Then he told me that he did not believe

I just came up with the idea of taking my grandpa's car out on my own, that my buddies must have influenced me. He said, "I should be more careful about who I ran around with." I did tell him that it was my idea, but he didn't believe me. He totally surprised me, no whipping and no restrictions. The next day when my grandparents got home, I was really dreading facing them. My grandpa's reaction surprised me also, he just said, "I hope you learned your lesson and I'm glad you didn't get hurt." I don't know why I was surprised at his response because even though they had 10 grandchildren, I am convinced I was always their favorite.

I have a lot of fond memories with my grandparents, but none better than eating breakfast with them practically every morning before I went off to school. My grandma would make a homemade breakfast of; eggs, bacon or sausage, biscuits, gravy, and all topped off with honey or sorghum every morning. Grandma would get up about 5:30, half an hour after grandpa, to roll out the dough for the homemade biscuits. We would eat at 6:30, which worked out perfect for me, since I had to be at school by 7 o'clock for free throw shooting practice. Maybe those breakfasts had a lot to do with me going from a little skinny 5' 8" and 130 pound freshman to a 6' 1" and 167 pound senior. My grandparents never went anywhere after dark, including to any of my basketball games. I know that they were proud of me and they loved me, but they never saw me play a game. The morning after a game, over breakfast, they would ask me about the game and how I played.

I finished my high school career in style. My childhood friend Lenny Duane had three older brothers. One of them, Sammy, was a good basketball player at Galatia and went on to play at Southern Illinois University. After he graduated from SIU he became the basketball coach at Vienna High School, about 40 miles from Galatia. He and I became good friends. He would come to my games, and invite me down to play against his players during the summer. He had a new beautiful convertible automobile that I loved. One day when I was just hanging out with him I asked him if I could borrow his car on Prom Night. He knew I was responsible and without any hesitation he said yes. There was only one condition: I had to promise I would not drink any alcoholic beverages and drive. Sammy went on to become a great high school basketball coach in Arizona. He was elected to the Arizona high school hall of fame. But what is really interesting to me was that he became good friends with my old nemesis, Clem Haskins, from Western Kentucky, who played several years for the Phoenix Suns in the NBA. I had been dating a girl from Eldorado during my senior year, and when I showed up on prom night in Sam's shiny, new convertible she was flabbergasted. We went to the prom in style. I think we got home around two in the morning. We had an unbelievable time and a night to remember. Now, I was ready for the next chapter of my life.

CHAPTER 3

Brief Stop at Mizzou
before MTSU (1962-67)

In those days the NCAA allowed a recruit to take six paid visits to colleges and universities. I visited Illinois, Memphis State, Dayton, Southern Illinois, Western Kentucky and the University of Missouri. I had never been on an airplane before I began making those visits. It was an exciting time for me. I really wanted to go to the University of Illinois. My interest in going to UI went back to when I was in the ninth grade and my parents took me to Champaign to see the Fighting Illini play the Ohio State Buckeyes. Ohio State had a great team with Jerry Lucas, John Havlicek, and Mel Nowell. They beat Illinois by 20 points, but it was a great game. I sat there in packed Huff gym thinking how good Lucas and his team was, and thinking one day I would love to play in a game like that. The Buckeyes went on that year and won the NCAA national championship with a 25-3 record. We went to an Illinois basketball game every year that I was in high school. Bob and Mary Lou Peyton were friends of ours, who had moved from Galatia to Champaign. Bob refereed high school and junior college games and a lot of the Illinois basketball inter-squad games so Coach Combs gave him game tickets. Going to see an Illinois game was always a highlight of the winter for me. I did make a visit to see the campus and talk to Coach Combs, but he wanted me to "walk on" and earn a scholarship. Even in those days, a four year scholarship was worth $25,000 or more, there was no way I was going to pass on a full ride scholarship to walk on at UI. Besides, my parents could not afford to pay for me to go to the University of Illinois for even one year.

Mom and dad inside the grocery store. Notice all the soot on the ceiling from the coal burning stove that was used to heat the store in the winter, Circa 1960.

I narrowed my choices down to Western Kentucky and Memphis State when the coach at Memphis State, Bob Vanatta, left Memphis to become the coach at the University of Missouri. I really liked Coach Vanatta, and at the last minute I changed my mind and decided to go to Missouri. Missouri was a great school, but from the very beginning, I just didn't feel comfortable there. It was a football school in those days, with an enrollment of over 20,000 students. It was just overwhelming to a boy from a little town like Galatia. I didn't know anyone there, and I rarely saw Coach Vanatta. In those days, freshmen were not allowed to play on the varsity, and the freshmen coach had never been involved in recruiting me. I would later regret not going to Western Kentucky, I had a great visit the weekend that I went there. I liked their players, and felt really comfortable with their coaches, including their Hall of Fame coach, Ed Diddle. Coach Diddle was an icon in college basketball, and even thou he was in his 70s, he was considered one of the best college basketball coaches ever. The Hilltoppers, as Western Kentucky was called, had recruited a great freshman class. All four of my college years, they were ranked in the top 20. As seniors, led by a great player named Clem Haskins, they came within one point of beating the University of Michigan, and going to the Final Four. I ended up playing against Haskins all three of my years at Middle Tennessee State University where I eventually ended my college career. If I would have followed my first intuition and signed with Western Kentucky, I would've been a part of those great teams. I realized after a couple months at Missouri that I had made the wrong choice, but I was determined to stick it out, at least through my freshman year. However, a bad experience in our last freshman game when we went to St. Louis to play St. Louis University changed all of that, and I decided to leave at the end of the first semester. The Big Eight Conference, the conference that Missouri played in, only allowed their freshman teams to play six games. I was having a miserable time, on and off the court, and my basketball play reflected it. I had started every game until we went to play in St. Louis. Ironically, our game was played in Kiel Auditorium, where the St. Louis Hawks and my childhood hero, Bob Pettit, played. St. Louis is only about two hours from Galatia and several people from Galatia, including my parents, drove up to see me play in our last game of the season. It was the only game all year that my parents were able to see me play and for some non explainable reason, the freshman coach decided not to start me. I ended up only getting to play about 10 or 12 minutes and scored 8 points. I was so disappointed and humiliated that on the two hour bus ride back to Columbia, I didn't speak to anyone and decided I was leaving. For the first time in my life, I had lost my enthusiasm and confidence in my basketball ability. It was January, and the second semester had just begun, I couldn't see myself staying at Missouri until school was out in May. I called my parents and told them of my decision. They came out to Columbia the next weekend to get me. They wanted what was best for me, and they knew the University of Missouri was not where I wanted to be. I went in to see Coach Vanatta and tell him of my decision to leave. He said he understood and wished me well. Ironically, this would not be my last encounter with Bob Vanatta. Coach Ken Trickey hired him to be the assistant athletic director at Oral Roberts University during my time on the coaching staff there. We remained friends for several years.

I needed a break from basketball, and I wanted to make some money. I got a job with a construction company that was laying cable for a telephone company. It was hard work, but the pay was good and I was getting my mind off of basketball. I didn't mind the manual labor, but I learned a valuable lesson. I needed to get a college education so I would not have to work like that for the rest of my life. Besides, I still loved basketball and knew that if I found the right school, I could play at the college level. I called a couple schools that had tried to recruit me out of high school, but they would only offer me a tryout and a chance to "walk on" the first year. I never doubted my ability to play and knew that sooner or later, I would get another opportunity. I had been back home for about two months when I got a call from an assistant coach at Middle Tennessee State University, Ken Trickey. Coach Trickey was from Cairo in Southern Illinois. He had recruited several high school players from our area, including Tom Whittington and Terry Thomas from Benton. They were on the team that beat us two years earlier in the regional. He had also recruited a 6' 7" center from Harrisburg by the name of Ed "Boom Boom" Cannon. A former coach at Harrisburg and good friend of Coach Trickey's, by the name of Gene Bland, had told him that I had left Missouri and was back in Galatia. Coach Trickey asked me over the phone that day, if I would be interested in MTSU? He told me that they had a scholarship for me if I was interested. Naturally, I was and since I knew of these other players from Southern Illinois, I thought it could be a good place for me. Coach Trickey and the head coach at MTSU, Bill Stokes, drove up to see me. A few days later they arranged for me to go to Murfreesboro, Tennessee to see the school.

MTSU was a beautiful school of about 4000 students. They played in the Ohio Valley Conference. (Today, the school has over 25,000 students and is the largest university in the state.) I liked the school and really felt comfortable there with the coaching staff and the other players from Southern Illinois. In the fall of 1963, I enrolled at MTSU and began a new chapter in my life. I was a transfer student; therefore, I had to sit out one year before I was eligible to play. It was a long year for me, but a good year because it gave me an opportunity to focus on my academics. I didn't realize it at the time but like Missouri, MTSU was a football school. My roommate that first year in the dormitory was another Illinois recruit, Barry Jackson. Barry was a 6' 8" player from Belleville, Illinois and a really smart, good guy; we got along great. Unlike at the University of Missouri, the coaches were always coming around and making sure everything was going good. Our 'dorm dad' was Coach Jack Deere, who was on the football staff and a really nice man. I became good friends with the southern Illinois gang of Tom, Terry, and Ed. Tom and Ed both had cars, so we had a way to get back and forth from home. I didn't go home nearly as often as Ed, Tom and Terry, but there was one weekend that I did go home and wished I hadn't. The most boring days were on the weekends when the basketball team was playing on the road and I was left in the dorm with hardly anyone around. It was on one of those weekends that I decided rather than stay in Murfreesboro, I would hitchhike home. It was about 200 miles from the campus to Galatia, we could make the trip in about four hours, sometimes faster if Boom Boom was in a hurry. I finished my last class on Friday at noon and headed for the highway to Nashville and home. I got to Nashville by 2 o'clock in the afternoon and got a ride with a salesman from Paducah, Kentucky, which is only about 60 miles from Galatia. I thought this trip home would be a piece of cake, and I would be home long before dark. He told me he had a "few" stops to make in Kentucky before we got to Paducah. Well, those few stops, turned into about eight or nine stops, and when he finally let me out on the side of the road in Paducah, it was already dark. It was winter time, so it got dark by 5 o'clock. Now I was on the side of the road, 60 miles from home, and it was dark. It was almost impossible to get a ride after dark on a two lane highway, especially when no one seemed to be going that way. I waited there for over three hours, past 9 o'clock, and decided the only way I was going to get home was to either walk or call my parents to come and get me. That meant over 100 mile round trip for them but it was getting late, and I was out of options. They actually were upset with me that I had not called them earlier, which is what I should have done. It was midnight before we got home. That trip from Murfreesboro to Galatia that typically took 4 hours took me 12 hours. This was the second time I had hitchhiked home, and it would be my last.

I practiced with the varsity that first year and realized that taking a break from basketball for five months, and putting on about 20 pounds had affected my game. I had a lot of catching up to do and needed to spend a lot of time in the gym. The year before I transferred to MTSU, a couple other players, Mike Milholland and Ray Kempf, had also transferred to MTSU. Mike, a 6' 6" forward, had transferred from Tulane University and Ray, a 6' 7" center, had transferred from the University of Tennessee. Both were good strong inside players, but both were "quick tempered." One of the things I remember most about Milholland was how fast he would eat. We would stop someplace for a team meal and be amazed that he would finish his plate before most of us could even butter our bread. He was embarrassing to eat with, so we just tried to ignore him. Boom Boom actually coined a phrase related to Milholland's eating habits. He would say if he saw anyone eating fast, "you sure did Milholland that down".

Coach Stokes, after a really tough year, winning only eight games, was forced to resign. I liked Coach Stokes, but

I don't think he was tough enough or strict enough with the players. Coach Trickey, his assistant and a former outstanding player at MTSU, took over as the head coach. That was fine with me since he is the one who really recruited me to MTSU. He was a much stronger disciplinarian and related to the players much better than Coach Stokes. Coach Trickey had recruited several players from Southern Illinois so it was like Southern Illinois at Murfreesboro, Tennessee. Coach Trickey wanted to make several changes and create a new culture around the basketball program. I was a victim of this new found "hard, no non-sense" discipline. One afternoon about a month before school was out, a bunch of us decided to get some beer, some coeds and go to this creek not far from the campus and party. It was a hot afternoon and we were swimming, drinking, and having a great time when we noticed a car on the bridge stopped. At the time, we didn't think anything about it and didn't bother to hide what we were doing. We later found out that it was the golf coach, Coach Patty, and that he was taking names of who he saw drinking beer. Of course, he told Coach Trickey what he had seen, and Coach Trickey immediately called a team meeting. At the meeting, Coach Trickey asked who had been at the party drinking. No one obviously raised their hand, so he begins to call off the names of those that Coach Patty told him were there. My name was one of those that he called out. He asked me if I had been at the party drinking, and I admitted that I had. He said that everyone who was at the party drinking would start the next year without their meals on the scholarship plan. That amounted to about seven or eight hundred dollars for the semester. That ended up being a very expensive party. I understood what he was trying to do to gain control of the program and to show he was going to run the team much differently than Coach Stokes. Several years later, when I went to work for him as one of his assistants, I asked him what if I would have denied I was at the party drinking. He said he appreciated me being honest, and if I would've lied, he would've taken my entire scholarship, not just the meals. He also said that the way I handled that situation made an impression on him, which would eventually lead to him hiring me. So now, I had a big summer in front of me that I needed to get in shape, step my game up, and make enough money to feed myself the first 4 1/2 months of the school next year. Coach Trickey actually relented and restored our meal plan after about a month; hence, I only had to eat off of the other player's trays at the cafeteria for a few weeks.

During the summer after my first year at MTSU I got in touch with my longtime friends, Harl Cockrum and Lenny Duane. They were working in Chicago at a Ford automobile plant, so I asked about the chances of getting on at Ford and living with him. Harl told me I was welcome to stay with him in Peotone (located just outside of Chicago) in a motel that they rented by the month. I went up to Chicago a few days after school was out in May and by June I was working at Continental Can Company making cans. It didn't pay as good as Ford but it was a good job and another friend of mine from Galatia, Jerry Malone, worked there so I had a ride to work. We all worked nights and pretty much slept all day. We got off work at mid-night so we were up until 2 or 3 in the morning drinking beer, playing music and cards. Everyone, except me, had a new very fast "muscle" car and everyone of them drove very fast. The weekends when we didn't come home were crazy around the hotel; actually the weekends we came home were crazy, too. There were no inter-state roads back then from Peotone to Galatia, so we drove two lane roads thru several small towns to get home. It was always a race to see who could get home the fastest and I mean fast. We would be driving down those two lane roads at night literally a hundred miles an hour. Everyone knew the roads, every curve, but it was a miracle we didn't get killed. Actually, one of my older friends, Larry Paul Lewis, who was my grade school girlfriend's brother, did die in a car accident. Harl, was a good roommate, we had a lot of fun those 7 or 8 weeks we lived together. I managed to save a few dollars to help get me through the school year. However, there were a few weeks when I would run out of money before pay day and end up just chewing gum and eating a peanut butter sandwich. We got paid on Thursday, so after work on Thursdays it was often a big steak or big late dinner for us. I came home in August for a couple weeks before it was time to go back to school. I was really looking forward to getting to play competitive basketball once again. It was going to be a little more challenging than I thought.

Sophomore at Middle Tennessee State University in 1964. I started on Coach Trickey's first team and played for him all 3 years at MTSU. Later served as an assistant coach on his staff at ORU.

The Ohio Valley Conference (OVC) was a very good basketball conference which included: Murray State, Morehead State, Eastern Kentucky, East Tennessee State, Tennessee Tech, Austin Peay, and Western Kentucky. MTSU had never finished higher than fourth in the conference but we had a good nucleus coming back from the year before. I was excited about finally getting to play again. We had four or five transfers, and every one of them were good players. One of those transfers was a great high school scorer named Jay Cole. He led the state of Tennessee in scoring his senior year. Jay was a transfer from Auburn, who just like me had three more years of eligibility. Jay was a good-looking guy, funny, and spent as much time chasing the coeds as he did playing basketball. Jay and another player by the name of Phil Meadows were the team clowns and kept us all loose. We had Milholland, Kemp, and Whittington returning along with a good shooting guard by the name of Billy Martin. Cannon was moving up from the freshman team and a couple of other junior college players named Phil Meadows and Bobby Gardner, made up the varsity. I had worked hard to get back in good shape, but I struggled to regain the shooting touch that I had in high school. We were all anxious to get the new season started. I had been out of basketball competition for almost 2 years, and it showed. Shots that I could make in high school did not fall for me now, so I tried to make up for it by being a play maker and playing good defense. Bobby and I started at guard with Martin, Kempf, and Milholland on the front line. We got off to a good start winning four of our first five games. I was really inconsistent; I would score 15 points one night and five the next night. I was frustrated and actually felt like I was letting Coach Trickey and the program down. The highlight or maybe the low light came for me in December, just before

Christmas, when we went to Louisville to play in the OVC tournament. Coach Trickey was always promoting his players and our team to the press. I was this rookie "hotshot" defensive player that was going to guard Clem Haskins from Western Kentucky in the first round of the tournament. Haskins had made Allstate three times and was named player of the year his senior year in Kentucky. He was recruited by everyone, including the University of Kentucky. He was 6' 3" but had a vertical jump of about 40 inches and was a terrific jump shooter. Western Kentucky had a great team, going into the tournament they had only lost one or two games. There was a lot of hype in the Louisville paper about our game and pictures of Haskins and me. I was really excited and looking forward to guarding Haskins and seeing what our team could do against them. About three minutes into the game I realized that I was way out of my league trying to guard Clem. Our team was overwhelmed with their talent and skills. We were behind by 20 points in the first half. Haskins had over 20 points at halftime. He ended up scoring 52 points, and I fouled out trying to guard him. That was a record for the most points in a conference tournament game, and I think it still stands today. Clem Haskins, was the best college player I ever played against, and the second best player I ever played against behind only Jerry Sloan. I wasn't the only one that couldn't guard him. He would go on to be three time MVP in our conference, and the 3rd overall draft pick in the NBA draft by the Chicago Bulls. He played for 6 years for the Phoenix

Suns and averaged over 15 points a game. I still catch some grief to this day from my so called MTSU "friends" about my great defense on Haskins that game. Except for Haskins, I was a pretty good defensive player for the Blue Raiders, and was voted the best defensive player two different years.

The first year under Coach Trickey, MTSU began to play some heavyweights in college basketball and get recognized as more than just a football school. We played at Dayton, Loyola of Chicago, and DePaul, and even though we lost all three games, we were definitely on the major college basketball stage. I vividly remember our game against DePaul on Saturday night. My uncles and cousins drove over from Kalamazoo to Chicago to see me play. I scored 5 points and to put it in Charles Barkley terms, I was "turible". I was so disappointed that they had driven two hours to see me, but they weren't as upset as I was. Our practices were always exciting. No one ever knew when Kempf or Milholland were going to "go off" and get in a fight, kick the ball into the bleachers, or get chased out of practice. Coach Trickey and I began a lifelong partnership that year. I was his point guard; he expected a lot from me. Sometimes I would get frustrated with him because he thought that I should "just know" what he wanted done on the court. It wasn't always easy to play for him, but he was a very positive person and always encouraging. We finished the season with a losing record, but you would never know it by listening to him. He wanted everything about our program to be first-class, just like Western Kentucky. He was

jealous of Western and hated that they thought they were better than everybody else in the conference, even if they were.
He was relentless in his recruiting. He was determined to get
the kind of players that it would take to beat Western.

Besides at Western, there weren't many African-American
basketball players in the OVC. Murray State had a couple black
players but that was about all. MTSU had never recruited an
African-American until Coach Trickey did in his second year.
Art Polk from Kansas City and Willie Brown from Nashville
were outstanding players and outstanding young men. Art, at
6' 3," was very smart and could practically jump out of the gym.
Willie, also 6' 3," was an outstanding guard, extremely quick,
and a great athlete. Freshmen were still not eligible to play on
the varsity then, but those two (along with a couple other recruits) actually beat our varsity in a scrimmage. We were not
that bad, they were that good. Coach Trickey caught some flack
from some in the community and around the conference, but
he integrated the basketball program at MTSU with these two
exceptional players. I had never been on a team with a black
player. I had only played against a half a dozen in high school.
I didn't know an African-American personally, but I understood perfectly what Coach Trickey was doing. He was on a
mission to beat Western Kentucky and win the OVC. Art, graduated with honors and eventually served on Coach Trickey's
staff at Oral Roberts University with me. Willie became a cop
in Stamford, Connecticut. Tragically, he was killed while on
patrol by a motorist who ran a red light and hit his motorcycle.

We had some great times at MTSU off the court. The basketball players hung out together quite a bit, and generally we all got along great. We would go out into the country and party or just play cards half the night in the dormitory. The most annoying thing, before we moved into our new dorm, was living in the same dorm as the football players. We would be asleep at two or three in the morning, and some of the drunk football players would come in and start banging on our doors. One night, one of the football players beat on the wrong door and got his butt kicked by Kempf. We hated living with the football players. My junior year we moved into a brand-new dorm with the entrances to our rooms on the outside. There were four rooms that connected to one bathroom, so there was only eight of us in a quad with other basketball players. One of the highlights of my junior year was going to a big concert in Nashville at the fairgrounds to see James Brown. One of the players on our team, Ken Shulman, loved James Brown. He was always playing his records, usually so loud you could hear them in your room even with the door closed. Ken got a group together to go see him. Tom, Terry, Ray, Bobby, our manager, and I were all excited to go. We were about the only white people at the concert. We were upfront, close to the stage acting all crazy, just like the other 10,000 mostly black people at the concert. It was a great show! James Brown was one of the greatest entertainers I ever saw. I had an interesting and fun Sophomore year at MTSU even if the basketball season did not turn out quite the way I had hoped it would.

My second summer working in Chicago would be much different than the summer before with Harl and Lenny, and living in Peotone. I got my old job back at Continental Can Company. My friend Jerry, who was still working there, had moved into a house closer to the plant. I had to live where he lived to have a ride to work. It really didn't matter too much to me, I was only going to be there a couple months before heading back to school. It was much different than living with Harl, there were eight or nine guys living in the house, some I didn't even know. We all worked different shifts, so there was always a bed or couch to sleep on. It was pretty crazy at times and very messy all the time, but Jerry and I got along great. One of the best experiences of that summer of 1965 was getting to know a former basketball rival, David Lee. David was an outstanding guard on the McLeansboro team that we played when I was at Galatia. He was a year older and was playing at Southern Illinois University when we were living in Chicago. David had an outstanding career at SIU, and we became lifelong friends. Several times that summer we would go to the local park and play basketball. I was able to save a few dollars again, but I was glad when it was time to go back to school.

My junior year was going to be a breakout year for me. I knew what to expect, and I felt more comfortable running Coach Trickey's offense. I had a year of competition to get my game back together, and Gardner and I had played together for a year now. Billy, Ray and Mike graduated, but we still had some good players and more importantly we all liked each other. Our biggest problem was we were not very big. Cannon was our tallest player at 6'6". Tom at 6' 4" and either Jay at 6' 3" or Phil at 6'4" were our front line players. Bobby was the shooting guard and I played the point guard most of the time unless Coach Trickey got a "brain freeze" and started a little point guard from Nashville named Billy Boner. Boner was about 5' 6" and not a very good player, but for some reason Coach Trickey liked him and at times would start him over me. Billy annoyed me because he could not play, and because he was a politician, always talking. Ironically, he would later get elected as the mayor of Nashville; however, he would also get removed from office for some shady dealings. Terry and Barry would come off the bench and play quite a few minutes as did Shulman and a guard from Indiana named, Chuck Fielder. Our team really played hard every night and despite our lack of size we were competitive in the OVC. We finished the season with a losing record but Art and Willie were about to rescue us.

There were three games that I remember from the year. We lost two of them but it was how we lost them that stuck out in my mind. We were playing Murray State at home after they had beaten us by about 20 points at their place. We were behind by 20 points at halftime, and it looked like a blowout. They were the second best team in our conference behind Western. They were big and very talented so at halftime Coach Trickey decided to start all of us "little guys" the second half.

We were going to press them all over the floor and just try to "wreak" havoc. We figured we didn't have anything to lose at that point. About seven minutes into the second half, their 20 point halftime lead had shrunk to 10. They begin to turn the ball over and play real shaky. With less than a minute left in the game, we went ahead by one point on a steal and basket out of our press. We had been behind so much that Terry, not realizing we were ahead, committed a foul in the back court against their best free-throw shooter, Billy Chumbler. Chumbler, who had led the OVC in free-throw shooting the last two years, made both free throws. We missed a shot at the buzzer and lost by one. Many of our fans had left at halftime, but the ones who stayed said it was the best game they had ever seen. It certainly was one of the best come back games I have ever played in. Another game I remember we also lost but we gave 11,000 fans heartburn for about 30 minutes. It was the last game of the year at Western. They were ranked in the top 10 in the country and had only lost two or three games all year. They had beaten us by 30 points earlier in the year on our floor. They were head and shoulders above anyone else in our league, including us. This was their first season in their new, beautiful 11,000 seat arena. In addition to it being the last game of the season, it was also senior night, and the place was standing room only. It was so loud that I remember during timeouts it was hard to hear Coach Trickey in the huddle. Coach Trickey decided we didn't have a prayer if we went into Bowling Green and tried to run up and down with them and play their style.

So we went into the game to play a spread, slow down offense, and make them chase us and spend a lot of time on defense. We made a couple baskets early and got the lead. There was no shot clock in those days, so we held the ball for two or three minutes before we took a shot. They got frustrated, their fans booed us, and went nuts. I remember missing a shot at the buzzer that ended the first half. We would have been ahead by one, instead of down by one. I don't remember the exact score but it was in the 20s. Western had been averaging over 80 points a game. The second half started out okay. They started pressing us and trying to get the ball before we could get down and start running our spread offense. We missed a couple of good shots and finally their talent just took over. We played a great, smart game but finally ended up losing by 20 points. We had finished the season with a "moral" victory, and the two hour ride home didn't seem so long. The best game, for me, came at East Tennessee State University in Johnson City where we won by 2 points. We played exceptionally well and upset a good ETSU team. I had my best offensive game of the year, scoring 22 points. I also made 2 free throws in the last 5 seconds to ice the win. I had another very inconsistent season, offensively. I think it was at the end of the year that I began to realize basketball was a means to an end, and there would not be another level for me. I had one year left. I was going to have fun and, most importantly, I was going to get my degree. I decided that this next summer between my junior and senior year, my focus was going to be on making money and not basketball.

I wanted to have enough money so I could enjoy my senior year and be able to do whatever I wanted, including go to Florida over spring break. Bobby and a couple other guys had talked about going to Fort Lauderdale during the break of our senior year, and I had told him to count me in. My cousin, Clyde, and his wife, Joan, lived in Highland Park, Michigan, a suburb of Detroit. I called them and asked them if I could come up and live with them during the summer. I was pretty confident I could get a job at an automobile factory. This was in the summer of 1966, and factory workers, even then, were making 140.00 dollars or more a week. I went up to Michigan a couple weeks after school was out, and by June I had a job working nights at Chrysler. My shift was 3 pm to 11:30 pm on the assembly line putting water pumps on car engines. It was a monotonous job. It seemed like the engine line moved at the speed of light, and "most" of the time I kept up. The foreman in charge of the assembly line did not like for anyone to stop the line so we had to work fast. I did get to sit down but my back really got tired by the end of the eight hour shift. I was making money, and by working the second shift there really wasn't much time to spend it. My whole objective was to have money when I went back to school, so I was good with that. I enjoyed living with Clyde and Joan and, living in the city. After a few weeks at Chrysler, I decided that if I really wanted to bank some money I should get a second job. I responded to an ad in the paper and got a job at an A & P grocery store stocking shelves from midnight until six in the morning. I left my job at Chrysler and drove about 30 minutes and clocked in at the A & P. Between the two jobs I was working over 70 hours a week. The only night that I had off was Saturday night. I enjoyed my work at the grocery store and after a few weeks the store manager made me the foreman of the night crew. I had a really long, tough work week so my weekends were spent mostly in bed or laying around on the couch. I was making money and Clyde and Joan, let me stay with them for free so I was building up my bank account. At the end of the summer I had over $1500 in the bank and figured that would be enough for me to really enjoy my senior year at school, and make it down to Florida for spring break!

In spite of working all those hours I did have some time to enjoy Detroit. I liked Detroit, and since I had never spent any time in a large city it was quite an eye-opener, in many ways. I had never been around African- Americans. I never even knew any African-Americans until Coach Trickey re-cruited Art and Willie. Now I was living in the city that was predominantly black, and I was working in the factory where half of the workers were black. I learned lessons that summer that would prove to be very valuable to me later when I came back to Highland Park to teach. These lessons would serve me well throughout my entire life, especially in the coaching profession. The most memorable moment of my summer came one July night when I was working at the A & P store at about three in the morning. Detroit had a history of violence and race problems. At one time it was the crime capital of the US. It was also in the forefront of the civil rights movement. The city was very volatile in the early and mid-60s, and I got a firsthand experience at just how volatile. Our store was located on a major street in a part of Detroit that was about 90% black. On this particular night in July, we were stocking shelves when we heard firecracker-like sounds outside and saw a lot of commotion with people out in the street in front of the store. I went to the front of the store to see what was going on and saw some buildings on fire off in the distance toward downtown Detroit. There were a lot of cops out and while I was standing at the front window, an army tank rolled down the street right in front of our store. As I stood there, like some five-year-old kid looking into a candy store in astonishment, a cop came to our front door, and motioned for me to come over. I fumbled through my apron for the key to the front door. I was very concerned, but didn't really know what to think. I had never seen anything like this before. The police officer asked me what we were doing and how many were in the store. He told me that there were race riots breaking out all over the city and for me and my crew to get out of the store and go home. Detroit would riot and burn for a week before the police, and the National Guard would restore order and the city would calm down. I didn't return to work at the store for over a week, and then I only worked in the daytime. Several stores were looted and burned along that street, but fortunately, the A & P was not harmed. I don't even want to think about what could have happened that night. God was looking out for me.

I got back home at the end of summer in time to spend a couple weeks with my parents and my buddies in Galatia before it was time to go to school. My senior year at MTSU was very special in many ways. Tom and I roomed together that year and as a result became lifelong friends. We were both ready for college to be over so we were just going to have fun and get through it. Our last week of school during final exams, we pretty much went out every night and drank beer. We both had met all of our requirements for graduation, and neither one of us cared what we made on the final exams. There were a lot of really great experiences that year and a few surprises, as well. My first surprise should not have been that big of a surprise at all considering how my basketball play had been over the last two years. Willie and Art were very talented basketball players that Coach Trickey recruited to start as sophomores. Willie was going to be the new point guard and start along with Bobby. Art was a small forward who ended up playing with Cannon and another junior college recruit named Frank Harris. Jay also started some games as a small forward. For the first time since I was a sophomore in high school, I was not in the starting lineup. I decided to make the best of it and not pout or be negative instead just enjoy playing my last year. I set my mind on being the best sixth man I could be and to help the team as best I could. Little did I know at the time that by making that choice, and playing with that kind of attitude I was paving the way for an opportunity to one day coach in college. I knew Willie was a better, bigger, and more talented basketball player than I was. If MTSU was going to compete in the OVC, Coach Trickey had to play Willie and Art. We ended up winning more games my senior year than in the previous two years. With another outstanding recruiting class coming in behind Willie and Art, MTSU could compete with Western and Murray. I ended up coming off the bench as the sixth man, and averaging about 8 or 10 minutes a game. I led our team in free-throw percentage for the third straight year. My most memorable game that year was against Austin Peay at their place in what was called the "Little Red Barn." Their gym was very old and only seated about 1000 people. We had beaten them by several points earlier at home, but it was never easy to beat them in their gym. They were not very good, but they played really physical and borderline dirty. During the game, I was going for a loose ball, and one of their players tackled me from behind to try to get to the ball. I usually played under control and with composure but not this time. I grabbed the player and while on the floor took a couple swings at him. He also swung at me, but fortunately we both missed. Ironically, neither one of us got kicked out of the game, but my action seemed to spark our team and helped to turn up our intensity. After the game, Coach Trickey recognized me and said I had been the difference in the game. We played every game tough and close that season, and for the first time in my career at MTSU, we won as many games as we lost. Three years later I would get a call from Coach Trickey to come to Oral Roberts

University and be an assistant on his staff. There was no doubt in my mind that I had been rewarded more by being a "good" sixth man on that team than if I would have been the star. Coach Trickey told me later that he always said that one day he would try and hire me.

I lived in the new dorm, in the quad, with a great group of guys. We were always hanging out together, playing cards, and sometimes even studying. Tom and Ed had nice new cars, which worked out good for me because I was always "bumming" a ride with them when I needed to go someplace. It was especially nice for me on the weekends when Tom rode home with Ed and left me his car to drive. I dated a couple different girls, so that gave me a way to get around and have some fun on the weekends. One was a Southern Belle, as Boom Boom liked to call her. She lived on a farm not far from Murfreesboro and raised Tennessee walking horses. She won a county fair beauty contest and was a really sweet girl. We had a lot of fun, but I was a long way from getting very serious with a girl. I think Boom Boom liked her more than I did and actually went to her house more than I did. We went to Nashville quite often to go to the Grand Old Opry or just hang out. I didn't go back home nearly as often as Tom and Ed because there really wasn't a whole lot for me to do in Galatia. Tom was dating a girl named Sue that he had gone to high school with and who was attending Southern Illinois University. Sue and Tom would end up getting married soon after we graduated. They became very good friends of mine and later lifetime friends of Diane, my wife, and me. It was a great year, academically, for me. I only needed about 25 credits going into my senior year to graduate, so I didn't have to study much. The highlight was doing my student teaching with an outstanding teacher named Mr. Jolly. He really prepared me for my first real teaching job in Highland Park, Michigan.

We did make that trip to Fort Lauderdale, Florida over spring break in Bobby's big old Buick. There were four of us that ended up going. There was a couple nights we ended up sleeping in that big old Buick. We got a room in a hotel for maybe half of the nights we were in Florida. The rest of the time we bunked in with other college kids or slept in the car. We had a great time.

Middle Tennessee State University was the perfect place for me to go to college. It was not that big when I went there in 1963, and with all the other Southern Illinois boys there I felt right at home. MTSU was a good academic school and I received a good education. The best thing that happened to me was playing for Ken Trickey. We developed a mutual respect and a great player-coach relationship. I would end up working for him at ORU and, best of all, meet my future wife there. Maybe not going to Western Kentucky University worked out for the best after all! I was so blessed to have been able to play Division I basketball. I had gotten a free college education with the talents God had given me, along with countless hours of practice and dedication to the game I loved. I started two of the three years I played at MTSU. I was voted MVP of our team as a junior and best defensive player as a sophomore and junior. I led the team in free throw percentage all three years I played. I averaged about eight points a game over my college career. I took great pride and satisfaction in being the leader and point guard on our teams. There are about 350 schools in the country that play NCAA, Division 1 basketball, and I got to play at one of them.

I played a few more years in Detroit in an industrial/recreation league against other former college players. My love for playing had run its course. I had started shooting a basketball when I was eight years old and now fourteen years later it was time to move on with my life.

CHAPTER 4

My First Teaching Job:
Highland Park, Michigan (1967-70)

When I graduated from MTSU I was 23 years old and a prime candidate to be drafted into the Army and go to Vietnam. That war was really heating up at that time and a lot of young men my age were being drafted. I wasn't opposed to the war, but I wasn't anxious to go to Vietnam either. My cousin, Clyde, who I lived with the previous summer, was the assistant superintendent of schools for the Highland Park, Michigan school district. Highland Park was an inner-city school district made up of 90% African-American students. Clyde called me and told me if I would come to Highland Park and teach he could get me deferred from military service. I had enjoyed my summer in Detroit with Clyde and Joan, in spite of the riots. The fact that I would be teaching in a school district of predominantly African-American kids didn't concern me at all. My first teaching job was at Liberty Elementary school teaching PE in grades K-5. Before the school year even started, the teachers had gone out on strike for higher wages. The teacher's union, like all the unions in Detroit, was very strong; no one messed with the union. However, because I was a new teacher and not in the union I was allowed to cross the picket line and go to work. Liberty was a great school with an outstanding teaching staff run by a very good principal. On the staff was an African-America named John Maxey who taught a class of special needs children. John did a great job with those kids, and they loved him. He was about my age, and he and I got to be close friends. Many weekends we would hang out together and go to all-black nightclubs. John had grown up in Detroit and knew a lot of people around the city. A lot of times I was the only white person in some of the establishments. It was a long way from Galatia to Detroit; much further than the 500 miles I had travel by automobile to get there. I was working and living in a whole new environment and culture than I had grown up in. I was beginning my teaching career in a much different culture and environment than I had lived in the first 23 years of my life.

John was an aspiring music producer looking to grab the brass ring and become the next Berry Gordy of Motown. In addition to John, there were a couple of women teachers that I got to be good friends with. We had an hour for lunch, so we went to a local cafe about a block from the school and had lunch together practically every day. During my three years at Liberty, I took over the school safety patrol and because I was out on the streets checking on my kids all the time. I got to know a lot of the parents in the neighborhood, and they got to know me. Liberty had a swimming pool, not a very big one, but big enough that one day a week, I gave all of my PE classes a swim lesson. I taught stunts and tumbling and started a gymnastics team. I also started a basketball team at Liberty. I was single and liked to stay busy. The principal and parents at the school really appreciated what I did for the students. The principal relied on John and I to provide a lot of the discipline around the school. He would send a student to one of us to be disciplined as we saw fit. John and I both had a reputation for being no-nonsense. We stressed to the students that they act like ladies and gentlemen. We spanked our share of students. Neither one of us ever got challenged or in trouble with any of the parents for giving those spankings. They knew we cared about the children at Liberty and wanted the best for them. I would, occasionally, allow the boys to settle their differences by boxing. I brought them into my office, closed the door, and had them put on these big boxing gloves. I told them if they didn't fight I would spank them both. After a few minutes, I would make them shake hands and tell them that was the end of it.

I was beginning to find my way around Detroit and enjoy the night-life. Detroit has a rich history of great places for entertainment and dining. One of my favorite establishments was a club where Denny McLain performed several nights a week at the organ. McLain was a great pitcher for the Detroit Tigers and the last pitcher to win 30 games in one season. He was an outstanding organist. I enjoyed living with George and Joan, but after a year I needed to get my own place. I moved into a one-bedroom apartment about 10 minutes from Liberty school. I bought a new car, my first, a Plymouth Fury that was baby blue. Between the car payment, the apartment, and the money I needed to "cat" around, I stayed broke. It took me over a month to save enough to buy a bed for my apartment. Clyde gave me his big overstuffed recliner and that is what I slept on the first month I was in the apartment. I actually slept well and dozing off watching TV was pretty handy because I was already in bed. It took me several months to save enough money to buy a dining room set. Even after a couple years in the apartment, I still didn't have any furniture. I liked living alone and being independent, besides, I was never home anyway. I was always doing something at the school or out running around. It was also about this time that, with the encouragement from Clyde, I enrolled in a graduate school program at Eastern Michigan University. I thought I might like to eventually be an Athletic Director or a Principal in a high school so I needed to get a Master's Degree. I began taking night classes and Saturday classes to earn a Master's of Education Degree in Administration. It took me a couple years to finish the 32 hours I needed, but I was single and it was the perfect time in my life to pursue the degree.

My last year in Highland Park, I met this young lady whose parents owned a nice dinner club. Gloria had graduated from college with a degree in teaching but had decided to help her parents run the club. She had to work most every weekend until late, sometimes until after midnight. On most weekends, I would show up at their club around 10 o'clock and have free drinks until they closed. Gloria was pretty and personable so she made a perfect bartender. Often she would invite me to come early and eat dinner with her at the club. As a bachelor, I loved it. Gloria's parents were from Poland and worked hard. They had good food, a nice club, and a good business. I never talked to her mom or dad much, I don't think they ever quite knew what to make of me. I dated Gloria for about a year, and in spite of Clyde's encouragement to get more serious about our relationship, I just wasn't ready for any lifetime commitment. Clyde and his colleagues at work went to her club quite often for lunch so he got to know Gloria quite well. I remember one night picking Gloria up after work to take her home. It had been snowing all day and the roads were pretty slick. I was on Woodward Avenue, the biggest and busiest street in Detroit. I hit a patch of ice and slid off the road and hit a parked car. I "might" have been a little distracted, but fortunately neither one of us got hurt. I dinged up the front of my car a little and put a pretty good scratch and "bump" on the parked car. No one was around, but I decided I should leave a note on the windshield of the car with my phone number. I never got called about that incident.

Besides my job and school I would always find time to go over to Clyde's to help him do yard work, paint, clean out the gutters or whatever else he needed me to do. Our relationship was more like brothers than cousins. He had gotten me the job at Liberty and the deferment that I needed to stay out of the Army, and I was grateful. Clyde always had a problem controlling his weight, so there were things like getting up on a ladder that he just couldn't do. He and Joan liked having me around, and besides that, Clyde was a good cook.

Clyde was a big Detroit Tiger baseball fan and I have always been a big St. Louis Cardinals fan. They met in the 1968 World Series and after jumping out to a 3 games to 2 advantage over Detroit, the Cardinals lost the last two games and lost the series. I was heartbroken, but Clyde, Joan, and the city of Detroit went crazy. After the Tigers won that seventh game, Clyde, Joan and I rode from Highland Park down Woodward Avenue in his Oldsmobile convertible with the top down. There must have been over 100,000 people out in the streets, half of them trying to jump in our car, as we made our way downtown. I wasn't nearly as happy as they were, but it was quite an experience that I will never forget.

I was loving my job, having fun, and perfectly content with where I was in life. That all changed one evening when I got a phone call from Coach Trickey asking me if I would be interested in coming to Tulsa, Oklahoma, and being one of his assistants at Oral Robert University. It was a call that I didn't expect but a call that changed my life! He told me that I did not have to make a decision right that minute, but he wanted me to come out to Tulsa, see the campus, and spend some time. The minute we hung up I knew what I was going to do. I was 26 years old and had an opportunity to coach college basketball. I was going to finish my obligation at Liberty, finish getting my master's degree at Eastern Michigan University, and go to ORU. I went out to Tulsa on a weekend when the team was playing a road game in Texas. ORU had its own plane that the team flew on to all away games.

President Oral Roberts and me, 1973.

I got on the plane with Coach Trickey, and in the first seat sat Oral Roberts, the founder of the university and the evangelist that I had seen several times on TV. Ken introduced us and told him that I was one of his former players, and that he wanted to bring me out to ORU to help him build the program into a national contender. I remember shaking hands with him and thinking how soft his hands were, and how many people they had touched at his healing crusades all around the world. His greatest reputation was as a "faith healer." I remembered watching him on TV on a Sunday afternoon conducting his tent revivals. In the four years that I would spend at ORU, I discovered that he was truly a great preacher, teacher, speaker, and he loved his basketball team. I really didn't know what to expect during the weekend I went to Tulsa, but Pres. Roberts had a very powerful "slogan" that was everywhere around campus: "Expect a Miracle". I guess it applied to me, too. The whole weekend in Tulsa was unbelievable. It was 1969 and the basketball program at ORU was relatively unknown. The University was only four years old, but the buildings on campus were very futuristic. There were already plans to build a beautiful 10,500 seat basketball arena. Pres. Roberts had founded the university based on three principles that he said he received from God. His students would spend four years developing their body, their spirit, and their mind. What impressed me the most was that the president of the university was traveling with the basketball team to play a regular game in the middle of February against a small college in Texas. I now knew firsthand what Coach Trickey told me about Mr. Robert's love of the game. He saw the basketball program as being an avenue to bring more attention and notoriety to the university and his ministry. He was always referencing how many millions of men read the sports page of the newspaper every day. ORU won the basketball game that night, and we were back home about two hours after the game. ORU had some outstanding basketball players, but to get to the next level "we" would have to get bigger and better. It was going to be a challenge, but it was going to be a "great ride". I told Ken that I would be back in June after school was out and I finished my master's degree.

However, before I got to Tulsa a lot was about to happen in my life. In May, a couple weeks before school was let out and I was going to leave for ORU, I got sick. At first I thought I had some kind of flu bug or stomach virus. But a week later I still wasn't feeling well and decided to go see a doctor. He also thought that I just had the flu. One morning I got up and began vomiting up blood, and that scared me. I called Joan, who had been a nurse for several years in a hospital. She didn't want me to stay alone, so I went over to their house. I got feeling better over the weekend, feeling good enough to get up on the roof of their two-story house to clean the gutters. But while I was up there I got lightheaded and actually felt like I was going to pass out. On top of a two story house would be a bad place to pass out. Fortunately, I didn't pass out, and when I got down I went straight to bed. This all happened on Sunday and on Monday I had a temperature of 104. Joan decided to take me to the emergency room. I had never been this sick in my life, and the doctors were not sure what was wrong with me. Rather than giving me some kind of medication to reduce my fever, they packed my bed with ice. I was sick and miserable before I got to the hospital. Now, I was packed in ice, the doctors were not sure what was wrong with me, and I was more miserable than when I checked in. During the night my fever broke, and by Tuesday morning I was feeling a lot better, but they still didn't know why I was sick or why I threw up blood. The doctors ran some test but didn't find anything until Thursday when a urologist ran this wire with a camera through my penis to look at my kidneys. The doctor discovered that I had a dysfunctional and deteriorated kidney. Basically, I had one functioning kidney. The doctor could not believe that I had never experienced back pain or had not experienced other health issues during my life. He speculated that the kidney had never fully developed and over time it just atrophied. The damaged kidney had to be removed. On Monday of the following week, they scheduled the operation. Clyde and Joan called my parents, and my mom came to Detroit to be with me. The surgery went well, but I was in intensive care for a few days. I have a pretty strong threshold for pain, but I needed a lot of pain medication those first two days after surgery. I rubbed my heels so much on the bed sheets that the nurses had to put heel cups on my feet because I was rubbing the skin off of them. I remember being in such pain that I would ask for pain medication and after I would get a shot, I would feel so good that I would actually try to stay awake so I could enjoy the feeling.

This was way before the days of non-invasive surgery. I still have a ten inch scar from that procedure. I was concerned about my quality of life with only one kidney, but the doctor assured me that I would do just fine. I actually had pretty much been living with one kidney my whole life already. By Friday, eleven days after Joan had taken me to the emergency room, I was feeling good again and ready to go home. Coach Trickey had called me to reassure me that I still had a job in Tulsa. He said the ORU people had been praying for me, which really meant a lot to me.

I taught in Highland Park, at Liberty Elementary School, for three outstanding years. During those three years, I met some wonderful people. I enjoyed my time with Clyde and Joan, experiencing the nightlife and activities of Detroit and my courtship with Gloria. I am not sure that I would have left my job for any other job other than a college coaching position. In those three years I had gained a lot of experiences of life. Even when I went back to Galatia to see my parents, I was always ready to get back "home" to Detroit.

I only got back to Galatia during holidays and the summer. I spent time with my mom and dad, and enjoyed visiting my high school friends and spending time with Sharon, my grade school girlfriend. Lenny was working in Chicago at the same time that I was in Detroit, so I didn't get to see much of him. Harl and Fred had joined the Navy, and were serving their tour of duty. After Fred was discharged and before he went back to work for Anheuser-Busch in St. Louis, he came to Detroit to stay with me for a week. It was on our drive back from Galatia to Detroit that I experienced a miracle. Fred and I had been out on a Saturday night until about three in the morning. I had to get back to Detroit by Monday to go back to school. We left Galatia Sunday morning about 9 o'clock, after about five hours of sleep. I thought between the two of us we could drive the nine hour trip and be okay. I started out driving the first couple hours, while Fred slept. Somewhere in Southern Indiana, I woke him up to tell him he would have to drive that I was really getting sleepy. He drove for about an hour and told me that he was afraid he was going to go to sleep while he was driving; I needed to take over again. I was so tired that one hour of sleep did not help me much. We were on the interstate north of Indianapolis, in a flat wide-open part of the state, and I was really struggling to stay awake. I remember seeing a car ahead of me in the right hand lane. I moved over into the passing lane to pass, and the next thing that I saw was that car in my rear view mirror. To this day, I do not remember passing that car. I pulled over at the next rest stop, woke Fred up, and told him if he could not drive, we would just have to stay there for a couple hours. I am convinced that one of my guardian angels got me by that car on the interstate that day. Fred stayed with me one week before he caught a bus back to Eldorado, Illinois where he was living with his brother. He went back to work in St. Louis at Anheuser-Busch for about 15 years before he was transferred to Austin, Texas. He bought some land in Texas to build a home. One day while he was clearing some of that land, he began to have some pain in his back. He thought nothing of it until it wouldn't go away, so he finally went to the doctor and discovered that he had cancer. Fred died about three months later. He was only in his 40s. I think of him quite often, and all of the good times we had together, beginning back in the fourth grade.

I finished my Masters Degree at Eastern Michigan University in May and finished the school year in early June. I gave my bed, dining table and chairs, and the recliner (that I had once used as a bed) to my friend, John Maxey. I left Highland Park for Tulsa, Oklahoma in June of 1970. I was in for an exciting four years, storybook years. Little did I know that my first teaching job would bode well for me in the future. I would use many of those experiences in my new job at ORU. In five years, I would return to Highland Park to be the Athletic Director, but I would not be alone: I would be bringing my new wife.

Welcome to My World

CHAPTER 5

The Oral Robert University Years (1970-75)

In Coach Ken Trickey's first year at Oral Roberts University, 1969-70 season, ORU won 27 games playing mostly National Association of Intercollegiate Athletics (NAIA) schools. To get to the next level, which is where President Roberts had hired Ken to take the program, meant he was going to have to get better athletes and a much better schedule. ORU was a unique and special place with unique student rules and student standards. President Roberts had founded the university on three basic principles of developing students: Body, Mind and Spirit. ORU also required the students to adhere to a different set of standards than most schools. One of the university rules required that all male students wear ties to class, the cafeteria, and to chapel services on Wednesday and Friday. President Roberts liked basketball and everyone knew the basketball players were put up on a pedestal. However, that did not exempt them from the same set of standards that everyone on campus had to abide by. Mr. Roberts wanted the basketball players to set an example for the rest of the students. At first, I wasn't real sure how all of this would go over in recruiting. I soon discovered that being in a strict and disciplined environment worked in our favor with the parents of these young men. They liked the idea of supervision, and Christian principles to keep their sons on the right track. At ORU the coaches were expected to do more than just coach the students on the field or on the court. Ken recognized that he needed a talented, energetic, and committed staff if he was going to be successful at ORU.

To help reach the goals of the university and the basketball program Coach Trickey hired a former assistant coach at North Texas State University, Dwayne Roe. One of Coach Roe's main responsibilities was to make sure the players were getting to their classes and doing what they should be doing off the court. "Moose" as he was affectionately known was a former three sport letter winner in college and was drafted by the Detroit Lions. He came by his nickname honestly; he was 6'4" and weighed about 260 pounds. Coach Roe and his family moved into an apartment in the athletic dorm where he was put in charge of supervising and running the dorm. He spent a lot of time with our players, and they soon learned that even though he could be tough, he wanted them to succeed off the court as well as on. Moose was also one of the funniest people I have ever met. He could and did tell stories until the wee hours of the morning, since he was often up walking the halls late at night checking on the student-athletes. Moose was also very recognizable on campus not only for his size, but for the trench coat that he always wore even if it wasn't cold enough to be wearing a coat. Some of the players began calling him Colombo, after Peter Falk, who played the role of a detective on TV. As part of my job and to help my salary compensation, I was the assistant dorm director. I lived in the dorm on the opposite end of the players in a one-bedroom apartment. All the assistants had offices on the first floor of the dorm before our new basketball arena was built. Having our offices around the player's dorm rooms proved to be helpful in us getting to know our players better and develop a better rapport with them.

Oral Robert University basketball staff from 1969 – 1974. L/R: Me, Dwayne "Moose" Roe, Ken Trickey, Art Polk

We would play ping pong and pool with them in the dorm recreation center.

The third assistant coach hired was a young African-American and former teammate of mine at Middle Tennessee State University: Art Polk. Coach Trickey recruited Art out of Kansas City. Art was one of the first black student athletes to play at MTSU. He was smart, helped identify with our black players and was an outstanding recruiter. We had a great staff, each coach bringing something special and unique to the program. Ken was a great head coach to work for because he delegated responsibility. We each felt like we were contributing to the program. We all recruited, we all participated in practice, and we all had a say in "game planning". However, the one facet in the game plan that never changed was playing up-tempo "run and gun" basketball. Coach Trickey had been hired away from Middle Tennessee State because President Roberts had been at the game in 1968 when MTSU came into ORUs gym and beat them 115-94. After that game Mr. Roberts talked with Ken about how enjoyable and exciting a game it had been to watch and how he would like to see his Titans play that way. We had great athletes who we recruited to play that style of basketball. It was fun to coach and fun to watch. There were occasions when I would get aggravated at Ken because he would be so cavalier about the role that we as coaches played in the success of the team. He would tell fans at a luncheon or other gatherings that the players win the games, and that coaches get too much credit. I understood what he was saying, and that great athletes make great coaches. However, there are programs that have great athletes but did not have the success that we had. I remember sitting on the bench next to him during a game that we were winning by several points and him leaning over to us and saying "how do you like playing this NAIA school with NCAA players?"

Our basketball program, with the full support of Pres. Roberts, was "rocketing" toward the "big time" in college basketball. Our players were talented, got along great, and played extremely hard. We played in our little gym called, "The Round House." It would seat about 3000 people. There was an Olympic size pool on one end and everyone that first came into the building was met with the smell of chlorine. We sold out every game, if you didn't get to the game an hour early, you probably would not get in. The students loved our team and wildly supported them. We definitely had a home court advantage. We won every game we played in The Round House the last two years before we moved into Mabee Center. The city of Tulsa was beginning to take notice that there was another basketball program in town, besides the "old" school, Tulsa University. ORU basketball became a popular topic among news media outlets all over the state. We were not winning with smoke and mirrors; we had great athletes who could have played at Oklahoma University, Oklahoma State University and Tulsa.

Winning basketball games in college depends on recruiting the best athletes, which was not a secret. Ken had established some close ties with several high school coaches in Tennessee during his coaching tenure at Middle Tennessee State University. One of those high school coaches was Dorsey Sims, coach at Chattanooga Riverside High School. Coach Sims was a highly respected and very successful coach whose teams were in the state tournament about every year. In 1968 and 1969, his teams won the state tournament and went undefeated. Those teams were led by a great player by the name of Richard Fuqua. Richard was our first recruit from Riverside but he would not be our last. He was a four-year starter for us and was the first All-American to play at ORU. Richard averaged over 34 points a game, finishing second in the country in scoring as a junior. He was a great shooter with unbelievable range. If Richard would have played with the three point line, he might have averaged 40 points a game. On that same Riverside team was another outstanding player by the name of Larry Baker. Larry was a 6'4" forward with great leaping ability and great athleticism. Also, on that team was a player by the name of Jesse Traylor. Jesse was not good enough to play at ORU but he was Richard's buddy and Coach Trickey liked him, so he gave him a scholarship too. The center on that team was a 6'6" junior named Eddie Woods. Woods played like he was 6'10"! He dominated around the basket. We signed Eddie the following year, and he started for us for three years. Woods was small for a Division I center, but he had unbelievable timing and could jump as well as any college player I ever saw. He set school records in rebounding and in blocked shots. In one game, he had 15 blocked shots and 25 rebounds. Woods was also one of the meanest and toughest players I have ever coached, which played to his favor when he went up against much bigger front line players. We developed a pipe line, a "gold mine," of high school players out of Chattanooga Riverside high school. In my first year at ORU we ended the season with a 21-5 record. We beat several Division I schools and led the nation in offense, averaging 95 points per game. In one game we beat an NAIA school, Union University of Tennessee, 154 to 110. One of the funniest lines I have ever heard came from one of the funniest college coaches of all time, Abe Lemons. When a reporter told Coach Lemons that ORU beat Union 154-110, he said, "Was that the AFL or CIO."

The construction of our new arena, Mabee Center, was ahead of schedule and being pushed to get completed by Mr. Roberts. The new arena would seat 10,500 and would be a state of-the-art building. All of the seats in the arena were plush theater seats. The arena had an auxiliary practice gym and a beautiful dressing area for our team. Also, we had a hand ball court, and a sauna and sunken whirlpool to help players recover from injuries quicker. The building was also equipped with the latest in sound equipment and a (first of its kind) electronic scoreboard. President Roberts wanted a first-class facility for his basketball team, but also a place to hold large ministry events. We also needed a nice arena to attract Division I schools to come to Tulsa and play us. The future was bright for ORU basketball. We needed a couple more players and to schedule more games against the "big" name basketball schools. We soon discovered that it was easier to get the players then get the so-called "majors" to play us. The word was out around the country on just how good we were and none of the "majors" wanted to take the chance of getting beat by "little ole" Oral Roberts University.

One of the players that graduated from the 1970-71 team was our captain and one of our best players, Haywood Hill. I really admired and respected Haywood as a player but more importantly as an individual. He was an under-sized forward at 6' 3" but he played like he was 6' 6". He ran the floor like a deer and got rebounds that would cause you to scratch your head. He averaged almost 20 points a game, including a 41 point game against an excellent Southwestern Louisiana team at their place. He was a match up nightmare for teams as a small forward. He was a joy to coach and watch. He was one of the best to ever play for the ORU Titans. (ORU has since changed their mascot to the Golden Eagles.)

It was truly a memorable first year, but the best thing that happened to me during the 1970-71 season happened off the basketball court. The coaching staff and players were required to attend chapel services twice a week. If Pres. Roberts was in town and speaking he would make it a point to look for all of us. At one of these chapel services Coach Trickey was the speaker. He always did a great job speaking to the students. He was funny and personable. At this particular chapel Moose, Art and I were on the stage with him so we could be introduced. When Ken introduced me, he said something to the effect that I was single and 24, but off-limits to any ORU co-eds. I don't really think there was a written rule about staff dating students, but Ken made it sound like there was. Sitting in the student body section that day was a very pretty, smart, and mature senior girl by the name of Diane Dixon, "Dixie." Her aunt was the head of the Foreign Language Department at the University. Alice, her aunt, had encouraged her to come to ORU after she finished a one year mission trip to Mexico. Diane was finishing her degree in education and planned to teach third or fourth grade. During her senior year at ORU she became a dorm resident counselor and served on the Student Advisory Council. She had a great personality to go along with a great smile. Evidently, when Coach Trickey made that statement in chapel about me being off-limits to co-eds, Dixie wasn't listening or chose to ignore it. The Dean of Students wife, Jo Wallace, began playing cupid and began to arrange for Diane to have dinner with her and Jack, her husband. If I was in town I too would also eat dinner in the school cafeteria with Jo and Jack. Jo was trying to coordinate a "chance" meeting between Diane and me over dinner. Jo was always telling me I really needed to meet this sweet, cute girl name Diane. I knew who she was but for some reason we never made it to dinner at the same time, but Jo kept trying.

One night I was out jogging around campus and just happened to be going by the girls' dormitory when I rounded the corner and practically ran over this girl. It was Dixie. Now, I have heard of getting swept off your feet by someone, but in this case, I literally knocked her off her feet. We talked for a few minutes and I asked her if she would like to go out to get something to eat after our basketball game the next night. She accepted the invitation, but I had failed to mention that I was also going to be taking a recruit out to eat after the game. We were trying to recruit this 6'5" African-American kid from across town. He was going to be at the game, so I would be taking him out to eat after the game and then taking him home. So after the game the three of us went on a date. Dixie did a great job talking up the University and trying to help me sell the recruit on coming to ORU. We didn't get the recruit but I ended up with my best recruit ever. Diane and I started dating and got married six months later. Not every woman is cut out to be a coach's wife; it is a tough and sometimes lonely partnership. Diane was and has been the perfect partner for over 49 years.

All of this happened in late February. I had worked hard, and had long days and nights. I hadn't really taken care of myself like I should have. I begin to get tired easily and couldn't eat. I finally went to the doctor. They ran some tests and discovered that I had mononucleosis. He recommended that I do nothing except rest for a week or so. I stayed in my apartment pretty much isolated for a week since I did not want anyone to catch what I had, especially Diane. I actually didn't even tell her what I had, which was stupid of me. She just knew that I was sick and needed some rest. When I finally started seeing her again, I avoided kissing her for another week, which I admit was a bit strange. Naturally, she did not know what to think. She actually told her friends that she didn't think that I really liked her; she thought the relationship was probably going nowhere. Even to this day, she tells me how strange all of that was. She couldn't believe I kept her in the dark about what was going on with me.

In addition to the Tennessee high school connection, Ken also had a friend that he had grown up with in Illinois named Jimmy Bratton. Bratton was coaching in Fort Lauderdale, Florida. He knew a lot of high school coaches around the Lauderdale area. Coach Trickey always said you recruit through your friends unless you are coaching at Kansas, Kentucky, UCLA, etc. A "normal school" like ORU was never going to out recruit those "blue blood" programs unless you had an edge. But if we were going to try to compete against them and beat them we had to have the same kind of athletes that they had. One of the strangest and best recruiting trips I have ever experienced was a Florida trip we made after my first year at ORU. Bratton had arranged for us to talk to eight or nine outstanding high school prospects in the Lauderdale area. Since we were pretty much an unknown school in that area of the country, Ken thought it would be a good idea (and really impressive) if the whole coaching staff went down there in the school's private 40 passenger prop-jet. Bratton had made arrangements for these high school players, their parents and coaches to meet us at the airport. We were going to take them all up in the plane together so they could see how we traveled, and also get an aerial view of the Miami area. Many of them had never been on an airplane, at least a plane as nice as ours. We accomplished our mission, the Miami-Lauderdale area became a great recruiting hotbed for us. Through the years we signed six or seven players from that area in Florida.

Pres. Roberts had bought this plane to fly the ORU singers and other ORU staff out to California when he was taping for his TV programs. We were flying in our own plane to away games when most other schools, even a lot of the "majors" were flying commercial. The plane was a tremendous asset for us, and definitely made an impression on our recruits.

In 1970 we recruited a smart, solid point guard from a junior college in Kansas, by the name of Eldon Lawyer. Eldon was a 6' 1" point guard who was tough as nails and a great kid. He would be the perfect playing partner for Richard Fuqua. The final piece to the puzzle was another junior college named Sam McCamey "Sudden Sam" from Alabama. He was a 6' 5" small forward who could run the floor and play inside or out. Sam had been recruited by Coach Trickey to play at MTSU. However, when Coach Trickey left MTSU for ORU, Sam decided to go to Martin Junior College in Tennessee. Sam was a fierce competitor and a smart player. He had huge hands, and could score off the dribble or be physical inside with much bigger players. Sam would eventually go on to be drafted by the Boston Celtics. He might have made it in the NBA if it had not been for a heart murmur that sometimes sapped his energy and limited his playing time. With our holdover players like Ingram Montgomery a solid 6′ 6″ center, who averaged 15 points a game, and the new players we were bringing in, we were ready to play and win at the Division I level. The fact that we were not in the NCAA that first year helped us because we could sign as many players as we wanted and stockpile players for the future. Our practices would be more competitive than some of our regular games. Now all that was left for us to do was get the "big boys" to agree to play us. I had learned so much this first year at ORU; it had truly been a memorable and exciting year. But it was about to get even more exciting and memorable.

The 71-72 season was our last in our little 3,000 seat Round House. We would be moving into the beautiful 10,500 seat Mabee Center the next year. In addition to my responsibilities with the varsity, Ken had asked me to coach the freshman team. In those days, freshmen were not eligible to play on the varsity, so we had a 20 game freshman schedule. We played mostly junior colleges, which was quite a challenge for freshmen players. However, my biggest challenge in coaching the freshmen that year would be a 7 foot high school All-American from Nashville by the name of David Vaughn. We had recruited David away from Memphis State, the SEC schools, and pretty much everyone else in the country. David was a future NBA player who had tremendous talent. He was a very likable kid, but very immature with a delicate psyche. One of my biggest problems with coaching David was not really his fault; he simply did not want to play on the freshman team. He knew and we knew, he was good enough to play on the varsity, but we were in the NCAA now and freshmen could not play on the varsity. Our freshmen team was very talented, yet we did not always play like a team. It was a constant struggle to get and keep everyone on the same page.

The 1971-72 year would be a year full of firsts for our program. The Oral Roberts University basketball program that was started in 1966 was now competing at the Division I NCAA level. The basketball program, under the initial guidance of Bill White, had some success before Coach Trickey arrived. Coach Trickey's MTSU team had defeated Coach White's Titan team in 1968 when the Blue Raiders came to Tulsa. MTSU scored over 100 points with Mr. Roberts in attendance. That game and the way MTSU played made quite an impression on him. After that game President Roberts wanted to talk with Coach Trickey. He was so impressed that he decided that he was going to try and hire him. He was totally "taken" by the "run and gun" style of basketball and wanted to bring that kind of excitement to ORU.

Our first year as a Division I school, we played practically every Division I school on their campus. We played Illinois State, Murray State, Butler, Idaho State, Boston University and Harvard on the road. At least they agreed to play us, which was more than I could say for the Oklahoma schools OU, OSU, Oklahoma City and the school across town, Tulsa. In spite of us getting a lot of national attention they continued to ignore us. We would play anyone anywhere. We were trying to meet the NCAA guidelines that required over half of the schedule be against other NCAA schools.

We also had another reason for playing all over the country. Pres. Roberts ministry was global. He had what he called "partners" all over the country. These partners supported the ministry so he wanted them to have an opportunity to see "his" team play. The basketball team was great publicity for the university and the ministry. It certainly helped that we won a lot too. Trying to schedule NCAA, Division I, teams was a never ending and frustrating job. Ken, who was also the Athletic Director, was getting tired of hearing all the excuses of why they would not play us, so he gave Moose the "task" of working on the schedule. Even though we played most of the Division I schools on the road that year, we managed to win 26 of our 28 games our first year in the NCAA. Our success was a credit to the talent of our team, obviously, but the fact that we won a lot of road games could also be attributed to traveling on our own plane. We would fly to the game on the day of the game and come home immediately after the game. That really helped us keep our players from missing a lot of classes and helped to keep the players from getting worn out. Sometimes the away games would require as much as a three-hour flight. It was still better than flying commercial, going in a day early, and staying in a hotel.

One of the trips that stands out in my mind was the game we played at South Dakota State in January. It was so cold that

I remember the pilots stayed with the plane to keep the engines running and the plane warm. They always went to the games with us, but they didn't for this game. Our bench was really close to the student section, and as usual, they were yelling and giving us a hard time. We were always heckled about representing Oral Roberts, the faith healer. Finally, after 10 minutes of their heckling, Ken turned to them and said "we can put you in those wheel chairs as well as take you out!" A nod to some of the things they may have seen Oral Roberts do on television when someone stood and walked away from their wheelchair. The opposing students loved Ken's comment. They laughed and were "somewhat" cordial the rest of the game. We won the game, and some of the students came by to congratulate us. I remember getting off the bus to get back on the plane after the game, and it was so cold I thought my eyes would freeze shut before I could get in that warm airplane.

Back on campus our games were played before standing room only crowds most every night. We had a tremendous home court advantage with our students being so vocal. The students and our other 3,000 fans were right on top of the court. We started the ORU Classic Tournament, in December, with East Carolina, Loyola of California, and University of Connecticut as the first year participants. On the Connecticut coaching staff that year was a young assistant coach by the name of Jimmy Valvano. Valvano would go on to lead North Carolina State to the NCAA championship in 1983. We won that first classic and everyone after that. Coach Trickey, did a great job promoting the tournament. ORU provided upscale hotel rooms, meals for the teams, and a monetary guarantee. We also gave away watches and luggage to the players and coaches. Mr. Roberts number one destination for ORU was to play a game in Madison Square Garden. Fortunately or by divine appointment, Hofstra University in New York had an opening on their schedule for a game in MSG. Moose had been working for months to try and get us a game in the Garden, so when this opportunity came about Moose and Art were off to New York City to seal the deal. This was a dream come true for all of us to be playing in the mecca of arenas. The experience would take on even more importance as we were invited to play in the prestigious, National Invitational Tournament (NIT), back in the Garden at the end of the year. We beat Hofstra and made a very good impression on the New York media. At that time, the NCAA Tournament was only inviting 25 teams which meant some really good teams ended up going to the NIT. We played Memphis State in the first round and beat them by 20 points. We were the talk of the tournament because we had risen to the top of the college basketball world so fast and we played such a fast, exciting brand of basketball. Before our game with Memphis State, many so-called experts didn't think we had a chance against them. What they didn't know, was that our players from Chattanooga Riverside high school had beaten many of the same Memphis State players when they were playing in high school. We went into the game expecting to win. It also didn't hurt that Fuqua scored 40 points and put on quite a show. The New York media loved the way we played; they thought we may be the Cinderella team of the tournament, at least for a few days. Mr. Roberts was also pretty happy, he got to see his name on the marquee at Madison Square Garden. Unfortunately for us the local team and New York City's "darling" college team, St. Johns, was our second round opponent. They were good and really big, which proved to be our Achilles heel. Fuqua had gotten their attention in the game against Memphis, and their defense against him was outstanding. We lost by 10 points but we would take away a valuable lesson. We needed to recruit some bigger players for the future; we needed more muscle and bulk. Playing in New York was so exciting, and a great reward for our players for a great season and for winning 26 games. Coach Trickey let us bring our wives to New York for the tournament, so Diane got to enjoy the tournament and the city too.

We had taken the college basketball world by storm, but our main goal was still ahead. We were focused on getting into the NCAA Tournament and getting a chance to play for a national championship. We would have to wait two more years for that opportunity; we would be back to play in the NIT again in 1973. The NIT and playing in Madison Square Garden was like a fairy tale come true for me. I had grown up a basketball junkie, in love with basketball. I was from a little town in Southern Illinois and had watched games on TV played in Madison Square Garden. In these past few days, I had walked on the court where the NY Knicks and some of the greatest basketball players in the world had played. I even got to shoot a few baskets on that world famous court. I was living a dream come true. It can't get much better than that, can it?

During the season, Ken had added another coach to our staff: Coach Bloomer Sullivan. He was a Hall of Fame coach at Southeastern Oklahoma College. He was brought in to be an adviser to our staff. He was going to come in on different occasions throughout the season to evaluate what we were doing as a staff and work with our front-line players. Coach Sullivan was in his 70s, but his mind was sharp as ever. I have to admit, that our staff was somewhat skeptical at first about having another voice in the locker room. What did we need this "adviser" to do? We soon discovered why he had won so many games at Southeastern. He had a lot of basketball knowledge that would benefit us and the team. I spent a lot of time with Coach Sullivan asking questions and picking his brain about teaching post play. I learned so much from this man and enjoyed being around he and his wife, who always came with him. Our players also grew to respect and love him. The only downside to this relationship with Coach Sullivan was he was terrible at keeping up with his expenses. Ken told him we would reimburse him for his expenses and give him a stipend. I got the tedious chore of straightening out all his receipts, even the ones that were for two or three bucks, and making sure he got paid.

I hated to see this season come to an end; it had been so exciting and so rewarding. We had experienced many first, like playing in the NIT. We had played basketball games from California to New York. We had made an impact on the college basketball community. I hated the season to end for another reason, too. We graduated two of the best players that had ever played at ORU: Eldon Lawyer and Sam McCamey. These two players had played a major role in getting us to this point. They had come to ORU not really knowing what to expect but willing to try and help us put ORU basketball on the map. They believed in Coach Trickey and in what we were trying to do. I have to confess that at the basketball banquet I had to wipe away a few tears. Pres. Roberts, obviously a great public speaker, gave one of the most inspiring speeches I had ever heard as he talked about Sam McCamey. Sam had grown up in Alabama, the son of sharecroppers, the first in his family to go beyond elementary school. What he had been able to accomplish was truly remarkable. Pres. Roberts spoke for about 30 minutes, without notes, incorporating some of his childhood experiences, as a poor dirt farmer, who had a stammer as a child. Like Mr. Roberts, Sam had truly overcome some overwhelming obstacles. Sam was a joy to coach. He had such class and humility. McCamey received the President's Award for being the most outstanding student-athlete at ORU that year. Eldon had come to us from a small Kansas high school via Butler County Community College in El Dorado, Kansas. Ironically, I would coach there five years later. Eldon had been a "perfect match" as a playing partner with Richard Fuqua. He was our point guard and ran the offense. We as coaches, as well as Richard, would miss him the next year. Sam and Eldon reminded us all of what coaching was truly about, not W's and L's, but helping young men grow and reach their potential. They both were so competitive and a joy to coach.

Diane and I got married on Saturday, October 1st of 1971, only 15 days before basketball practice officially started. Needless to say, our honeymoon was rather short; actually it was an overnight stay in the local Hilton Hotel in the honeymoon suite. We had a small wedding in a big church. We were attending Boston Avenue Methodist Church and got married there. We had several out-of-town guests and most of the guests were leaving on Sunday. We wanted to spend some time with them so we arranged a big dinner for all of our visiting guest at the Hilton on Saturday night. The associate pastor for the Oral Roberts Ministry, Bob DeWeese, performed the ceremony. Rev. DeWeese was a friend of mine and a big basketball fan. It was a great, but very short weekend. On Monday, Diane was back to teaching fourth-graders and I was back to planning for the up-coming season. Did I tell you what a great coach's wife Diane was? She totally understood what being a college coach's wife meant. October 1st brought a reinvigorated focus on basketball as a new season was just around the corner.

Diane and me on our wedding day, October 1, 1971 in Tulsa, OK.

I would make it up to her after the basketball season was over. We would take a four week honeymoon trip that included driving back to see her family in Ogden, Utah. From Utah we went to Lake Tahoe, then to San Francisco, and down the scenic Pacific Coast Highway to Los Angeles. We spent a few days with my cousin in Santa Barbara and a trip to Disneyland in Anaheim. From LA we drove across the desert to Las Vegas ignoring sound advice to not drive through the desert in the daytime because your car might overheat, which is exactly what happened to us. We made it to Vegas and spent a couple of days there before heading to Phoenix where my older sister Judy lived. We were having a great time! It was a really great honeymoon until we got a phone call from my dad that my mom was very ill and had been taken to the hospital.

Circa 1970 mom and dad at Christmas. Mom liked her fake tree with the colored light that shined on it and caused it to change colors. We got the black and white TV when I was about 10 in 1954.

My mom, a beautiful, godly woman had been fighting can-cer off and on for several years. She had just retired at the age of 62 and was looking forward to not having to spend 9 or 10 hour days in the store. My sister, her daughter Lisa, Diane and I loaded up the car immediately and started for Illinois. Nor-mally the drive from Phoenix to Southern Illinois would take 2 to 3 days, we drove it straight through in about 24 hours. I had a new car that was pretty fast. The closer to home I got the faster I drove. We were just out of St. Louis and still 100 miles from home when this feeling came over me that I was not going to see my mom alive again. We got to Galatia mid- morning but mom had died that night in the hospital.

Mom had been the choir leader at Galatia Baptist Church for many years, now she would be in the choir in Heaven singing face-to-face for Jesus. I had not seen my mom since our wedding that first weekend in Oct. I brought Diane home to meet my parents before we got married. Diane always said, what a blessing it was that she got to spend a week with her. What a sad way to end a honeymoon. Diane and I stayed with my dad and my two sisters for a few days after the funeral. I had been away for eight years and had not seen much of my family or friends since high school. Staying those few extra days was bitter-sweet.

But by now it was the end of July and time for me to get back to ORU and back to work. Diane would be starting her second year of teaching and was ready to get back to school. When you are a college basketball coach you look at the years differently and the calendar differently. As a college coach, the year begins with the basketball season and in those days, we started official basketball practice October 15, and by August we are beginning to gear up for a new season. I was always excited with anticipation and eager to get another season started. I would get so caught up in the activities surrounding basketball and the preparation for the new season that the days would often run together. Even after Diane and I were married the basketball secretary would have to remind me to pick up my check. I never coached for a payday. I was still only 28 years old and living the dream of being able to coach in college.

Pres. Roberts had given the basketball program everything that we needed to be successful. The new year (1971-72) was going to bring new challenges and new excitement. We were moving into our new arena. We had recruited what we thought would be the players to take us to the next level, the NCAA Tournament. We recruited some great high school players like Al Boswell, from River Rouge, MI; Vincent Banks from Miami, FL; John Patterson from Hollywood, FL; and a junior college All-American from New York by way of Seminole Junior College in Oklahoma, Greg McDougald. We remembered the experience from the year before playing against St. John's in the NIT and getting pushed around and needing more size on our front line. Greg was a left handed, 6' 8", 230lb power forward, who was one of the most recruited junior colleges in the country. His previous year's success and playing in the NIT definitely helped with our name recognition throughout the country.

Detroit would become another great area for us to recruit. I had lived and worked in the Detroit area for four years prior to coming to ORU and had developed a friendship with several high school coaches in the area. One of those coaches was a great coach by the name of Lofton Greene. Coach Greene

coached at River Rouge for over 40 years and was the win-
ningest high school coach in the history of high school basketball in the state of Michigan. He was named to the Michigan
Hall Of Fame. Greene had sent players to Michigan State,
Michigan and several Division I programs. He ran a disciplined and solid high school program. On his 1970-71 team,
was a 6' 4" forward/center, Al Boswell, who was All State, but
because of his academics and his "tweener" size, Div 1 schools
were reluctant to recruit him. He was not big enough to play
forward and not a good enough ball handler to play guard. Al
was very athletic, a fierce competitor, with exceptional basketball instincts. I thought he could be a great two guard at the
Div 1 level. He had also played for an exceptional coach who
stressed sound fundamentals and a tough man-to-man defense. I wanted him at ORU and Coach Greene wanted me to
get him out of the Detroit area and into a good environment.
Boswell came to ORU knowing he was going to have to red-
shirt (meaning sit out a year) to work on his grades and improve his out side game. That year really turned out to be a
great blessing for him. His second year of eligibility he would
team up with a point guard we would recruit from Pensacola,
Fl. Named Sam McCants. McCants and Boswell would be one
of the best guard tandems in college basketball in the 1974-75
season. But I'm getting ahead of myself; we still had this season
to get through. Our recruiting was going great, with our name
recognition around college basketball, it was getting easier to
attract great talent. Pres. Roberts continued to be involved in

the recruiting; he was genuinely interested in what we were doing. Many times he would come to the basketball offices during the day, pull up a chair in front of our desk, throw his feet up on our desk and start asking questions, usually about recruits. He knew most of them by name and would want to know how we were doing, and if they were going to sign with us? He realized the basketball team was opening doors for his ministry and getting the university name out around the country in a positive way.

ORU basketball had skyrocketed from being an obscure little "Bible" college in the mid-to late 60s to a top 20 program in the NCAA by the early 70s. We were going into the 1972-73 season ranked #4 in the country by Sports Illustrated behind only UCLA, Florida State and Maryland. SI said in that publication "after finishing 28-2 last year the young Davids are ready to venture forth to play the Goliaths of college basketball." This was going to be Fuqua's last year, he averaged 35 points a game and finished the season as the second best scorer in the country, as a junior. We had added David Vaughn and Greg McDougald to our front-line, we thought we could match up with anyone. With Vaughn taking over the center position, we moved Eddie Woods at 6' 6" to forward. Our front line of 7' Vaughn, 6'8" McDougald, and Woods made a pretty impressive front line. We planned to move Larry Baker 6' 4" to guard to play with Fuqua, even by today's standards that would be a huge team. Vaughn was the most highly recruited player in our program, our fans and the coaching staff were anxious to see him play. Most everyone had thought that David was going to go to Memphis State because it was close to Nashville and he was dating Larry Finch's sister. Finch was the star guard on the Memphis State team. David would eventually marry Finch's sister. We got them both to come to ORU. Art got to know David really well, and practically lived in Nashville Vaughn's senior year. The entire staff was in Nashville on signing day, the signing was a big deal with the local media. But the "secret weapon" we used to recruit David was Mr. Roberts himself. David's dad was a Baptist preacher and a big fan of Mr. Roberts. Mr. Roberts had agreed to go speak at David's father's church in Nashville. It was a little country church that probably averaged less than 50 people at their Sunday services. But when Mr. Roberts came to preach there were over a thousand there, including our whole staff. Naturally, we "had" to take up an offering, it wouldn't be a true Baptist Church service without an offering. Mr. and Mrs. Vaughn liked the idea of David going to a Christian school that required students to go to chapel twice a week, and had strict student guidelines. Recruiting Vaughn was quite a coup for our program. David was a good kid, very personable but also very moody and very immature. Like many highly recruited high school athletes, he was spoiled from all the attention and notoriety that he had received. David was a can't miss future NBA player. We had to blend three new starters into that 72-73 team, in addition, we changed two other player's positions. On paper, we looked every bit as good as Sports Illustrated had predicted we would be, but you don't win games on paper, you win on the court. We opened the season in front of over 8000 fans, the largest crowd to ever see a basketball game in Tulsa, with a win over the University of Wisconsin. To play a Big Ten school in the dedication game of Mabee Center in front of that many fans spoke volumes about how far our program had come. Coach Roe had worked diligently for two years on our schedule; he had heard every excuse in the book, for why some of the DI schools could not come to Tulsa and play us. Getting a school like the University of Wisconsin to dedicate our new arena was not easy. It was not a particularly well played game on our part. We actually were behind much of the game. Fuqua had an off night, and McDougald didn't play well but Vaughn played well down the stretch, and that proved to be just enough for us to pull out a win. Woods did not feel comfortable in his new position at forward and Baker had a tough time playing guard. Little did we know at that time that this first game of the 72-73 season would be a harbinger of things to come. The chemistry that we pretty much had taken for granted with the previous two teams was sorely missing with this team. However, we won our first six games before playing Long Beach State in the finals of the Nassau Classic in New York. Long Beach State was coached by Jerry Tarkanian. They were very talented and very big, led by an All-American guard and future NBA player, Ed Ratleff. In spite of our size, we still got manhandled by their big front line. So we still were not big enough and strong enough up front to beat the "big boys." Tarkanian was an excellent coach who would go on to win the National Championship with UNLV.

Even though the season was only two weeks old we had already played games in Nevada, California and New York. Now we were going back home to play in our new "palace" in front of what was a growing fan base. We won the ORU Classic beating St. Mary's of California and Eastern Kentucky. We continued to win but every night seemed to be a struggle and honestly, no one was having a lot of fun. Woods was still struggling at forward and we began to look at other guards to play with Fuqua. Fuqua's scoring average was down 10 points from the previous year. He was having a hard time getting McDougald and Vaughn to accept their roles and play as hard as he did. Vaughn was so unpredictable: sometimes really good and sometimes not very good. He also had some issues off of the court like missing classes and struggling with his marriage. At one point, Coach Trickey had to suspend him to try and get his attention. David would apologize, work hard, go to class, but after a few days we would be back in the same place again with him. There seemed to always be some kind of drama going on with the team.

We continued to win even in tough places to play like Marshall and Rhode Island. The Marshall game in Huntington, West Virginia left an indelible memory with me. Our game at Marshall was in early January on a cold, foggy, snowy night. We were making our typical game day trip, flying in to play the game on the same day. Mr. Roberts had two excellent pilots who flew the four engine prop jet for him; we knew we were in good hands. Huntington Airport is on or near the side of a mountain, not an easy place to fly into even in good weather conditions, and this was not a good weather day. As we approached the runway to land the pilots didn't like the speed or something, so they decided to pull up and make another pass. I can tell you there was some extra praying happening on that plane. Mr. Roberts was not with us on this trip, but we were all wishing that he would've been. We could have used the extra help. I have flown many times to a lot of places here and overseas, but that was the most "concerned" I have ever been. Fortunately, the players were not as concerned as I was because they played well enough to win the game. Marshall will always be a team that I remember for another reason. We played them again in Tulsa two weeks later. When they came back to Mabee Center to play us we had a 52 straight home game winning streak that stretched back several years to our days in the Round House. We had beaten them at their place in spite of that scary landing at the airport. In the early going of our game, in Mabee, we were ahead by 20 points and playing well. In the second half with 10 minutes to go in the game we were up by 25 and coasting. I was sitting in my usual spot on the bench beside Coach Trickey. I leaned over to him and suggested that we start substituting. We could look at some different combinations, and maybe discover something off the bench that would make us better. We still had several question marks about our team and I thought maybe this would be an ideal time to try some new combinations. He was reluctant because there still was a lot of time left in the game. Ken liked to play as many players as he could, and reward them for their hard work in practice. So with my encouragement, he began to sub out the starters, after about five minutes that 25 point lead had shrunk to about 15. We did have good players on the bench, but this particular night, they were not very good. So this "sure" win for us to extend our home winning streak, began to look shaky. Before he began putting the starters back in, the lead was less than 10 points and momentum had changed teams. The starters were cold now and not able to regain the momentum. Marshall tied the score in regulation and we lost in overtime. That is how our 52 straight home game winning streak came to an end! I would never suggest anything like that to Ken again during a game. Coach Trickey loved to tell that story, how the win streak ended and how it was my fault. He didn't really blame me, I don't think.

As the season "wore on" we continued to win, but things on the team, especially with Vaughn, never really got much better. There was always something with David and more than once we, as a staff, had second thoughts about recruiting him. Woods was not happy playing forward and Fuqua was frustrated. But with talent like Vaughn, you just hope that he matures and you can get over the hump. He never did, even after he left us and signed to play in the American Basketball League. There were still some highlights of the season, like playing in a doubleheader against Northern Illinois in the Chicago Stadium, where the Bulls played. Mr. Roberts had gotten his name on the marquee in New York, now it was Chicago. We were not the "feature" game, which was Loyola vs. Dayton. We were the "preliminary" game. Although, there were actually more people that came to see us than to see the "old established" schools. We lost to Northern Illinois by four or five points and again did not play very well. After this game, we only had one more game away from Mabee Center, at Rhode Island in the Providence Civic Center. Rhode Island was good and Providence Center was a tough place for a visiting team. We played extremely well that night in front of a crowd of over 12,000 and won our 15th or 16th game of the season. We finished the season with the last five games at home. Another 20 game win season was pretty much a certainty, our fourth in a row. There were still two big games left on our schedule against Illinois State University (ISU) and Southwestern Louisiana. We had played ISU every season since the 1970-71 season. ISU had one of the best scorers in the country, a young man I had known from my days back in Galatia, Il. Doug Collins was an All-American, an Olympian and an All-Pro in the NBA with the Philadelphia Sixers. Doug was a 6' 1" guard, who played at Benton High School, the same high school that my college roommate at MTSU, Tom Whittington, played at. Doug only had a few Division I schools recruit him out of high school, but he grew 5 inches in college and became a great college player. He played for the first African-American coach of a Division I program, Wil Robinson. Coach Robinson was a great high school coach from Detroit. He and I would butt heads over several high school recruits from that area. He won most of the time, but I got one of his former recruits after he went to ISU and became disenchanted with his playing time. Duane Fox, was a 6' 6" jumping jack, who would be one of our starters on the 73-74 team that got to the NCAA Tournament Elite 8. ISU had never beaten us and in spite of Collins 40 points (Fuqua had 35) we beat Illinois State for the third straight year.

Our next to last regular season game was against Southwestern Louisiana of Lafayette (the Cajuns). They had a great basketball team, and had started the season ranked #6 in the country. We had played them in Lafayette the year before and lost 124-115 in what was one of the best and most exciting games I have ever seen. Haywood Hill lead our team in scoring with 41 points, but Bo Lamar scored 47 for the Cajuns. Lamar led the country in scoring the year before, averaging 35 a game. The return game in Mabee was televised on NBC; it was promoted as the game of the week. The fact that a major network was going to televise the game was a pretty good indication of how far our program had come in three years. In those days, before cable, the only college games on TV were games in the Big Ten, ACC, SEC, etc. Mabee Center was standing room only, the atmosphere was electric. The game was as good as advertised, great players and a lot of scoring. Fuqua and Lamar lived up to their All-American billing, Fuqua scored 35 points and

Lamar scored 39. We lost 89-104 but it was a closely played game with two outstanding teams. No one asked for their money back and NBC loved it. We finished the season 21-6 and were invited back to the NIT. Unlike the previous year, our trip to New York would be short. We were disappointed we did not get invited to the NCAA Tournament but there were only 25 teams invited and the teams that won their conferences made up the majority of the participants. Our first opponent in the NIT was North Carolina, coached by a legend in college basketball, Dean Smith. They defended us really well; our guards had a tough time getting us into our offense. We lost by 17 points, and were never in the game. We had more talent than we had ever had but the chemistry just was not there. As a staff, it was frustrating; we could not put all the pieces together. By most anyone's standards, we had a great season. We had won 20 games and gone to the NIT. We had led the nation in scoring, averaging 97 points a game. But we had raised the bar so high at ORU that it felt like we had let our team, our fans and ourselves down. We were just one year removed from a blockbuster year, and things would be different in 73-74. We were losing the best player to ever play at ORU, Richard Fuqua, and the most publicized recruit we had ever signed in David Vaughn, but we were going to have an opportunity to play for a national championship.

I have to admit that I was glad when the season was over. It had been a roller coaster ride and I was ready to get off. Diane and I had been married two years and were very happy in our cozy little one-bedroom apartment. A funny thing about that apartment, it was a really nice, new apartment complex, but it was built behind a seven-eleven store. Several times when Ken was talking about me, at a civic club luncheon, he would mention that I lived behind a seven-eleven. We took a few days off but the players that were returning were back in the gym a few days after our loss to NC. The staff was working on our recruiting and getting ready for our basketball camp. Our summer basketball camp had grown from 50 or 60 campers to somewhere over 200 each week. Coach Trickey had put me in charge of organizing the camp, which meant getting the dorm rooms for the campers, getting camp brochures out, planning the court activities for the campers, and getting high school coaches to come in and help us coach. The camps were a lot of fun but a lot of work.

Our number one recruit for the year was another player from Chattanooga Riverside, Anthony Roberts. Roberts was one of the best players in the state of Tennessee, and was recruited by a lot of Division I schools. "Woosie," as he was called by his teammates, would be the best sixth man in college basketball, his freshman year. Anthony would go on to break a lot of Fuqua's scoring records and become the schools second All-American. Anthony was drafted by the Nuggets in the NBA and played there for several years. We also signed a 6'9" center, Willis Collins, from the Miami area. Another signee was Duane Fox, a young man from the Detroit area that I had tried to recruit out of Inkster, MI high school but had signed at Illinois

State and Coach Robinson. Duane called me when he decided to leave Illinois State to see if we were still interested, we were. Duane had sat out the 72-73 season as required by the NCAA transfer rules but would end up being a three-year starter at ORU. Our fourth recruit and perhaps the most important was a point guard, out of Pensacola, Florida by the name of Sam McCants. McCants was Mr. Basketball in the state of Florida his senior year and had averaged over 30 points a game. He scored 60 points in a state tournament game, a game Coach Trickey attended. He was going to be our "quarterback" and the leader on the team that would get to the Elite 8 in the NCAA Tournament. Sam was a left-handed guard, who reminded me of Walt Hazzard, of UCLA fame. Sam would be the perfect partner for our returning guard Al Boswell. We "convinced" a skinny' 6' 7" outstanding high school player from Cleveland, Tennessee to come to ORU, Alvin Scott. Alvin, was Terry Scott's younger brother, Terry was a graduate assistant on our staff. The following year he took over Coach Polk's position on our staff after Art decided to go to Columbia University in New York to get his MBA. Even though Alvin was highly recruited out of high school, Terry had pretty much "guaranteed" us that he could "deliver" his brother. Alvin, would go on to have a great career at ORU and be drafted by the Phoenix Suns in the NBA. We had three starters coming back from the 72-73 team, and were adding two great players. Our bench was about to get a whole lot better, especially our front line. Looking back now on all the expectations for that 72-

73 team, the predictions by Sports Illustrated and others, was just a year premature. The 73-74 team would end up being the best team Oral Roberts University had ever had. Not only were our players talented but they had all come from successful high school programs that had won a lot of games. They had a special ere about them that bordered on cocky, led by McCants and Boswell.

Several years later, I ran into Collins, the Illinois State All-American, at the Final Four, he still was lamenting about them never beating us. He recalled our game with them at their place in 1971 when Lawyer hit a shot at the buzzer and beat them by one point. He said everyone in the building that night "knew" that Fuqua was going to take that last shot. They left Lawyer open and covered Fuqua with two guys, Lawyer hit a 20 foot jumper at the buzzer and broke their heart. In that 70-71 season Fuqua would finish second in the nation in scoring, averaging 32 points a game, Collins finished third with a 31 ave. It seems like every game with Illinois State came down to the wire, they were a fun team to play.

It is hard to even know where to start when talking about the impact that Richard Fuqua had on the Oral Roberts University basketball program. I count it a privilege and a blessing to have been around him for three years. He was equally great off the court as on the court. He was humble, a fierce competitor, and hated to lose at anything and he rarely did. He was great around kids who idolized him, and equally as cordial around so many adoring fans. He, more than anyone else, put ORU on the college basketball map. He was the first player that Coach Sims, at Riverside High School, had sent to ORU. Richard, was one of the main reasons, Mr. Roberts built Mabee Center so more fans could see us play. He would've been a great NBA player if he had had two healthy knees. In spite of playing with pain, Fuqua always gave 100%. He was a phenomenal shooter with unlimited range. There was never a moment to big for Richard Fuqua. My favorite personal story about Richard is how I taught him to drive a car. He was 20 years old and a junior at ORU but did not know how to drive; he had never been interested in cars or driving. He decided he wanted to drive, so in the parking lot of the basketball arena, he was most responsible for being built, he learned to drive. I had a few tense moments in the car with Richard, we had a few laughs. In spite of his excellent teacher, he couldn't drive as good as he could play basketball.

Being a coach in college is a wonderful blessing that few get to enjoy; I was still only 29 and living a dream. I was fortunate enough to get to enjoy several benefits of being a coach at that level. One of those benefits happened during the 72-73 season in Los Angeles when Ken and I were out there recruiting. The Super Bowl between the Dolphins and the Redskins was going to be played in the LA Coliseum during the week we were there. We decided, at the last minute, that it would be fun and a great experience to go to the game. We actually bought tickets at the ticket window on the day of the game.

This was only the fourth Super Bowl to ever be played so obviously it had not caught on like today. I think we paid $20 a ticket to set in the upper deck. Things are just a little different today. We left at the end of the third quarter to get to the airport to catch our flight back to Tulsa.

The greatest experience for me that week we were in Los Angeles was not going to the Super Bowl but getting a chance to meet my coaching idol, John Wooden of UCLA. President Roberts had a quarterly television program on a major network. He would always have a special celebrity guest on each one of the specials. On one of those programs, Coach Wooden came on and shared his faith, and talked with Mr. Roberts about some of his experiences. It was during the taping of this program that Mr. Roberts asked Coach Wooden if Coach Trickey and I could come to one of his practices. Coach Wooden generally did not allow visitors to his practices, but because of his friendship with Pres. Roberts he agreed to the request. He was very cordial and spent about 30 minutes with us after practice. I had never seen a practice quite like his; he would sit in a chair on the side of the court while the assistants conducted the practice. He did not have a whistle but when he stood up and began to speak everyone stopped immediately, you could hear a pin drop in the place. My only regret was that I didn't get Coach Wooden to autograph his famous Pyramid of Success lithograph for me. Several years later I would get an autographed lithograph from a former player, Sam McCamey, who had gotten

Coach Wooden to sign one for him. I still cherish that autograph to this day, he was the greatest.

Another fringe benefit to being on the coaching staff at ORU was getting "dibs" on tickets to special events in Mabee Center. The first year Mabee opened, they were fortunate to get my all-time favorite entertainer, Elvis Presley, to do a concert in the arena. I had some "connections" that I used to get Diane and I tickets on the fifth row, right in front of the stage. Elvis was the only person to get more people into the Mabee Arena than us.

We had stockpiled talent, we knew we were going to need to step our game up; we were not going to sneak up on anyone anymore. We may have been in the NCAA only three years, but everyone in college basketball knew about our program. This 1973-74 team had five legitimate NBA prospects. Our starting lineup of Woods, McDougald, Fox, Boswell and McCants was really good offensively but maybe even better defensively. McCants and Boswell would average 40 points a game, McDougald was capable of 20 on any given night, Fox was a solid defender and rebounder and Woods was as good as any 6' 6" inside player in the country. We had 6' 4" Roberts and 6' 8" Collins coming off the bench. We started off the season winning seven of our first eight games, losing only to a very good and highly ranked Jacksonville team on their home floor. We were playing the best schedule we had ever played, schools like San Diego State, Houston, Southern Cal, Virginia Tech, Long Beach State and, finally, cross-town rival Tulsa.

We no longer had to play all of the so called "big boys" on the road, which meant we were getting crowds of over 7000 in Mabee Center most every game. We were averaging more fans at our home games than any Oklahoma school, including OU and OSU. One of our fans who attended several of our games was the governor of the state. That should not be so surprising since most politicians like to be where the crowds are. No matter how hard he tried, Coach Roe, or even the governor could not get OU or OSU to play us. Our biggest test would come on December 29 when we played #14 Southern Cal at home. USC was led by All-American and future NBA star guard, Gus Williams. USC would go on to win 24 games that season and finished second in the PAC 8 behind #1 UCLA. We lost by eight to USC, but that game was a great barometer on what we needed to do to compete at the top level. Our next big test was a couple weeks later when we went to Blacksburg, Virginia to play Virginia Tech. Virginia Tech had surprised everyone the year before by beating Notre Dame in the finals of the NIT. Blacksburg was a tough place to play, their Coliseum would seat 10,000 and it felt like they were all sitting right on top of you. We would get the typical "cat calls" from students such as: "Why do you need a trainer?" don't expect any miracles tonight!" It was a tough defensive game, but we won on a last second shot. I guess you could say there was a miracle for us that night.

We would go back home and score over 100 points in seven of our next eight games and pretty much coast to our

13th win of the season. We still had eight games remaining on our schedule, so another 20 win season was a good possibility. Our next game was back out to California to play Long Beach State for the second straight year at their place. Long Beach was ranked #10 and had two future NBA players. They were big, talented and almost unbeatable in the Long Beach Arena. They were coached by Lute Olsen, a future Hall of Fame coach. Coach Olson would win an NCAA championship as the coach of the Arizona Wildcats. Our paths would cross again a few years later when he became the coach at Iowa and I went to Iowa State as an assistant. The game was like a heavyweight fight and was decided in the last couple minutes when they pulled away and beat us 98-89. They finished their season 24-2, won their conference, and would get invited to the NCAA Tournament. Five of our last seven games were at home in Mabee. One of our "away" games was across town against Tulsa University. Tulsa, like all of the other Oklahoma schools, had refused to play us until the media and the fans put so much pressure on them. They soon could no longer dodge us. The game had been promoted and "talked up" for pretty much the entire season. They had a good team (17-8) and had finished third in the very tough Missouri Valley Conference. They had their own All-American candidate and big scorer, Willie Biles, who was averaging 27 points a game. He was 6' 3" and not bashful about shooting the basketball. He proved to be a good test for Boswell. The Expo Pavilion, where Tulsa played, would seat a little over 7000 and it was completely sold out for this game. The game was back and forth with neither team leading by more than 4 or 5 points. It was a tremendous basketball atmosphere. Woods got into foul trouble down the stretch, and fouled out with about four or five minutes left in the game. Tulsa took advantage of our loss of Woods, out rebounding us down the stretch and scoring a couple baskets inside. They beat us 85-84. We finished the regular season 21-5, good enough considering our schedule, to get an invitation to play in the NCAA Tournament. Tulsa was good enough to be invited to play in the NIT.

It had been a great season for our team and very rewarding for us coaches. The chemistry on the team had been great, the players really liked each other, and they were enjoyable to coach. We averaged over 90 points a game, led by McCants, Boswell and McDougald but all of the starters averaged double figures. Anthony came off the bench and gave us great minutes; he was like having a sixth starter. And as I had said all along, our guards were the best tandem in college basketball. In those days, ORU was not in a conference, we were one of about ten independents. That meant that the NCAA selection committee did not pick any teams for the postseason tournament until all of the conferences had determined their representative. At that time conferences could only send one team to the tournament, which left a few spots for the independents. The tournament field had only 30 teams, so getting in was a really big deal. We did not want to go back to the NIT a third straight year. We wanted a chance to play for a national championship. We felt like we were good enough to make a deep run in the tournament and our players, coaches and fans were excited to get that chance. It didn't matter to any of us that this was only our fourth year as a Division I NCAA program, we felt like we had done our part and now we were truly "expecting a miracle." That miracle came, the selection committee extended the invitation and placed us in a first round game against another independent, Syracuse.

Syracuse, a great basketball school, had won their last five games and finished 19-7. We played them in Denton, Texas on the campus of North Texas State University. Coach Roe had coached at North Texas for four years before coming to ORU, Moose was going home. We didn't know much about Syracuse, I don't think anyone on our staff had even seen them play, but with no disrespect to them, we were so happy to be in the tournament that we didn't care who we played. We were going into the tournament with the idea that with a break along the way we could get to the Final Four. That had always been our goal from the very beginning. We were not "star struck" or overwhelmed with just getting into the tournament. Syracuse was led by a very talented guard by the name of DuVal. They were not real big upfront, so we matched up really well with them. We didn't need any additional motivation to beat Syracuse but we were fully aware that if we beat Syracuse, we were going to get to go back home to Mabee Center to play in the Midwest Regional. The NCAA had opened up the possibility of us getting to the Final Four by playing on our own campus. This would be the last year the NCAA would schedule a Regional in an arena as small as ours. From this year forward, all of the Regionals would be played in arenas that would seat over 18,000 and not on the campus of a participating school. There would never be a chance again that a school could have a "home game" in the tournament. Led by McCants and Boswell's 42 points we beat Syracuse 86-82 in overtime.

The game in Texas was on a Saturday afternoon, our next game against Louisville, who had won the Missouri Valley Conference, would come way too fast on the following Thursday. We began preparing for the Louisville game on Sunday; ironically, I had seen Louisville play when they came to Tulsa in January. The four days between the games was like a blur, there was so much going on with the media and the excitement of our fans, I barely remember it. Louisville was ranked 16th in the country and finished the season 21-7. Their top player was Junior Bridgeman, who averaged over 16 points a game and was drafted in the NBA. The most interesting thing about the Cardinals was they played fast and they had great leapers just like us. I had thought when I saw them in January that they were a mirror image of us. I also thought it would be ironic if they won the Missouri Valley Conference, and we played them in the tournament. Needless to say, with us in the tournament along with Louisville, Kansas and Creighton, the city and our fans were going "bonkers!" NBC was back in town to televise all the games, in those days the Regionals were set up like a four team tournament. Our players, however, remained characteristically focused; this moment was not too big for them. With a completely sold out Mabee Center of over 15,700 fans, including standing room, our game followed the overtime Kansas win over Creighton. Creighton, was coached by hometown son, Eddie Sutton. Sutton had started his coaching career after playing at OSU for Henry Iba, as the coach at Tulsa Central High School. What a great atmosphere for basketball with the fans, bands, and a lot of media. The first half was back and forth with the score 51-51 at halftime, I don't think either team was ever ahead by more than five points. Led by 30 points from McCants and 23 points by Boswell we won 96-93. It was one of the most exciting and best college basketball games I have ever seen, and I got to sit in the front row! Anthony Roberts came off the bench to score 14 points and get 14 rebounds. Only the freshman "Woosie", had done that all year long for us. A prelude to what he was going to do before his career was over at ORU.

It had been an exciting and exhausting five days since our game against Syracuse. I was very happy but drained. The biggest prize was still two days ahead when we would play Kansas for the chance to go to the Final Four. I got back to the apartment late after the game. I had turned down an invitation by Coach Trickey and some friends to go out to eat and celebrate. I wish they had not gone out either. About 2 o'clock in the morning I got a phone call from Ken telling me he had been arrested for driving under the influence (DUI). He had been stopped by Oklahoma highway patrol officer after pulling out of the parking lot of a club. I couldn't believe what I was hearing, it made no sense for several reasons: 1)Ken was not a drinker, I had never seen him intoxicated in the four years I was with him. 2) Why was his car singled out and stopped when there were several others leaving the club at the same time? 3) Why wouldn't the patrol officer after realizing who he was and what had happened that night in the tournament, allow him to get a non-drinking person to drive him home or even allow him to follow him home. We would later find out, at the court hearing, that Ken's breathalyzer test showed he was barely over the limit. To this day, there are many unanswered questions about that weird night. So with a very large contingent of media in town for the tournament, the big news on that Friday was not our win over Louisville or our upcoming game Saturday against Kansas, but on what happened after the game on Thursday night. There was talk of Coach Trickey stepping down and volunteering not to coach Saturday. For a few hours on Friday it looked like I would be coaching the team on Saturday, no pressure there. However, by Saturday morning, Pres. Roberts had decided it was Ken's team and he deserved a second chance. It was the right decision for all of us, especially for the players. One thing that also got lost in all of the rhetoric was that Coach Trickey had notified Pres. Roberts that he would be leaving ORU at the end of the season.

Mr. Roberts never considered firing Ken, he actually tried to talk him into not resigning and coming back another year. Our game on Saturday with Kansas was one of only four games that were played that day, the winners of those four games would be playing for a national championship. The "little ole" Christian school on the South side of Tulsa, in the fifth season as a Division I school, was one of them.

The Mabee Center was standing room only and a national television audience would guarantee we were going to play in front of our biggest audience yet. We started the game cold as ice and got behind 15 or 16 points in the first 10 minutes. Maybe the distractions of the previous day were on the players mind, but things begin to turn around just before halftime. I remember coach Trickey kept telling the players we were all right and there was a long way to go in the game. He was right, we really started playing well when we put Roberts in and by halftime, Kansas lead was only one (45-44). The second half was back and forth until we ran off several baskets in a row and took a seven point lead with about four minutes to play. McCants and Boswell were not having a particularly good shooting night but would still end up scoring 42 points, their average. Then Woods fouled out with about 5 minutes to go in regulation, and that really affected how we played down the stretch and in overtime. With about four minutes left in the game, Boswell took an ill advised long jumper. McDougall was called for a walking violation, which was a bad call, on a sure layup pass from Boswell. The basket by

McDougall would have put us up by five points with about a minute to play. After a made basket by Kansas, McDougald took the ball out against the Kansas press and threw the ball against the edge of the backboard for a turnover. We had established a program based on the philosophy of, run and gun, we were always on the offensive, but in this game that would prove to be our undoing. Kansas would tie the game in regulation and outscore us 11 to 8 in overtime and beat us 93-90. One of Kansas's guards hit all four of the shots he took in overtime. Some in the media, and even some of our fans, thought we had blown the game and that we had given it away. They forgot we were down by 15 points in the first half and had come back. They also forgot that in five years playing this style, we had won 118 out of 141 games. An average of winning 23 games a season and scoring over 90 points a game. That adds up to some great basketball, great success and exciting times. We were all very disappointed that we had lost and our dream of getting to the Final Four would have to wait for another year, which unfortunately would never come for any of us. But there are college basketball programs that have been around for over 100 years and never came as close as we did. McCants would be voted the MVP of the Regional Tournament and Boswell would make the All-Tournament team.. They were the best guards on the floor, in both games. Fox and Collins would be coming back along with our sensational freshman Anthony Roberts. Roberts had scored 26 points and grabbed 20 rebounds in two of the biggest games of the year. Also on that team, little used Alvin Scott, would go on to stardom at ORU. We were certainly not leaving the cupboard empty. The future of Oral Roberts University basketball was bright.

The ORU basketball program had skyrocketed to the top of the NCAA basketball world. We had stockpiled enough talent to stay there for the foreseeable future. Pres. Roberts could not change Coach Trickey's mind about leaving so the search was on for a coach to keep this program on the right track. There would be a lot of coaches interested in the ORU job because of what we had done and the talent that was still here. They say there is only one happy team at the end of the season, the one who wins the last game. However, that was not the case for me, I was so proud of what we had accomplished, and I was determined not to play the "what if" game. What if we had beaten Kansas? What if we had gone to the Final Four? I looked at the whole experience of the '73-74 season as being a positive learning experience for our program and for me as a coach. I really thought that we could repeat what we had accomplished. In my mind, there was no reason to think otherwise. I had let it be known that I wanted to be the next head coach at Oral Roberts University. My focus was on keeping the players happy, focused, and on track to get their degree. We were only going to lose two starters, Woods and McDougald. We could replace them with Collins and Roberts. We still had McCants, Boswell, and Fox, plus some very talented young players like Scott. I thought at the time and still do to this day that I was the right man and the most logical choice to succeed Coach Trickey. I had been there for four years, knew the ORU philosophy, married an ORU girl, and most importantly, had the respect of our players. Beside Fox and Boswell, who I had personally recruited, I had played a role in recruiting all of the other players. I was close friends with Terry Scott, Alvin's brother, and intended to hire him to be on my staff. I obviously would have tried to keep Coach Roe, as well, so as to not disrupt what we had going on with the program. Why "fix it" if it isn't broken?

Pres. Roberts had enough confidence in me that he asked me to stay on campus and not go to the NCAA Final Four in Charlotte, NC. He wanted me to stay on campus to be around our players and keep everything running smoothly. I agreed to stay out of respect for Mr. Roberts, but in hindsight I should have gone. The Final Four is a big weekend, not only because of the games but because of the coach's convention. It is also the one time of the year when all of the college basketball coaches are together. It is a time when a lot of assistant coaches can meet with the head coaches about openings on their staff. I wasn't looking for another job, I thought I had a job, the only one I really wanted was at ORU. I knew Pres. Roberts would ultimately make the final decision on the hire for the head basketball coach. I had met with him and some of his administrative staff several times over the week after the loss to Kansas. All of those meetings had gone very well, I felt totally comfortable and confident about being the coach that succeeded Ken Trickey. As a matter of fact, I felt like I had been "interviewing" for that job ever since I first shook Mr. Roberts hand and was introduced by Ken on the plane that day we were going to play a game in Lamar, Texas in 1969. He had been in my office many times since then talking about our players and basketball. I think he knew that even though I had been on Ken's staff these past four years that I was not just a "yes man" but had my own ideas about how to run a basketball program. Obviously, I agreed with a lot of Coach Trickey's philosophy, particularly on offense, but I had a different philosophy about playing defense. Ironically, when I played for Coach Trickey at MTSU, he chose me as the defensive player of the year. I learned so much from him about how to recruit, relate to players, and how to deal with the fans and media. In many ways, Ken Trickey was ahead of his time.

As time went on and March Madness began to fade, I began to sense that Pres. Roberts was listening to a lot of pundits about who he should hire to coach his basketball team. One of those so-called authorities was a "partner" from North Carolina that had followed the NC Tarheels more than he followed us. He had been to a couple of our games and thought he knew a lot about the game and who President Roberts should hire. The fact that I had never been a head coach seemed to be the number one argument, maybe the only argument, against me getting the job. Of course, my rebuttal to that line of thinking was that my idol, Wooden, or for that matter, Smith or Knight, had not been born into that position. Finally, either Mr. Roberts called Henry Iba, the Oklahoma State Hall of Fame Coach or Coach Iba initiated the conversation that resulted in the hiring of one of his former players. There was also the rumor that Mr. Roberts had tried to hire Coach Eddie Sutton from Creighton. He was looking for a much bigger job, like the University of Arkansas, where he ended up going. Sutton had also played at OSU for Coach Iba and had started his coaching career at Central High School in Tulsa. Sutton was a teammate of Jerry Hale, who was a junior college coach in Idaho. Hale had been a very successful coach at Southern Idaho Junior College the past three or four years. Sutton had coached there also. I learned later after Mr. Roberts hired Hale that he was presented to him as the "glue" that would hold our team together and be a strong disciplinarian. I had lived and died with these players for four years and wasn't aware that our program was coming apart and needed glue. Our players were more disciplined on and off the court than most programs or they would never have made it four years. Ironically, while Coach Iba was one of the best college basketball coaches ever, he never was a big fan of ORU. He had often made negative comments about the way we played and our program. Coach Trickey had stated publicly when he first came to ORU and began building the program that he could not duplicate Oklahoma State and Coach Iba's success. So the approach at ORU would be 180° different from what

Coach Iba had done at OSU. ORU would play a totally different style of basketball. Pres. Roberts asked me if I would sit down with Coach Hale and tell him about our players and answer any questions that he might have about our program. I agreed because I truly cared about our kids and wanted them to be successful the next year, even if I was not going to be coaching them. I was really disappointed that I did not get the job. I thought I was the most qualified and the best choice. Pres. Roberts had asked me in one of our many discussions if I would be interested in staying on as an assistant. I said no, perhaps I should have said yes to show my loyalty to him and the university, but my heart would not have been in it. I don't think I could have worked for anyone else and coached "my" players. Well, the "glue," for whatever reason, let the two best guards in all of college basketball leave the first year. Boswell and I had grown close and after I left I think he was not as focused. Al was a good kid who just needed someone to give him attention and direction. McCants was an independent and strong-willed young man that just needed to know that he was cared about as a person. They both were tough, hard-nosed players that hated to lose. In spite of losing Al and Sam, ORU (with Roberts averaging over 23 points a game) would win 20 games in the 1974-75 season. They started the season ranked #12 in the country and finished the season playing in the NIT. Illinois State University after four years would finally get some revenge by beating the Titans 107-98. I am sure Doug Collins got some satisfaction from that and Lawyer, well, he just probably got a good laugh. Finally, I will always believe that I could have kept all of those players together, focused, and we would have gotten back in the NCAA tournament. Who knows what would have happened? But that would be playing the "what if" game that I refused to play back then or now. God is in control and He does not make mistakes!

CHAPTER 6

Life after Oral Roberts University (1975-76)

oach Trickey began talking with several schools about their head coaching position after our loss to Kansas in the Mid-West Regional, but nothing had developed. I wasn't even sure he was going to take a job if one was offered. I knew he would hire me again to go to another school with him, but I certainly seemed to be in a bigger hurry than he was to find a job. Diane and I didn't know where we were going, but we both believed it was in God's hands. She finished the school year while Terry Scott and I pretty much hung out, had a few beers and sent out resumes. We developed a really close friendship during those two months. We had a lot of time to reflect on what had transpired, and think about where we might end up. I had not looked into any other jobs while I was at ORU. I was not interested in going anywhere. But now, in light of all that happened, I began to think I should have developed a better network like so many other assistants did, just for an occasion like this. I got an interview at McNeese State in Lake Charles, LA and another at Oklahoma Baptist University in Shawnee, OK.

The interviews went well, but they hired someone else. I really wanted to stay in college coaching, but by now most of the staffs had been hired and my prospects looked slim. There is a lot of truth to the saying that "the best time to get a job is when you already have one." I called my cousin, Clyde, once again, to see if there might be something in the Highland Park school system. Clyde hired me back in 1967 right out of college to teach physical education in an elementary school. In the three years that I spent in Highland Park, MI I got to know several of the administrators in the district because of Clyde. When I talked with Clyde about job opportunities, he mentioned that they might be looking for an athletic director, but he would not know until later in the summer. My job at ORU had ended in March, but the public schools still had two months to finish the year and then three more months before starting a new year. Those five months turned out to be five of the longest months of my life.

Diane finished in May and so did our paychecks. We didn't want to stay in Tulsa, and continue to pay rent. I called my dad in Galatia to see if we might be able to stay with him for a few months. He was more than glad and excited to have us come and live with him. The rent was really cheap. It was quite a change from Tulsa and what we were used to. Dad had only been around Diane that short period of time before our wedding and after my mom died. All of the people that she was going to meet were my friends and total strangers to her. She did great and soon fit right in. She convinced my dad that she knew how to cook and didn't need him in the kitchen trying to help her. Living in Galatia gave us a chance to save money and to renew a lot of old acquaintances. We were just biding time hoping that something would develop with Clyde or we would get a teaching job somewhere. It was pretty obvious (by this time) I was not going to have an opportunity to coach in college. Coach Trickey was still looking, and everyone else that I knew had filled their coaching staffs.

My college roommate Tom Whittington married his high school sweetheart after we graduated from MTSU. He and Sue were living about 20 miles from Galatia in Benton. During our years at MTSU and after, I had gotten to know Sue very well. Sue's parents had a cabin on Benton Lake where we would spend a lot of time skiing, playing cards, and drinking beer. I did get an interview for a teaching position and coaching job in Murphysboro, IL, which was only about 40 miles from Galatia. The interview went well. I was offered the job, but Diane and I just didn't feel like that was where we wanted to be. I declined the offer. Tom and Sue couldn't quite understand that decision, they had a good athletics program and I needed a job, but it just didn't feel right. Soon after I turned down the Murphysboro position, Clyde called me to offer me the athletic director position in Highland Park. It was a great job for me, making more money than I had made at Oral Roberts University. There were three junior high schools and one high school with over 3000 students in the school system. Highland Park school district was pretty much an inner-city school surrounded by Detroit. At one time it was the headquarters for

Chrysler and the first assembly line for Ford's Model T cars. I had great memories of my previous three years there. I was excited to go back. This time would be different because I was going back with a wife. However, Diane was not quite as excited about living in Detroit as I was. Because my job paid so well, Diane would not have to get a job right away, which made her feel a little better. She didn't know anyone except my cousin whom she had only met at our wedding. Detroit had a rough reputation at the time, deservedly so, but I felt comfortable there and kept telling her that she would like it too. We found a nice apartment just outside of Highland Park in Bloomfield. Bloomfield was an upscale Jewish community with a lot of places to eat and shop. Diane liked the area and the shopping potential. It was about the time we were moving to Michigan that Coach Trickey got a job as the head coach at Iowa State University in Ames, IA. It was such a late hire for a college that Ken was asked to keep the assistants that were there from the previous coach. That was okay with me, I was so thankful to Clyde for the job that I wouldn't have reneged and gone to ISU even if Ken had asked. I was actually kind of excited about being back in Highland Park.

Diane was in for a culture shock. She had never been in the north. Actually she had only been in Utah where she grew up and in Tulsa, Oklahoma. She had also spent a year in Mexico, as a missionary, the year after she graduated from Ogden High School. She would later say that she had never even had a bagel until we moved to Bloomfield. She had never taught in a school system that was 90% African-American. She was in for a lot of firsts just as I had been four years earlier in 1967 when I came there right out of college. She adjusted quickly to the new surroundings. Diane was always able to make friends easily and fit into most any situation. As athletic director, I was out several nights a week to different athletic events; Diane was with me most of those nights. All of the junior high athletic events were in the afternoon, which meant I was home some of the evenings. Diane was not comfortable driving in Detroit traffic, so when she taught I would drop her off at her school and come back in the afternoon and pick her up. She would just stay with me and go to the sporting event. She worked on her grades and did her lesson plans and school work in the bleachers. At least she did not have to cook that much; we ate out a lot. I finally convinced her that she could drive herself on the weekends to the grocery store or to shop. She had a little Chevy Nova that she bought when she was in college at ORU. (When we left Detroit in June 1975, we sold that car to a policeman that I knew, for exactly what she had paid for it five years earlier.) That car came in handy on several occasions. The first three months we were in Highland Park, we had our Thunderbird stolen twice. The first time it was stolen was in the middle of the day while I was inside one of my junior high schools visiting with the coaches. It was the strangest feeling when I came out of the building to go to my car and it wasn't there. The first thing that went through my mind was that I just forgot where I had parked. Then, in a few seconds, reality set in, and I realized that

I did remember where I parked, and I realized what had happened. The police found the car a couple of days later in an alley in Detroit up on blocks with the tires missing and my tape deck taken out of the dashboard. Yes, we had tape decks. The thing that really made me mad was that I had about $600 worth of clothes in the trunk that I was going to take to the dry cleaners. I had just bought and worn this nice, new gray suit once, and they took it. Fortunately, they just drove the T-Bird until it ran out of gas and didn't do any real damage to it. A couple months later the car was stolen again while I was at one of our high school basketball games. This time the police recovered it the next day. It had been used in a robbery. Again, I was lucky it was not damaged, but it was pretty obvious that I wasn't the only one who liked that Thunderbird.

There is a funny story about how I bought that automobile. Diane and I had been married a few months, when one Saturday morning I told her I needed to go to the sporting goods store and buy a new tennis racket. I drove by this Ford dealership and saw this beautiful brown Thunderbird, the one with the small porthole windows. Growing up I loved the look of the Thunderbird, it had a long hood, it was sleek looking, and had a lot of horsepower. I was gone for about two hours. I came home and told Diane what I had been doing. I told her we "had" to go back to the dealership and get this new automobile. She loved the car, too, but it was a very expensive tennis racket!

Highland Park was a great place to work, except for the car thieves; I got along really well with all of the administration. The superintendent of schools, Dr. Mitchell, was best of friends with my cousin. Clyde and Chuck, the superintendent, made a great team. They worked hard and they partied hard. Diane and I were invited to go out to dinner with Clyde, Joan, Dr. Mitchell and his girlfriend on several occasions. Another administrator that was close to Clyde and Chuck was a lady named Mary Lane. Mary was a sweetheart of a woman, very smart, and married to Hall of Fame Detroit Lions football player, Dick "Night Train" Lane. Another member of the "rat pack" was the principal at the high school, an African-American, Ed Martin. Mr. Martin was an outstanding principal and a great man to work for.

One of my closest and best friends was the head basketball coach at Highland Park High School, Darrell Pursiful. Darrell was from Kentucky, and it didn't take very long after I was around him to realize he was a Southern boy. He was an outstanding individual and a great high school coach. Coach Pursiful was a devout Christian, respected by his peers, and loved by his players. Darrell and his basketball players made this a most memorable year for me. Highland Park had been blessed with a lot of talent over the last three or four years, but to get to state they had to beat the best teams from the Detroit Public School League and that wasn't easy. Detroit high school basketball has been a great recruiting field for Division I schools for a long time. Darrell had an outstanding team led by a terrific shooter by the name of Terry Duerod. Duerod was the best shooter I have ever been around, other than Richard Fuqua. He averaged almost 30 points a game as a senior, and had unbelievable range on the court. He scored 45 points in the quarter finals of the state tournament. Deurod went on to play at the University of Detroit for Dick Vitale and then in the NBA with the Pistons. Coach Pursiful also had a 6' 6" center that went on to play at a Division I school, a 6' 5" power forward and an outstanding point guard, who got a scholarship to play in college. Darrell had a lot of depth; he played eight or nine players every game. That depth would prove to be a winning asset during the tournament, his teams liked to press and wear down their opponents. One of the things that I remember and admire about Darrell and his wife was they would have the team over to their house after every game. Often times, several players would stay all night. His players would do anything for him, including win a state tournament. Coach Pursiful coached at Highland Park for over 20 years. He was voted into the Michigan high school Hall of Fame. Darrell was also superstitious. His team got on a winning streak on their way to the state championship. He started eating liver and onions for his pregame meal, and that continued right on through the championship game. I was always thankful I wasn't in his huddles during timeouts!

They were good and their games were exciting to watch, but that success created my biggest headache. Highland Park's high school gym was built in the 30s. It was tiny and a horrible place to play basketball game. We rented a local Catholic school gym that would seat about 1500. As the season wore on and the team won more and more games, more people began coming to the games. Toward the end of the season, we had standing room only crowds, that is, until the fire marshal started limiting the number of fans we could allow into the gym. As athletic director, it was my job to supervise the home games and control our crowds. On several occasions, I had to lock the front doors and turn people away. I was afraid the fire marshal would close us down. I wasn't the most popular guy in the neighborhood on those occasions, to say the least. At one of our games, I locked the front doors and was in the lobby when I heard two or three pops that sounded like firecrackers. I soon realized someone had shot through the front doors. Diane happened to be at that game setting in the bleachers. I told her to stay where she was and not come out at halftime. At several other games, I caught students trying to sneak in to the gym through a basement window or through the back entrance. It was times like this, that even though I was getting paid well, I wasn't sure I was getting paid enough. The team captured the excitement of the entire city, which made for a couple of fun months for our school and our fans.

In spite of the cold and sometimes harsh winter weather, Diane and I enjoyed Detroit. The year we were there, we even had a 15 inch snowstorm on Easter. The food and entertainment was great. Besides our friendship with Clyde and Joan, and the friends we made in the school system, we also met a couple named, Denny and Susan Carlson. We met the Carlson's at Highland Park Baptist Church, which ironically enough, was not in Highland Park, but in Bloomfield. They were one of the couples that stayed around after church to meet and greet visitors. They had two small children, but we seemed to have a lot in common and hit it off right away. Denny owned a metal stamp business that made parts for automobiles. He was a very good businessman who had grown his business into an operation that employed over 20 people. We spent quite a bit of time with them, including trips up to their place on beautiful Lake Charlevoix, north of Detroit. Our friendship continued to grow for several more years, even after we left Detroit. We went with them on an adventurous three-week trip through Europe in 1978. The four of us rented a Volkswagen bus and traveled from Germany, through Austria, Switzerland, and Italy. It was a fun and crazy trip that I will detail a little later. Also, as a result of the Carlson's friendship, we became friends with a couple they had known for years, Tim and Diana Tomkinson. Tim would later play a major role in our move to Brandon, Florida. This friendship would prove to me that God does go before us planning our way. He does put certain people in our path. The whole work experience at Highland Park and living in Detroit was a fun time for both of us. We had our challenges, to be sure, but we would be leaving behind some great friendships. We would also be leaving with a soon-to-be new addition to our family. Diane was pregnant with our first, a little girl, we would name Amy. Coach Trickey, had called me in March to see if I would come and join his staff at Iowa State University. I had never hidden the fact from anyone at Highland Park that my heart was still in coaching at the college level. I felt like I had to take the job. In June 1975, we were once again on the move, this time to a place that neither one of us had ever been: Ames, Iowa.

Welcome to My World

CHAPTER 7

Short and Not So Sweet: Iowa State University (1976)

Neither Diane nor I had ever been in the state of Iowa, let alone to Ames. We actually had to look on the map to find out where it was. Yes, back in those days, people used a map to find their way around. After Tulsa and Detroit, it felt like we were going to the middle of nowhere. I had grown up in a farm community but not like this where there was nothing but miles and miles of cornfields. Ames was a nice community of about 30,000 people. The town revolved around the university. One of the things that we found out very quickly was that the people were very cliquish. We were outsiders; we didn't know anyone there besides Coach Trickey. I would soon learn that one of the reasons that people were so inhospitable toward Diane and me was that Ken had not exactly gotten off on the right foot with the community and particularly with an ISU vice president. When Ken went to ISU, he was in the middle of getting a divorce from Peggye, his wife of over 30 years. Ken had shown up at several community and university functions with his girlfriend who was about 20 years younger. That should not have made a difference but it did not go over too well in this very conservative environment. I don't think Coach Trickey was prepared for the scrutiny of his private life in the Ames community.

ISU thought Ken was going to show up in Ames with a wife and family. He was truly a big fish in a little pond. He was in a fishbowl, as were all of us coaches at ORU, but Ames was not Tulsa. Coach Trickey had been very successful at ORU and had pretty much free reign of the entire basketball program. At ISU, one of the vice presidents at the university had questioned Ken's decision on the direction he wanted to take the basketball program. That did not set well with Ken and he informed the VP that he had been hired to run the basketball program. Ken should have known he was not going to win a fight with a vice-president at the university but his ego got the best of him. That is not a recipe for success and for longevity. Coach Trickey, the "people person," was not exactly a hit with a lot of people in Ames, and going 11-16 the first year did not help. Diane and I were not aware of any of this prior to arriving in Ames. As much as I wanted to get back into college coaching, I would not have left Highland Park to go to ISU if I had known how much animosity there was toward Ken. One of the reasons that Ken had struggled so much that first year was he did not have his own people on his staff. As a head coach or any leader there is nothing more important than to have good people around you that you trust and know. I would learn this lesson the hard way a few years later. That first year, Coach Trickey was educating his staff as well as trying to coach a team. He was playing kids that he didn't know and had not recruited. He was trying to coach them with a staff that he had not picked, a formula that pretty much guarantees failure. He did end up keeping one of the assistants, an African American by the name of Gus Guydon. Gus was a good loyal assistant who wanted Ken to succeed. Gus and I would become good friends.

Diane and I found a really nice two bedroom apartment about five minutes from the campus. We would need the extra bedroom with the new addition coming in a couple months. I will never forget pulling up into the parking lot of the apartment complex and seeing what looked like parking meters. I thought, "What kind of management makes you pay to park at your apartment?" I found out that those "meter looking things" were actually electric heat plug-ins for your car engines. It would get so cold that the oil in your engine would freeze up. What had we gotten ourselves into?

We had only been in Ames a few weeks, and Diane was getting cabin fever. We had no friends. There was really not much for her to do except hang out in the apartment. I was busy with basketball, so it was much easier for me. Eventually, she became friends with the wife of Max Urick, one of the assistant athletic directors. They would go out to lunch or to shop, and Diane would babysit their four children. Fortunately for us, Iowa State furnished me a car so Diane could use the Thunderbird and get around. The one bright spot in this move was that we were able to find a good doctor, Dr. White. Diane liked and felt comfortable with him. He was "old school." He took time with Diane, and assured her that she and the baby would be fine. Everything for the next two months went just as Dr. White had promised. On October 27th, 1975 we became proud parents of a little girl, Amy Lee.

ISU is a nice university with one of the biggest basketball arenas in the country. The Hilton Coliseum held over 14,000 people and was a great selling point for recruits. ISU was in the Big Eight conference with Kansas, Kansas State, Oklahoma, Oklahoma State, Nebraska, Missouri, and Colorado. The Big 8 became the Big 12 in 1994. Today the Big 12 actually has 10 schools and only KU, KSU, OU, OSU and ISU are the only original schools still in the conference. The task of recruiting to Ames would prove to be much more difficult than getting high school players to Tulsa. Ames is about 40 miles north of Des Moines. Winters are long and cold, a tough sell to kids from Florida, Tennessee, or even Detroit where we had recruited most of our players for ORU. I still believe we could have made it work if we would have been given enough time, but time was something that we didn't have very much of. We needed to get out of the gate fast and win some games. I felt extra pressure as well, since I had been represented to the media to be this guy who would bring stability and consistency to the program. I wish it would have been that easy. The single most important key to winning is having good athletes. At

ISU, we did not have any Fuquas, Woods, McCants or Boswells on our roster. We only had two players that were skilled enough to play at this level, a 6' 3" guard named Hercle Ivy and a 6' 6" forward named Art Johnson. Hercle averaged 20 points a game; Art averaged 17 points and 10 rebounds a game. We lost the first 11 games of the season, including three games in the Big Eight tournament in Kansas City.

This was my first time to ever be in Kansas City at Christmas time; it was beautiful. We stayed in a five-star hotel and were treated like royalty. I didn't know it at the time but the trip and playing in Kansas City would be the highlight of the season for me. The worst part, other than losing three games, was that Diane and the baby were not able to be with me. In all the years that we've been married, Diane would say that this was the worst Christmas she ever had. She was by herself with a newborn on Christmas Day. Our kids were playing hard and doing everything we asked them to do, but we were undersized and just not talented enough. Attendance at our home games was way down. The media and fans were really giving Coach Trickey a hard time. Finally in mid-February, Ken was asked to resign. I was devastated. Ken was the only reason that I had come to Iowa State, and it seemed like we had barely unpacked and we were through. I knew as soon as the season was over we would be moving on. Mr. McCullough, the athletic director, who had hired Ken and supported him up to the end, asked Gus and I to finish the season as co-head coaches. In the short six months that Gus and I worked together, we had developed a mutual respect and close friendship. We both realized the best thing we could do for the players was to just try to keep them together and have fun.

The players responded really well to our coaching. We made it through those last four weeks without any problems. We won our last home game against Oklahoma and finished the season 3-23. I had never experienced a basketball season this bad; however, another one like it was in my future. Coach Trickey had a weekly ISU basketball show on a television station in Des Moines. Gus and I alternated weeks filling in on the show. It was during the taping of these shows that I became friends with Lute Olsen, the coach at the University of Iowa. He had a show on right before ours. I had met Coach Olson when I was at ORU, and we played at Long Beach State where he was the coach. The Sunday mornings that I went to tape the show we would talk, and he always had something positive to say to me about what Gus and I were doing.

Only eight months after getting the job at ISU, I was looking for a job again. A strange coincidence occurred just a few weeks after the season was over. Two years earlier, after I realized I was not going to get the coaching job at ORU, I heard about this high school coaching job that was open in Salem, Illinois, near where I grew up. I called the athletic director, Bob Eller, about the job, and on the day that I called, he was going to present the name of a man for the position that night at the board meeting. We talked for about 5 minutes and I had an opportunity to tell him a little bit about my background. Well, now that same position was open again, so I called him again about the job. He remembered our conversation from two years earlier and asked me to meet him in Champaign at the state tournament to discuss the job. The meeting went great, and he pretty much assured me the job at Salem was mine. He wanted me to bring Diane to Salem and meet with the school superintendent. Diane and I, along with Amy, drove to Salem to meet with Dr. Raver, the school superintendent. I was offered the job and Bob told Diane that he would help her get a job teaching in an elementary school. Bob had been around Salem all his life and was highly respected. We were not surprised that Diane was offered a teaching job soon after we moved. Bob and his wife, Annie Lou, became good friends. The last two years of basketball at Salem High School had not been very good. There wasn't much talent, and Salem had gone through a down cycle. I thought those could have been my first two years if Bob had hired me the first time. It would not be easy, particularly that first year, but we were on our way to Salem, a place close to home and my dad. In April of 1976 the three of us left Ames, Iowa. I was going back home.

CHAPTER 8

The Salem Years (1976-79)

I t was during one of our several trips to Salem from Ames that we found a lot in a new housing development close to the high school. We were going to move to Salem in three months and into our very first, brand-new house. We were excited about our three bedroom, two bath house, with a very small, single car garage. That little house of 1400 sq. ft. was like a mansion to us. The people in Salem were very hospitable, unlike what we had experienced with our move to Ames. The administration at the high school was very helpful and cordial. I couldn't wait to get to Salem, get into our new home, and get started with summer basketball. One of the first teachers I met was Greg Gruenkemeyer, who taught math. Greg had been an assistant coach and the freshman coach the previous two years. I liked Greg and decided right away to keep him as my assistant. He was a hard worker who believed in structure, discipline, and teaching the fundamentals. He had grown up in Salem and was liked by the students, as well as, the players. Coach Eller had spoken highly of Greg and thought that he would be an asset to me. Greg and his wife, Rae, lived just down the street from our new home. We would become friends for many years. I wanted Greg to work with me on the varsity and coach the JV, so I decided to look for another young teacher to coach the freshman team. Salem had won only 6 games in the previous two years, so we had our work cut out for us. Salem, at the time, was known more for its football than basketball. Lee Emery, the football coach had been the basketball coach up until the last two years. We would become good friends. I liked to tease him about switching sports when he saw the basketball talent getting thin. He was always coming around wanting to talk X's and O's. I think he really liked coaching basketball better than football. He left Salem a couple years later to coach basketball again at another high school.

My first year was a struggle to say the least, especially that first summer trying to develop the players and getting them indoctrinated into my style of play. The coach before me played a very deliberate style. I wanted to speed things up, even though we didn't have the talent to play that way, but I was building for the future. Salem high school had about 1200 students, and played in the largest school classification in the state. Some of the schools on our schedule had over 2000 students. We also played in a very tough conference with four of the eight schools having a rich tradition in basketball. The toughest thing about coaching at Salem was the travel; Salem was located on Interstate 57 about 60 miles from St. Louis. It was a great location, as far as, proximity to shopping and going to St. Louis, but not for playing sports events in the North

Egypt Conference (NEC). Salem was home to 8000 residents and famous for being the home of the great orator William Jennings Bryan. It was a beautiful little town. But it was tough getting to the other seven schools in our conference to play a sporting contest. We were the western most town in the conference; the closest school to us was 20 miles away. Three schools in our conference were 75 or 80 miles away. We had to leave school before dismissal time at 3 o'clock so the JV team would have enough time to warm up before a 6:00 tip off. The only consolation was that we did get to take a charter bus to the games that were farthest away.

In addition to our tough conference schedule, we played in one of the oldest and most prestigious Christmas tournaments in the state of Illinois. The Centralia Holiday Tournament was one of the first high school Christmas tournaments in the United States. The tournament, which was started in 1943, is still going strong, 76 years later. Centralia invited schools from Chicago, central Illinois, and teams from out of state to participate in the three-day, sixteen team tournament. Besides playing in Centralia, we had our own eight team tournament in January. The Salem Invitational Tournament was one of the first mid-winter tournaments in the state. We invited schools from the St. Louis area as well as schools from central and southern Illinois. Several of those schools had enrollments of over 2000 students.

The school system was outstanding and with both of us teaching, we made a nice income. The high school was beautiful, and the gym was one of the largest in Southern Illinois.

There were 1000 reserved chair back seats, and the gym held about 3000 people. We had great kids, just not very big or talented. We won our first game of the season, but ended up winning only two more games. It was my second year in a row to win only three games following the disappointing Iowa State experience. Even though we only won three games, we didn't play like we were going to lose. We began to change the mindset of the players and began to establish a sound foundation for the future. We had three seniors on the varsity and only one of them was a starter. Our tallest player, Jim Bookout, who was 6' 3," would be returning along with the best player that we had, Brian Skelton. Brian was a 5' 10" guard that had not even played much until we started playing him his junior year. Brian was a great kid and a hard worker, very coachable. He spent a lot of time the summer of his senior year working on his game and became a real offensive force. We were playing an exciting style of basketball and we were beginning to get fans back in the gym to watch us. The local newspaper and radio station were great about covering our games. I had a Saturday morning radio show to promote our program. We also had Saturday morning Pee Wee basketball games for kids ages 8 to 14. My varsity players coached the teams and my JV players refereed the games. We adjusted the baskets to 8 feet for the little guys, offered refreshments, and tried to make sure they had fun playing. The Saturday morning program would grow from 50 kids to over 100 in our third year.

I was willing to do whatever it would take to promote our basketball program. I encouraged the students to come to the games and asked our players to encourage all of their friends to come out. I became friends with the music director, who had one of the best music programs in Southern Illinois. The music program at Salem had won awards in the state for their marching and playing ability. I got the band director to provide a pep band at all of our home games. I wanted to make our gym into a real home-court advantage. Even during that first year (when we were not winning) Coach Eller would tell me how much bigger our game receipts were than from the year before.

Diane and I were happy in our new home. Amy, our new little daughter, was adjusting to her awesome babysitter, Lawanna Green. Lawanna's husband, Jim, was an English teacher at the high school. Jim and Lawanna were good Christian people who lived about two blocks from the high school. Diane could drop Amy off at Lawanna's house on her way to school. The Green's had two children, and they loved Amy like she was one of their own.

We joined the local First Baptist Church and the Country Club, and began making new friends. We were close enough to my dad that we could go to Galatia every few weeks and spend the day with him. He and his friend Charlie even drove up to our house a few times. In addition to coaching basketball that first year, I had agreed to coach cross-country and baseball. Cross-country was easy. I had run cross-country in high school, so I had a pretty good idea of what I was doing. Besides, how difficult is it to teach kids to run 1 mile, and turn around and run back? Baseball was a little different story. I had played baseball in high school, but I didn't know much about coaching baseball. I had grown up watching a lot of baseball and was a big baseball fan. However, contrary to what a lot of fans think, just because you watch a sport doesn't mean you know how to coach that sport. I was upfront and transparent with my players about coaching baseball. I was not trying to impress anyone, particularly them, with my baseball knowledge. Fortunately, I had a few seniors who were not only good players, but good kids, so they helped me a lot by "suggesting" things for us to do in practice and in the games. I didn't get paid much to coach baseball but half of what I got paid, I should have given to my senior players. I hated coaching baseball, it was damp, cold, and it took over three hours to get through a practice or a seven inning game. There was a lot of standing around, and most of the time I was cold and bored. Coach Eller, knew it was a real struggle for me so after that first year he found someone else to coach baseball. I had been coaching a sport since before school even started and baseball season ended in May so I had spent a lot of time at the school. I was tired and ready for summer.

Our players and staff really worked hard during the summer. We were determined to improve on our record from the year before. I knew the league and a lot more about our players going into my second year. We were so much better prepared and we had much better talent going into the 1977-78 season. Brian Skelton, who averaged eight points a game as a junior, averaged over 20 as a senior. Bookout, who could jump, became a physical, solid inside player for us. Another senior, Delmer McNeil, a 6'1" forward, was hard-nosed, and a good defensive player. But the kid that made us go was a 5' 7" senior point guard by the name of Steve Schmidt. Steve had been cut from the team as a sophomore. He loved to play basketball, and I saw that competitive spirit in him. He was also very smart and an excellent ball handler. We still were not very big, but we played bigger than our size. We also played hard and together. Everyone bought in to what we were doing, and everyone knew their role. We won a few games early, including a game in the Centralia tournament, which really helped to boost our confidence. That was the first time Salem had won a game in Centralia in four years. Brian made the All-Tournament team at Centralia and in our Salem Invitational tournament. He finished second in scoring in our conference and made the All North Egypt Conference (NEC) team. He received a four-year scholarship to play basketball at a NAIA school in Kansas. We had only won one game in our conference the previous year. This second year we were 6-8 and finished fifth in the eight-school league. We also won a game in the regional tournament for the first time in four years. Salem was no longer the doormat in the NEC. We lost to Lawrenceville, who won the conference, by two points in our gym. We ended the season, winning eight games but it was a "far cry" from what the season had been like the year before. The kids had worked hard, and basketball was fun again.

The most memorable game of the season was our game at Mt Vernon. It was not memorable because we won, because we didn't. It was the second game of the season. Mount Vernon is a school that had a long history of great basketball tradition including winning the state tournament two or three times. They had twice as many students as we did, including a large population of African-American students and players. Mount Vernon was only about 15 or 16 miles from Salem so we played them every year. We rarely beat them. We were in the dressing room before the game going over some last-minute pregame stuff when my dad and his friend, Charlie, walked in, totally unexpectedly. I am not even sure how they found our dressing room. After I finished my "speech" about playing hard and being positive, no matter what happened, Dad, without any provocation or an invitation, said "boys don't be afraid of those N..... they put their pants on just like you do so go out there and kick their ass." The players didn't know what to think or whether to laugh or not. I didn't either, but I think that it really relaxed them. We played really well and were behind by only two points at halftime. Mt. Vernon ended up beating us by 15, but we played about as well as we could. Dad and Charlie sat on the end of our bench and yelled the entire game. They had had a few beers before the game, so I was just thankful that they behaved and didn't say anything that would have gotten us in trouble. Greg, my assistant, thought that "speech" was one of the funniest things he had ever experienced as a coach. It was pretty funny.

Galatia High School retired my #34 basketball jersey in 1978. First number to ever be retired at the school. L/R: Coach JW Pulliam, Me, (only time I grew a mustache) and Principal Lester Gill.

I enjoyed teaching at Salem High School. The teachers and other personnel at the school were very helpful and kind. Jim Davis, the shop teacher, who could build anything out of wood, designed and built me a new score keepers table for the gym. One of the most important "team members" a head coach can have is a good, reliable custodian. I had a guy who was my right hand man; he was always doing special things for me, like mopping the gym floor and setting the gym up for our home games. The guys I taught with were fun to be around. We had a lot of fun playing golf, and just hanging out over a few beers at the local Elks Club. The most fun we had was going on "scouting trips" in Bill Morgan's customized van. Bill taught driver's education, coached golf, and was pretty much a nondrinker. He made for a perfect chauffeur. We would have a scouting trip about every week. Our scouting crew, included Greg, the two Hawley brothers, who did our radio broadcast, Darrell the football coach, and Tom who coached the freshman. We would get a case of beer, and a few tapes of the Bee Gees and the Beatles, and have a great time in the van traveling to the games. We might drive 60 or 70 miles to scout a basketball team. It never seemed that far sitting in the back of that van in those "captain chairs" drinking beer and listening to the Bee Gees.

During the summer of our second year in Salem, our friends from Detroit, Denny and Sue Carlson, asked us to go with them to Europe. Amy was only three, but Lawanna was so good with her that we decided we could leave her for a couple weeks and go with them. As great as Lawanna was with Amy, we probably would not choose to do that if we had it to do over. Amy, who is now in her 40s, said she thought we were never coming back and that we had "scarred" her for life. Denny had spent several months in Europe when he graduated from high school. He knew his way around and served as our tour guide. We rented a Volkswagen bus and toured Germany, Austria, Switzerland, and Italy. This was the first real vacation we had been able to take since we left Tulsa four years earlier. We had a great time traveling the countries and enjoyed being with our friends. We ended up spending four days in one of my favorite cities in the world: Rome. We celebrated Denny and Susan's anniversary in Rome by staying at the expensive and famous Rome Hilton Hotel. We had stayed at pensiones (bed and breakfast places) all throughout Europe, but they were not the Rome Hilton. We had a great time traveling throughout Europe in that bus, but we were anxious to get home and see our little girl. Before we left Rome, we went to the Trevi Fountains and just like thousands of other tourist, we threw three pennies in the fountain which is supposed to guarantee that you will be back. This was the first of three trips to Europe that we would make. One of those trips we took Amy and her husband, Darrin, hoping to make amends for leaving her when she was only three. In 2001, 23 years later, our whole family went to Rome. After we retired, Diane and I went back a third time with our travel partners and dear friends, Tom and Karen Ruggiero.

Our summer basketball camp had grown from 25 or so campers that first year to almost 100 campers. We also had open gym three or four nights a week for our players to play and work on their skills. Most nights I was there for at least an hour watching our players and doing a little individual work with them. As the 1978-79 season began, I felt good about where our program was and about the upcoming season. We added an auxiliary gym and new offices onto the current gym. The first two years, my office was a desk in the corner of the PE offices located in the basement of the gym. I had no privacy, no place to talk with a player, and no place to study game video. Diane and I were both pretty content with our jobs and with life in general. I had no idea, at the time, that this was going to be my last year at Salem. We lost three starters from the year before including our All-Conference guard, Brian Skelton.

I thought our conference was going to be weaker overall, so I thought we could win at least as many games as we had the year before. We were still a long way from having the talent that Lawrenceville and Olney had, but we were competitive. The non-conference schedule remained the same, much too tough for our talent level. I was working on getting a more favorable schedule for us. It was hard enough to compete in our league and in our own tournament without playing schools from Chicago or from out-of-state. I finally convinced Coach Eller, our athletic director, to get us out of Centralia and into the Breese Mater Dei Tournament playing schools that were our size; we had a chance at Mater Dei. Salem had won only a half dozen games in the 20 years they had played in the Centralia tournament. Those 6 or so wins included our win the year before.

I did not win many friends in Salem when word got out that I had been the one responsible for the change in tournaments at Christmas. Even my good friends, the Hawley brothers, did not want us to get out of the Centralia Tournament. I totally agreed with them that it was the best Christmas tournament in the state, but we had no chance of ever winning that tournament. We were pretty much guaranteed two losses every year we played there. They continued to bring in teams from all over the state, and most of them were much bigger than we were and a lot more talented. As they say, "old habits die hard"! Interestingly, two years after I left Salem, they were back playing in Centralia again. I guess everyone has their own idea about what prestige is, and obviously to a lot of people around Salem thought that just being in that tournament is good enough for them. They were not the ones who had to deal with the kids' egos and practice for games we couldn't win.

We started the season winning the first two games, but lost in a close game to a good Mt Vernon team, again. No "speeches" this year from my dad, he and Charlie did not come up this time for the game! We were good enough to compete in our conference and finished fourth with a 7-7 record. To no one's surprise, including me, we went 0-2 in the Centralia tournament. We did win a game in our own tournament for the second year in a row. We lost to Lawrenceville by one point, who won our conference for the third straight year. We actually had them beat in our gym before the officials took over and decided the outcome. The game ended with a very controversial call. We had the ball in under our basket and a one point lead with just a few seconds to go. The officials called a charging foul on one of my players as he was going over to set a screen on another player to free him up for the in bounds pass. (I don't think I have seen that call two times in my over 20 years of coaching.) Lawrenceville was this "big" state power with an All-American by the name of Jay Schiedler and coached by Ron Felling, a Hall of Fame coach. I am convinced that the referees let that influence their decision making at the end of the game. Scheidler, went on to play at Kentucky and Felling later won a state championship and went on to coach on Bob Knight's staff at Indiana. None of that should have been a factor in this game on this night, but I really believe it was. Their kid hit both free throws with a couple seconds left and they beat us by one. I "went off" on the officials after the game and committed the cardinal sin in a coach/referee confrontation. It would be the one and only time I would ever make this mistake in my 20+ years of coaching. The referees' dressing room was just down the hall from our players' dressing room. I had yelled at the officials all the way down the hall and until they went into their dressing room. Then, as if I needed to say more, I went down to their dressing room and barged in. I already had told them how terrible the last call was, that they had "determined the outcome of the game, and not the players." I told them "that they had stolen the game from us and my players had played their heart out, and didn't deserve to lose like that." They asked me to leave the dressing room and warned me I was going to get "written up" if I stayed in their locker room. I was already in trouble, but what I said to them just before I left would cause me a lot more grief. I told them that just because it was Lawrenceville with their winning tradition, they did not have to "F-- us!"

That was a Friday night game, and by Monday the officials had filed a report with the Illinois High School Association and sent a copy of the report to my superintendent at Salem. I had a great relationship with Dr. Raver, our superintendent, but good relationship or not, I had stepped over the line on Friday night. Dr. Raver was a good Christian man, soft-spoken, who saw the best in everyone. Coach Eller came down to the gym mid-morning and told me that Dr. Raver wanted to see me in his office right away. Both he and Dr. Raver gave me an opportunity to present my side of the story and explain what had happened. I could not justify my behavior; I apologized and agreed to write an apology to the referees. I was willing to accept whatever consequences were going to come my way. Both of them expressed their disappointment in me for what I had done, but they were both satisfied with my remorseful attitude. It was what I said as I was leaving Dr. Raver's office that makes for a legacy and lasting memory even though I didn't think about that at the time. What I said to them as I was leaving made a tough situation a little lighter. With my buddies, it made for a good story about my coaching career in Salem. Just before I walked out of the office, I stopped, and said I was sorry that I had used the F-- word, but at that moment in time, in the heat of the battle, telling the referees that I thought they had "screwed" us just didn't sound strong enough.

I had a good group of boys to work with and playing soft or easy was just not in their DNA. I tried to coach as hard as they played. Our home attendance had gone from maybe 500 to over 1,000 almost every game. Our tournament games and the games against our rivals were played before 2,000 or more spectators. We made basketball at Salem High School fun again and exciting to watch. All of the Saturday morning Pee Wee basketball games and all of the kids that participated in our summer camps were now paying off. We had a pep band and excitable students which gave us a home court advantage, and the chance to win every game at home. We had changed the culture. The basketball program was on solid footing. We finished the season with a 10-15 record. The record, however, does not tell the whole story. A lot more things go into a successful program besides just how many games are won. The schedule was way too tough for the size of our school. Playing in a conference where we had to travel over two hours by bus to play four of the seven schools was tough. I was leaving Salem better than I found it and satisfied that whoever would follow me would have it better than I had when I came three years earlier.

A couple years after I left Salem I got a call from one of my former players thanking me for what I had done for him and the basketball program at Salem. He had grown-up in Salem and still lived there. He told me I was just ahead of my time. He wished we would have won more games, and had had better talent, but I had made basketball fun and exciting again in Salem.

I will never forget the many great times I had with my fellow coaches at Salem: those fun scouting trips, playing golf, and hanging out at the Elks Club. The best time was the trips that we made to the Illinois state basketball tournament in Champaign every year. Our whole staff and our radio guys would leave on a Wednesday after school and drive the couple hours up to Champaign. We would get two or three rooms at a local hotel, and by 6 o'clock on Wednesday, we had started a three day party. Actually, the party started in Bill's van on the way to Champaign. We had the Bee Gees pumping and the beer flowing before we even got out of the city limits. Assembly Hall on the campus of the University of Illinois was a great basketball venue. The arena held over 16,000 and every seat was full for the tournament. If you love high school basketball, this one weekend in March called, March Madness, was like heaven on earth. Actually, that phrase that is so popular now, was coined by an Illinois sports writer, who was describing high school basketball in Illinois in March. There was only one classification in Illinois high school basketball, during this time, so schools with enrollments of 50 students might be playing a school with over 3000 students. Of course, everyone except the people from the Chicago area pulled for any school from downstate to beat the Chicago schools. Between sessions, we would walk to the Ramada Inn to eat, drink and catch up with old friends we hadn't seen since the last state tournament.

It was a great time, a fun time to renew old acquaintances, and talk about the past season. What wasn't fun was the half-mile walk on a windy, cold day (sometimes in the 30s) from a warm arena to the hotel. We watched basketball from noon until 10 o'clock at night. By the end of the tournament on Saturday night, we were pretty much "spent" and ready to head back home. I always wanted to take Andrew, our son, back during March to experience what I had, but the tournament was moved from Champaign to Peoria a few years after I left Salem.

The Illinois High School Association (IHSA) also changed the classification from one class to three classes. There are no more David versus Goliath basketball games in the tournament. Hebron High School (the David) was a school with an enrollment of just 98 students. They beat Quincy High School with enrollment of over 2,000 to win the state championship in 1952. In 1964 a little school from near my hometown by the name of Cobden finished second in the state. Cobden was a school with only a hundred or so students. The Appleknockers, as they were called, beat several schools with enrollments of over 2000 to play for the Illinois state championship. They lost to Pekin with an enrollment of 2500 students but there was over 14,000 fans pulling for them that night. The venue change from Champaign and the added classes have contributed to the drop in the size of the crowds. They now have crowds in the six or seven thousand range, about half of what I witnessed. I have never been back to the Illinois state tournament since I left Salem. I want to remember it from the "good ole" days.

CHAPTER 9

Butler County Community College (1979-85)

The best thing that came from our three years at Salem was the birth of our second child, Andrew. Andrew was born in April of 1979 in Centralia, Illinois. Just like before when I left Highland Park to go to Iowa State, I had always had the desire to be a head coach at the college level. It is very difficult to go from high school to college coaching unless you have a special connection or a great player that the head coach is recruiting. Soon after our season was over at Salem, Mal Elliott, our Sports Information Director (SID) and my friend from my days at ORU called me. Mal was the Sports Editor of the Wichita Eagle-Beacon newspaper in Wichita, Kansas. Butler County Community College (BCCC) in El Dorado, KS was looking for a head basketball coach, and he wanted to know if I was interested. He thought it could be a good juco (junior college) job and he could help me get an interview for the job. I, also, had a couple friends with a great deal of influence in Kansas. Jack Hartman, the coach at Kansas State and Gene Stephenson, the coach at Wichita State. These men were coaches that I had

217

known and been friends with since my ORU coaching days. I thought I had a chance at the job. It was my opportunity to get back into college coaching once again. Butler County, located in El Dorado, was in one of the best juco basketball conferences in the country. BCCC had only won only 7 games the year before I went there. Curt Shipley, who was the coach, was giving up coaching to focus on the athletic director's job. I knew that they played good high school basketball in Wichita and I thought I could recruit out-of-state players to come and play in El Dorado, 20 miles from Wichita. There were over 25 coaches that applied for the job at BCCC, but with my experience at ORU, and a phone call from Hartman and Stephenson, I was invited out to interview for the position. My interview with Coach Shipley went so well that he asked me before I left El Dorado if I would take the job if they offered it to me? I liked Coach Shipley and thought he would be a great person to work for. I had planned to stay overnight and look around El Dorado at houses that were for sale and to just get familiar with the town. Coach Shipley arranged a meeting with the school president, Dr. Carl Heinrich and the Dean of Students, Bill Cummins for the morning after my interview with him. That meeting lasted about 30 minutes, and I left the meeting knowing that I was going to be the next basketball coach at Butler County Community College. They liked my background at ORU, but the deciding factor was the phone call and recommendation that Coach Hartman gave me. Curt was a graduate of Kansas State, and like practically everyone else in the state, he admired Coach Hartman. Coach

Hartman, who had coached at Southern Illinois University with Walt Frazier and won the NIT would become a Hall Of Fame coach and a legend at KSU.

After accepting the BCCC job, Coach Eller and Dr. Raver were great about allowing me to take days off so I could travel back and forth to El Dorado to recruit and work at Butler. They had been so good to me, I wasn't about to jump out and leave them before the school year was over. I made several trips out to Kansas from late March until school was out in May. Besides traveling I was calling my coaching friends in Illinois and the St. Louis area trying to find players to take with me to Butler. Even though we had recruited Eldon Lawyer (who played for us at ORU) from Butler County, I really didn't know any high school coaches in the state of Kansas. I certainly had my work cut out for me, but I was back coaching in college. I was looking forward to moving to El Dorado.

It was a tough time for Diane because I was gone so much. She now had a baby to take care of as well as a four year old. We had a house to sell, packing to get done, and a move as soon as school was out. Fortunately, I had a good assistant at Butler that had been there for over 20 years, Gene Arnold. Gene had been the assistant coach for Coach Shipley for the 10 years that he had been the coach. He had been the assistant coach before Coach Shipley during the 1968-69 season when Butler won 27 games, the most in their history. Coach Shipley had had some good teams at Butler, but the last couple years, they had really struggled. Curt, who was from Kansas, had a great reputation around the state and knew a lot of people. That first year at Butler I picked his brain about the conference and some of the high school coaches. Even though Gene had been in Kansas for over 20 years, ironically, he was born in Grayville, Illinois which is about 40 miles from Galatia, my hometown. Butler County had won a National Championship in basketball in 1953. The school had produced two juco All-Americans, Tony Andre in 1977-78 and Robert Cox in 1976-77. They had sent seven players to Division I schools. One of those players was Eldon Lawyer. BCCC had been a contender in the Kansas Jayhawk Conference but the program had slipped in the last several years. There was a lot to get done at Butler before the season even started. My number one focus was on trying to recruit players. It was going to be tough to win in the Jayhawk Conference, and it would take awhile to recruit the kind of players that I would need to win. It didn't take long for me to discover that every team in the conference, all 20 schools had one or two Division I prospects. Coaches in Texas and California might argue about who plays the best Juco basketball in the entire country, but Kansas has to be in the top three. The Jayhawk Conference was split into a West and East, BCCC played in the West, the toughest division. Hutchinson, which hosts the National Junior College Tournament each year, is one of the schools in the Western division. The conference had a rule that a school cannot have more than five out-of-state basketball players each year on their team. I liked the rule but it made it tough on me. As the newcomer in the league, it was hard to get the kind of Kansas kids that it would take to win. It also put a premium on what five out-of-state players a coach brought in; I could not afford to make many mistakes. These were Kansas colleges, so Kansas kids should make up the majority of the teams. Kansas high schools played a good brand of basketball, especially in the Wichita and Kansas City areas. Wichita high schools were going to be my main focus for two reasons: it was close, and they played good basketball.

Coach Sutter and Coach Arnold talk to the team during timeout at Butler County CC. 1983

I also knew that the African-American kids we recruited from Wichita would be close to home and a large African-American population. It wasn't going to be easy because everyone in the Jayhawk Conference recruited Wichita. We had a nice school and a nice dorm, but Butler was recognized more for its football than basketball when I arrived in 1979. The high school kids in Wichita were not thinking about going to BCCC to play basketball. Coach Arnold knew a lot of high school coaches and that certainly helped.

One of the things that I did not realize about Butler was that it was the farthest east in the Western division. Just like at Salem, the travel to play the other schools in the conference was not easy. While the proximity to Wichita was an asset to us when it came time to recruit and fly in out-of-state players, it was a real liability during the season when we had to make three hour bus rides to play a game. There were 10 schools in the Western division, and all but two of those schools would require at least a two hour bus ride. It just seemed that I was destined for long bus rides. Dodge City, Garden City, and Seward County were all over three hours from El Dorado. In the middle of a Kansas winter with blowing snow and temperatures in the teens those bus trips were long and sometimes treacherous. I remember several times getting home at one or two in the morning and the doors on my car were frozen shut.

Our gym seated about 2000 but was bland, simple, and had no atmosphere. There wasn't even a separate dressing room for the basketball team. Everyone used the PE dressing area with the little lockers. There was an office for the men PE teachers and an office for the women PE teachers, but no coaches' offices. I had to share an office in the library with the cross country coach. Needless to say, I didn't have much privacy or a very impressive office to sell recruits when I brought them on campus. Before I even moved my family to El Dorado, I had already started getting the gym painted and a "special" area in the back of the PE locker room, closed off for the basketball team. Coach Shipley was great about letting me do things around the gym. He increased my budget and was willing to help me in any way he could. He wanted me to succeed. He knew that Butler had some catching up to do to compete with the other basketball programs in the league.

While I was occupied with getting things done in El Dorado, Diane was busy getting us packed up and getting our house sold. Selling the house turned out to be one of the easiest things that we had to do. We had built a small, three-bedroom house on a really nice street in a new subdivision behind the high school in Salem. One of the advantages to being the basketball coach in a small town like Salem was that everyone knew that I had resigned and was moving. Before we could even hire a real estate agent or put a For Sale sign up in our front yard, a lady came to the house and asked us how much we wanted for the house. We had not even done any research or comps for our neighborhood. We just threw out a figure of about $5000 more than we had paid for it. She made the decision to buy the house that same day, so naturally, we thought we probably sold it too cheap. We were moving as soon as school was out and needed the money to buy a house in El Dorado. We were fine with the quick sell and being able to move on without worrying about selling a house. Diane only had one weekend that she could leave the kids and come to El Dorado to look for our new house. Our real estate agent, who was the wife of the football coach at Butler, had heard that a house in a nice area "might" be coming up on the market. Angie Henson, our agent, knew about everyone and everything that went on in El Dorado. She was very nice, personable, and aggressive. The week before we were coming to town Angie had talked with the lady, a schoolteacher, about selling her house. She wasn't 100% sure she wanted to sell, but Angie worked her magic, gave her our offer, and the lady agreed to sell her house. We bought the house based on Angie's advice. It was perfect for our needs: three-bedroom, a little over 2000 sq. ft., two bath, large garage, and a huge half acre lot. The house was on a great street that had several kids for Amy and eventually Andy to play with. We had great neighbors on both sides of us. Looking back on the whole transition, Diane and I could see God's hand in all of it. It was one of the easiest moves that we have ever made. I will never forget driving the U-Haul from Salem to El Dorado, and getting outside of Kansas City into the open spaces of Kansas at about 9 o'clock in the evening. A storm began off in the distance, and the sky began to light up like a special Fourth of July fireworks display, courtesy of God. Lightning danced all over the sky; it was spectacular and like a welcome to Kansas from God. One of my former players, Steve Schmidt, had decided that he was going to help Diane drive so she would be able to take care of Andrew, our infant son. Steve was the 5' 7" point guard that had gotten cut from the varsity the year before I got to Salem, but ended up starting for me and being one of the best point guards I've ever coached.

El Dorado was a town of about 12,000 people who made their living from the two oil and gas refineries located just outside the town. Besides the oil, the biggest source of income for El Dorado was the community college, which at the time I was there, had about 5,000 students. Like most jucos probably 80 percent of those students commuted. The businesses and townspeople support the college and are proud of the school that is located just on the outskirts. The locals were very hospitable to Diane and me. We felt right at home soon after we moved. Diane didn't have too much time to socialize; she had her hands full with a four-year old and an infant son. I couldn't wait to get going at the college with all the things I saw that I wanted to do to get Butler to a first class program.

It is always about the talent when it comes to winning and Butler didn't have much of that when I arrived. We were able to recruit six freshmen that first year, but only three returned the second year. Coach Shipley left me a solid 6' 5" center from Washington DC by the name of Tom Brozell. Also returning was a 6' 2' guard, Rodney Winston, also from DC. Rodney had undergone a knee operation halfway through the 77-78 season and never fully recovered. Brozell had a very good sophomore season for us, leading the team in points and rebounds.

He made the all-conference team and went on to play at Morgan State. That first year was a struggle, to say the least. Every team in the Jayhawk Conference was well coached and had good players. The biggest surprise, however, was the travel in our conference; I would never get use to those long bus rides. We finished that first season 5-21. Our players competed, and we began to change the culture around the campus and the town. The year before I arrived, less than 200 people showed up at the home games. We got a lot of positive publicity from our local radio station that broadcast all of our games. I developed a good relationship with our play by play announcer, Steve Moberg. Steve did an outstanding job, and was always promoting our games on KOYY, the local radio station. Steve and I have remained friends, even today. Mal Elliot, my friend and the sports editor of the Wichita Eagle-Beacon newspaper, would also give us some positive publicity. Mal was an outstanding writer and had been the SID at ORU so he knew all about how to put a media guide together. He volunteered to write and put together a Butler County basketball program and media guide for me. No one would ever guess that we had only won five games that first year from all of the publicity that we received. That publicity made a big impact on our future recruiting. We also got great support from our local businesses, which bought advertising in our game program and sponsored our broadcast. Coach Shipley and the administration recognized how hard we were working and were very supportive. I developed a good friendship

with the music director at BCCC, Doug Talbot. Doug recruited about 10 kids to play in the Pep Band at our home
games. Doug became quite a fan and did a great job helping
us develop a "home court" atmosphere. The band played and
the fans would stand and clap until we scored our first basket
at each home game. That first year, sometimes we were standing and clapping for several minutes.

The interest of high school players coming to Butler got
considerably better. We out recruited everyone in the conference, including the big three of Barton County, Dodge City,
and Hutchinson. Gene and I went all over the state recruiting
every week. I was also making a trip to East St. Louis, Illinois
every chance that I got. My last year at Salem I had seen this 6'
8" center, James Douglas, from East St. Louis, playing in the
Centralia tournament. James was good enough to play at most
Division I schools right out of high school but did not have the
grades to qualify for a scholarship. James was not only an outstanding player but also an outstanding person. I developed a
great relationship with his high school coach, Coy Nunn, who
was like a father to James. I thought James would make us an
instant winner. With a couple good players to go with him, I
thought we could win the Jayhawk Conference. He became my
number one recruit and my main focus. Every weekend (if we
did not have a Saturday night game) I was driving the 400
miles from El Dorado to East St. Louis. I knew every rest stop
and fast food establishment between my house and East St.
Louis High School. The East St. Louis Flyers had won a lot of

games with James. My focus was not only to get the best players I could, but players who had played on high school teams that had won.

I needed to change the mindset at Butler, and what better way than to bring in a bunch of proven winners. For that reason, Gene and I also focused a lot of our attention on Wichita South High School. They had won three straight state championships under an outstanding coach by the name of Coach Gus Guice. They played great defense and were very disciplined. They had a 6' 3" outstanding leaper who could play guard or forward by the name of Stephen Foster. Stephen was a great kid with great parents and a solid student. Another "winner" we went after and signed was a 5' 9" point guard who played for Topeka High, the runner-up to Wichita South in the state tournament. Andre Barber was a strong, quick and smart player that ran Coach Nicklin's team at Topeka High School. Coach Nicklin's teams were always in the state tournament. Also, on that same Topeka team was an all-conference player, Rodney Nickerson. Rodney was 6' 3" forward that averaged 16 points and seven rebounds for his team that finished the season 20-4. Our best signee was a small, slim 6' 2" forward from Junction City, Kansas by the name of Major Craig. Major was coach Arnold's "pet recruit." He loved the way he played even as an undersized front line player. Gene drove the two hours from El Dorado to Junction City a half-dozen times to watch Major play. Craig was very quick and almost impossible to guard small forward. He was a "slasher" scorer with an uncanny ability to get in the lane or to the basket and score. He led the conference in scoring with 22 points a game. There are shooters and there are scorers in basketball, and Craig would be a tremendous scorer for us. A lot of schools did not recruit Craig because they thought he was too small to play forward and did not shoot the ball well enough outside to be a guard. He would prove them all wrong.

We had a great in-state recruiting season and with the signing of James we were well on our way to being able to play with anyone. We had 6' 7" Eric Coley and guard Joe Buntyn returning as sophomores, so we had some depth and were excited to get our second year in the Jayhawk Conference started. But first, I was looking forward to a little down time since I felt like I had been in overdrive since getting the Butler job back in March of '79. We had accomplished a lot in only one year, but we still had a long way to go.

Diane and the kids had made several friends in the neighborhood. Amy became really good friends with a little girl that lived two houses up the street. Mendy and Amy were always at each other's houses. On one side of our house lived Mike and Attcha Nolan, and their two daughters. The Nolan's were both school teachers and became life-long friends. Diane also had two good, dependable babysitters right next door with their teenage daughters. On the other side of us was a sweet, older couple that loved Amy and Andy. Russ was a handyman who was always offering to do things for Diane since I was gone a lot. We loved our new house with the big back yard. We even decided to create a big garden and grow our own vegetables. The only thing missing, I thought, was a dog. So I got a beautiful cocker spaniel puppy named Hopper for the kids to play with. I soon learned a dog was not the best idea. Amy was five years old and did not like animals. We tried for a couple weeks to make it work but if the dog was in the house, she was outside. If Hooper was in the backyard, Amy was not going back there. So after a couple weeks we found a new home for Hooper.

Down the street from us lived Tom and Beverly Wilkinson. Tom was in the oil business and a big supporter of the college. We became good friends, and Tom would help me a great deal with his support of the basketball program. The best thing that he did for me and the program was give James Douglas a job that paid him very well. James brought a car with him to El Dorado and needed a way to make some gas money and have spending money. Tom took care of James but made it clear to James that he had to show up to work to get paid; there were no phantom work hours. Up the street from us lived the Lattimers, who had five kids. He was a dentist and his wife and Diane became good friends. We were very happy with our new home and neighborhood. We joined the First Baptist Church and became good friends with Steve and Linda Clark, who had two kids a little older than our two. I didn't really have many hobbies or distractions from basketball, at that time, but Steve helped me develop one. He bought a new catamaran, Hobie Cat, which he liked to take out on a nice lake about 2 miles from town. Sailing a boat in Kansas is pretty easy because the wind blows about every day. I enjoyed going out with Steve and sailing, having a beer, and getting away. The constant wind is nice if you are into sailing but it can be annoying if you're a golfer and not use to it. I remember one day out playing golf and it was really windy. I was complaining about the wind and my playing partner, a Kansan, told me that I had two choices, get used to playing in the wind or quit playing. After that, I never whined again about the wind.

We started the 1980-81 season by winning three of our first four games, losing only to a good Allen County team by five points on their home court. We won five conference games including a win against perennial powerhouse, Hutchinson. Those five wins were four more then we had won in the conference the entire year before. We finished the season 8-17 but we were competitive, and I felt like we had turned the corner. We just needed another good recruiting class to go with the six or seven freshmen that we would have coming back as sophomores. Douglas, Foster, and Craig had good years and gained some valuable experience. James led us in scoring with 15 points a game and averaged nine rebounds. We got some very positive publicity in the Wichita paper and around the league. The coaches were saying that Butler County was no longer a push over. We averaged over 75 points a game and attendance at our home games was double what it was the first year. We again capitalized on being close to Wichita by adding an outstanding point guard from Wichita South,

Butch Berry. South was 42-6 and won a state championship with Butch as the point guard. He had been a teammate of Stephen Foster the year before. Butch went on to be one of the best team leaders and smartest players I have ever coached. Now we had two outstanding point guards in Barber and Berry. Butch played for BCCC for two years and then signed a scholarship to play at Oral Roberts University, just like Lawyer had done in 1972. We also signed a good prospect from Douglass, KS, named John Ford, one of two Fords we recruited that year. We had signed some good Kansas high school players but we needed some outstanding players from out-of-state if we were going to win the conference.

Our number one out-of-state recruit came from Alabama and was the step brother of Sam McCamey, who was a great player for us at ORU. Henry Ford, no relation to the automobile icon, was only 6' 3" but was the Alabama state champion in the high jump. Henry set an Alabama state record with a jump of 7' 3/4". Henry was 190 lbs., of muscle. He was a great athlete, who could rebound with guys four or 5 inches taller and could score by jumping over and out muscling players inside. We also signed a 6' 6" forward from Florida by the name of Earl "Magic" Walker. Earl was in All Broward County high school player who, like James, was good enough to play at a DI school right out of high school but needed to get his grades up. Earl led our team in scoring as a sophomore and made the Jayhawk All-Conference team before signing a scholarship to play at Mercer University in Macon, Georgia. Several years later, after we had moved to Tampa, FL, Earl called me to invite me to come and see him play. He was playing professional basketball in the Continental League, for the Albany Patroons. Albany was coached by future hall-of-fame coach of the Bulls and Lakers, Phil Jackson. Andrew and I went to the game and met Coach Jackson after the game. We also signed a teammate of Henry's from Scottsboro, Alabama, Byron Green. Byron was a 6' 3" forward, who had originally signed to play at Northeast Alabama Junior College, but decided to transfer to Butler and play with Henry.

I felt like we now had enough depth, size, and experience to not only compete in the Jayhawk Conference, but to win it. The new recruits had all come from winning programs just like the players we had recruited the previous year. We had great chemistry, thanks to the sophomores. We started out the season winning our first seven games. That was only one game less than we had won the entire previous year. We won our own tournament and a four team tournament in St. Louis at Forest Park Community College. There were several highlights to our season, and one of those was winning the tournament in St. Louis. I wanted to take James back "home" to play, so his family and friends could see him. It was also fun for me because my Salem friends drove over to see us play in the championship game on Saturday. Just like old times, they planned a "scouting trip" in Bill's van. They had a few beers on the drive over but that didn't stop us from having a few more at *Stan and Biggies* famous St. Louis restaurant after the game. We had a great time after the game reminiscing and telling "war stories" until they ran us out and closed the place. I had been to St. Louis many times but had never been to my hero's restaurant, the great St. Louis Cardinal, Stan Musial.

We split games that year with the three best teams in our conference: Dodge, Barton and Hutchinson. We beat Hutchinson at their place for the first time in five years. While we had many highlights our loss to Dodge City on their court by two points in overtime in the playoffs was very disappointing. We finished third in the conference behind Barton County and Dodge City. We had beaten them both during the regular season, and our players and I were confident we could beat them again. In the play-off game, we had a two point lead going into the last couple minutes but turned the ball over and lost by two in overtime. We finished the season with a 22-8 record, the second best record in the school's history. For the first time in 12 years, Butler was ranked in the top 20 in the country among junior colleges.

Sideline coaching "Position"
Butler County CC. 1981

Every team and every year takes on its own unique iden-
tity, this was one of the most satisfying seasons I have ever
had as a coach. We had come so far in three years, and I was
so proud of our players. They had demonstrated their confidence in me and what we were trying to do by signing on to
play for me at Butler. There were very few "hiccups" during

the season, and if a problem crept in, the players addressed the situation before it got to be a serious. Berry and Barber, our point guards, were great leaders on and off the court. James Douglas was just incredible; he became only the fourth Grizzly, our mascot, in school history to be named to the All Region VI first team, which included junior colleges in Kansas and Oklahoma. He was a two-time all Jayhawk Conference selection, a unanimous pick as a sophomore. Ford and Craig were also chosen All Jayhawk Conference. James was recruited by several D1 schools and decided to get back closer to home and play at the University of Missouri. It was his choice; he was 20 years old, but I really wanted him to go to Kansas State and play for Coach Hartman. All those seven-hour driving trips from El Dorado to East St. Louis were definitely worth it. James would come over to our house all the time, unannounced, and eat with us and hang out. He was great with our kids, particularly with our four-year-old son, Andy. Tom and Beverly Wilkinson had also played a major role in James success and happiness at Butler. We were losing, not only James, but Barber, Foster and Craig, as well. They had all played a major role in putting BCCC on the juco basketball map.

We had gone from five wins my first year to 22 wins three years later. Going into the 82-83 season I felt confident, but we still had to replace an All Region player in Douglas and make up for over 40 points of our team average of 78 points per game. I always thought that coaching in junior college was unique in that every two years you have a totally new roster. Sometimes you don't even have a player two years because the good ones leave in one year. As a coach at the juco level you are constantly recruiting, replacing and reloading. I was finding out firsthand just how difficult it was going to be to consistently win. We had established a good reputation in the state of Kansas, so recruiting was getting easier. However, we were still recruiting against two or three small four-year colleges and 19 other junior colleges for the best high school players in Kansas. KU, KSU, and Wichita State, the three Division I programs in the state, got whoever they wanted.

I was able to recruit and sign another really good big man from St. Louis, Tony Dye. Tony was 6' 8" class 5A All-Stater from St. Louis Northwest High School. He averaged 20 points and 20 rebounds a game his senior year at Northwest. He knew about the success that Douglas had had at Butler and knew we would help him academically as well as develop his basketball skills. We signed a 6' 3" outstanding scorer from Julian High School in Chicago, Gwayne Lambert. Lambert led his high school to a sectional championship and a 20-7 record. We signed another 6' 8" center from a little town called Olpe, KS. Fittingly, our players nicknamed, James Redeker from Olpe, "Opie." We also signed Greg Allen from Derby, Joe Howard from Wichita, and Jerry Kruger from Topeka who were outstanding guards. Jerry was the younger brother of Lon Kruger, who at the time was the basketball coach at Pan-American University in Texas. Coach Kruger went on to coach at his alma mater, Kansas State and four other D1 schools, as well as coach in the NBA for the Atlanta Hawks. Lon and I became friends; he recruited one of my high school players to the University of Illinois, several years later when I was coaching in Florida. Andy, our son, attended his basketball camp at the University of Florida. We started the season with the same identical record as the year before going 7-0. We lost game eight and game nine on the road to a really good Coffeyville team and at Allen County. We came back home and played six straight games, including a return game with Coffeyville, and won five of those games. We lost in the finals of our tournament to a very good Cloud County team by 2 points. Our game with Coffeyville was a classic; the game went into two overtimes before we finally won 105-104. We finished the season 5-7 and fifth in the Jayhawk Conference, just missing out on making the playoffs. We got upset at Garden City by a team that we had beaten by 15 points at our place, that loss knocked us out of the playoffs. We won 19 games and were disappointed. Our perspective had certainly changed from a couple years earlier. Walker had a great year; he led us in scoring with 18 points and over eight rebounds a game. He made All-Conference along with our outstanding point guard, Butch Berry. Both received D1 scholarships. Ford, who had made All-Conference as a freshman, did not have the same kind of year as he had in 81-82. He never felt as comfortable playing with Dye as he had the year before playing with Douglas. Dye and a couple of our other freshmen struggled and did not play as well as we had hoped they would.

The Jayhawk Conference was a tough league and a big step up from high school. We continued to grow our home attendance, averaging close to 500 fans a game. Because BCCC was a commuter school, it was hard to get a lot of students to the games. Our big rival games with Hutchinson, Barton County, and Dodge City, were sell outs. Doug and the pep band were awesome; we had truly created a home-court atmosphere. Everyone that came into play us knew it was going to be a dogfight. The attendance at our basketball games was not the only increase, our residence also went up; our third child was born in April, 1981. Ashlee would complete the AAA club: Amy, Andrew, and Ashlee. We had three kids, all born in different states, no surprise since dad was a college coach. Perhaps one of the reasons for our increase in home attendance was the halftime show. In addition to having fire flaming baton exhibitions and gymnastics exhibitions, we had kids from my camps play during halftime. But the star was Andy, who was four years old. He loved to get out on the court to shoot baskets and play. He was a cute little kid, and the fans enjoyed seeing him.

I was always promoting our program and raising money to try to take care of our players and to subsidize our budget. Curt had increased our basketball budget and had given me what I needed to have a successful program. However, there was always "extras" that I needed to help our players with certain needs, like getting home at Christmas. I started a golf tournament as a fundraiser for our program. We had about

100 golfers who were willing to pay $50 to play and to spend money on mulligans and other "fringe" benefits. I could raise enough cash from this one activity to support our program for a year. I always felt an obligation to do what was right and necessary to take care of my players, especially the ones who were hundreds of miles away from home. I have always believed that the athletes that generate so much money for their programs should get a fair stipend. Coaches and schools make a fortune off of the skills of these great athletes, and oftentimes they do not even have enough money in their pocket to go on a date or go out and get a meal. A scholarship and a "free" education are great, but there should be more for the athlete than just that. I am happy that the NCAA has finally gotten around to making it legal for college athletes to benefit monetarily from the use of their name and likeness.

Before the basketball season started in 1983 I got word that my dad had passed away. I was in the gym working out some of our players when Coach Arnold came in and told me that the nursing home, where my dad had been for a few weeks, had called the athletic office about his death. Dad had been struggling with diabetes for several years. I had gone to see him in August shortly after he had to have a foot amputated due to the disease. After he lost his foot I think he kind of gave up on life. He never left the nursing home and just wasn't interested in rehabilitation. The first day I saw him in the nursing home after he had left the hospital was the first time he fully realized that his foot was gone. I remember him saying

"I thought that is what had happened." I think he was in denial. It was less than a month after I left him that he died from congestive heart failure. My dad was a tough man who had worked at manual jobs since he was 8 or 9 years old. He was 75 years old when he died on September 1, 1983. I admired my dad's work ethic, and while he could be harsh and "strong headed," he also had a soft and compassionate side that not many people saw.

Also before the start of the 1983-84 season, Coach Shipley made a decision that would affect my coaching career at BCCC. Curt decided that he no longer wanted to be the athletic director. He would just continue on as the head of the physical education department at the college. Curt was not only my boss and the person that had hired me but a good friend. The school year wasn't getting off to a very good start from my perspective. Losing my dad and now losing my boss was just the beginning. Coach Shipley had the respect of Dr. Heinrich, the school president, and Bill Cummins, the Dean of students. They allowed him to run the athletic program the way he saw fit, without any interference from them. He, in turn, allowed me to run the basketball program as I saw fit. Tom Spicer, a graduate of Fort Hays State University in Kansas and a former football coach in high school in Oklahoma became our new athletic director. Coach Spicer and I seemed to hit it off okay those first few months after he came to Butler. That all changed about a month before basketball season was about to start. Tony Dye, my 6' 8" center from St. Louis who averaged over

nine points and seven rebounds a game as a freshman was ac-
cused of breaking into the dorm director's apartment and steal-
ing $50. The only evidence that anyone had that it was Tony
was that whoever kicked the door in had a big foot. Tom and
Mr. Cummins had decided that it had to be Tony because he
would have known where the money was and he wore a size
15 shoe. There were about 100 other boys who lived in the
dorm, and also knew where the money was kept. Tony did
have a big foot but there were also some football players living
in the dorm who had a big foot. I seriously doubt that those
facts and their theory would've held up very well in a court of
law. Tony emphatically denied that he was the one that had
broken into the apartment. After a day or two of back and forth
with Coach Spicer, I was "informed" that I had to send Tony
home. Tony was a street kid from St. Louis, but he had been
with us for a year and had gone to class and done everything
that we had asked him to do. I liked Tony, and told Coach
Spicer and Mr. Cummins that I thought he deserved a second
chance. Neither one of them was willing to reconsider, so I really had no choice but to send Tony back to St. Louis. Tony had
the potential to be all conference and a Division I player. He
would make us competitive in the Jayhawk Conference by
himself. Now, a month before we are to start the season, my
biggest and best player was gone. I don't believe this would
have happened if Coach Shipley would have still been the athletic director. This would also be a harbinger of things to come
in my dealings with our new athletic director.

My friends on the basketball staff at Wichita State tried to help us, after I lost Dye, by sending us a 6' 9", 250 lb player from Springfield, Illinois. Charles 'Junior' Ray was leaving Northern Michigan University and rather than set out a year, he was looking for a junior college. He would still have to set out one semester to get his grades up and qualify, but he was a big inside presence and we needed some help. We signed a good 6' 5" forward, David Miller, who would start for us as a freshman but we would start the season very under sized. David had made All-State at Derby, KS, and had been recruited by every school in the Jayhawk Conference. Tony Brinkley and Anthony Edmonds, both at 6' 4" and both from Indianapolis, would give us some much-needed help on our front line. The best recruit of this freshman crop was a 6' 5" forward-guard from Urbana, Illinois. Eric Smith, was an All-State and All-Conference player who played for a good friend of mine, Hal Wertich. Hal was an excellent coach who had been very successful coaching in a very tough confer-ence in central Illinois. Eric was a great kid as well as player. He was good enough to play D1 basketball, but just needed to improve his grades. After two years with us he would get another opportunity. We had good perimeter players at But-ler, we were just missing a big man, like Tony Dye. We had won 41 games the past two years, and due to our success, we were invited to play in junior college tournaments outside of Kansas. One of those invitations came from Phoenix, Arizona, and an opportunity to play in the Valley Of The Sun

Classic over Thanksgiving. It was a prestigious tournament and a great opportunity for our players and our program to get some national publicity. A friend of mine from back in my days at ORU was the basketball coach of the Phoenix Suns, John MacLeod. MacLeod had been the coach at the University of Oklahoma before moving on to coach the Suns in the NBA. I called John and told him we were going to be in Phoenix over Thanksgiving and asked if I could bring the team to one of his practices. I thought it would be a great experience for our kids to see an NBA team up close and personal. He invited us to their practice and spent 30 minutes talking to our team after practice.

During the tournament we beat Phoenix Community College in the first game. However, we lost in the finals 86-96, to a very good nationally ranked team, Ricks CC from Idaho. We struggled through the first 13 games without Ray, we did not have a player over 6' 5". We were going into the conference 6-8. We had a good group of kids who played hard and were trying to do everything we asked of them. Junior gave us an instant boost with his inside presence, but he was really out of shape and couldn't play more than about five minutes at a time. Eric was having a great year as a freshman, but we were lacking a solid floor leader. We had recruited several guards, but none of them had the leadership abilities of a Barber or Berry. Eric ended up leading our team in points and rebounds. Ray, who only played half the season, ended up averaging 15 points and 9 rebounds a game. Had we had him all season, he would really have made a difference in the number of games we won. The truth of the matter was had we had Tony Dye we would have certainly won more than 12 games. Tony would have made us competitive in our conference. He was good enough to have influenced the outcome of several games. It was a tough year, the toughest for me since that first year in 1979-80.

One of the best things that took place beginning with the 83-84 season was the school embarked on a gym building and extension program. Finally, after five years, my players were going to get a nice, private dressing room and I would have my own office. We added an auxiliary basketball court on to the back of the gym so the kids had a place to play during the day when the gym was being used for volleyball or PE classes. The project was completed in the summer of 1984, just in time for my last year at Butler.

Coach Spicer and I had managed a professional relationship after the Tony Dye incident. Tom, unlike Curt, was a micro manager who thought he should be involved in the basketball program. He was a former football coach, who had been around Butler for one year, and had never coached in college. I had worked tirelessly for five years building the BCCC basketball program into a competitive and respected program. I never pretended to know it all about coaching college basketball, but I had been doing it for 10 years now at the D1 level and at Butler. I certainly knew more than Tom did about running a college basketball program. Before the end of the 83-84 season, the women's basketball coach, Tonya Kershner, was "nudged" out for a man Tom knew and wanted as the coach. Steve Kirkham and Tom had developed a friendship when they both were at Fort Hays State University so Tom hired Steve to coach the women's team. I began to see the writing on the wall.

Soon after Steve came on board, he began to promote a young man he knew to be my assistant coach, a guy by the name of Dick Clark. He thought I needed someone who was young, energetic and would be a good recruiter. Supposedly, Dick had contacts all over the country and had recruited players for Dallas Baptist, Fort Hays State, and Jackson Community College in Michigan. Steve was always talking up the attributes of Dick Clark to me and to Tom. It was the perfect storm for me in my basketball coaching career. I was still upset over losing Dye and having a losing season. Coach Arnold had been with the college over 20 years and had been my assistant for the last five years. He was honest, hard-working, and most of all very loyal. But in the five years with me, he had never recruited outside of Kansas and while the players liked him, he did not do a lot of teaching in practice, which was my fault in some ways. He was in his 50s and I felt like I was doing everything within the program alone. We had one player coming back, Eric Smith, who could compete at a high level. Davis Miller, who averaged eight points a game as a freshman, was a solid player. I had began to wear down a little from all of the out-of-state recruiting and felt like I needed someone who could help me get some players. I decided to make a change. That decision would turn out to be one of the worst decisions that I have ever made in coaching. It would turn out bad for everyone involved, and it would doom my coaching career at BCCC.

I decided to replace Gene Arnold with Dick Clark. Cardinal rule number one in hiring an assistant: never hire anyone you do not know. Cardinal rule number two: if you don't really know someone you probably can't totally trust them. I never knew Dick Clark until Steve Kirkham started talking him up to me and Coach Spicer. Dick was a nice guy who was in his late 20s, but he really didn't deliver on any of his so-called great out-of-state players. Even though he was closer to the player's ages then Gene, he didn't have as close a relationship as Gene had with them. Cardinal rule number three: before firing an assistant coach, take the time to analyze and evaluate what that person brings to the table. In this case, with Gene, he had been at the college for a long time and had some strong ties with the administration. They liked him and appreciated his loyalty and work at the college. He was also very close friends with Tom Wilkinson, the same Tom Wilkinson that had helped me by taking care of Douglas over the two years he was at Butler. I realized as the year went along that I had pretty much isolated myself and was on an island. Tom had the upper hand and it would be just a matter of time before he could get rid of me and hire his own man. As they say, "winning covers all sins," we needed to win, and it wasn't going to be easy. Dick had found a 6' 4" forward, who was looking to transfer from Henderson County Junior College, Willie Ashley. Willie was a good player, a great leaper but would have to sit out the first semester. We had gone through that scenario the year before with Junior, not an ideal situation. It was tough enough to win when I had the players two years, a half a year was almost impossible. We also brought in a kid from Macon, Georgia, who had not played basketball for two years. Al Goolsby would also have to sit out the first semester. Al was 6' 6" and strictly an inside player who did not shoot the ball very well but could rebound and play defense. I signed two players that I had never seen play, and was going strictly on Dick's recommendation. More importantly, I was also getting away from my basic philosophy of getting players who had won in high school. I signed another one of Coy Nunn's players from East St. Louis, a guard named Deundre Spraggins. Teddy, as he preferred to be called, was a tremendous athlete who at 5' 10" could dunk the ball with both hands. He was quick and could score off the dribble or from outside. We signed a couple solid Kansas kids, but neither one of them was good enough to make an impact in our league as a freshman. We basically had Eric and David the first semester to carry the team. Fortunately, our pre- conference schedule was not as difficult as in the previous two years. As expected, we struggled through the first 12 games but managed to go 5-7. We finally got everyone eligible and on the court on January 5th, but still lost to Cowley County on their court. Al and Willie showed the signs of rust from not playing. It would take a few games for them to really hit their stride, but we were running out of games. It was a struggle every game and not having the whole team together for the entire season proved to be too much to overcome. One of our few highlights was a win over Hutchinson, who would end up winning the conference. The game was in our gym, and half of the gym was filled with Hutchinson fans. They had beaten us by 20 points earlier in the year at their place. We played our best game of the year and led most of the game until one of their players threw in an off-balance jump shot with about two seconds to go to take a one point lead. We called timeout, threw the ball to the top of the lane, and hit a 22' shot at the buzzer to win by one. It was the biggest win of the long season for us.

For the second straight year, we only won three games in the conference and finished the season 10-18. I felt totally responsible for the outcome of the season. I did not recruit the type of players that we had had in the previous years. They were not as good athletically nor was the chemistry and mental aptitude what we had in our players in the past. I really felt sorry for Eric, he had played hard every night, most nights getting double teamed. In spite of finishing last in the conference, Eric was picked to the All-Conference team and the All Region VI team. James Douglas had achieved that honor two years earlier, but considering our record over the last two years, that was quite an accomplishment for Eric.

I knew going into the year that I was on a short leash. I never thought Tom totally supported me. Maybe it was because I never sought him out and ask for his opinion. The truth of the matter was I looked at him as a football guy. He seemed to be more comfortable and engaged with the football staff. I think that any chance that I had of saving my job went out the window on a cold, snowy, horrible February day. The winters in Kansas could be brutal, with the blowing snow, the ice, and temperatures into the teens. It was on one of those days in February that we were scheduled to go to Dodge City to play. Dodge was a three-hour bus ride from El Dorado on a good weather day, and this was anything but a good weather day. It had been below freezing with blowing snow for two days and the weather report was not sounding much better. I talked with Tom about rescheduling the basketball game early on the morning of the game. That would give the Dodge City authorities plenty of time to make other arrangements and notify the referees. I was not interested in taking my twelve basketball players, managers, and anyone else on the road in this kind of weather just to play a basketball game. Instead of working with me and understanding, he said that if we left in the morning we should be there in plenty of time to play a 7:30 game. He didn't say anything about getting home after the game, which could have been a 6 or 7 hour bus ride. I explained to him that it was the prerogative of the travel team to decide if it was safe or not to travel. For some reason, he thought we should go to Dodge on this particular day and play. Finally, I told him that I wasn't taking the team to Dodge, if he wanted Butler County to play Dodge City he would have to take the team. That was the final straw. I guess that could be interpreted as insubordination, but there was almost a month left in the season and we had plenty of time to make up the game. It wasn't a week after this encounter that I began hearing from my friends around the league that I was in "trouble." At this time, there was only one other coach in the Jayhawk Conference that had been in the league longer than me. I was finishing my sixth year, and as I discovered, coaching in junior college is like "dog" years. I have a lot of respect for those junior college coaches that have spent 15 or 20 years coaching at that level. I was worn out, mentally and physically, and while it was not my choice to leave Butler, I was ready to turn the page and move on with my life. I was "given" the opportunity to resign. I wasn't about to give Tom the satisfaction of a resignation. I was let go less than a week after the end of the season.

Just like at Salem I left BCCC in much better shape than I found it. We didn't win as many games as I would've liked, nor did we ever win the Jayhawk Conference. Nevertheless, we were competitive and changed the culture and atmosphere around the basketball program during those six years. I had the privilege of contributing to the development of over 70 young men. Of those players that stayed in our program two years, 90% got their associates degree. Seven of our players got scholarships to four year schools.

Off the basketball court, our family had enjoyed our six years in El Dorado. We developed some friendships that have endured even to today. Diane taught in an outstanding school and worked for one of her all-time favorite principals, Mr. Nutley. We had some harsh winters and a hailstorm or two, but outside of the constant wind, Kansas was a nice place. There had been a couple of times when Diane had to grab the kids and run down the street to the Wilkinson's house to get in their storm cellar because of a tornado warning. Dick and Linda Clark were great friends that we had spent a lot of fun time with. The Nolan's, who lived next door, are still on our Christmas card exchange list. I have never been one to look back and question why things turn out the way they do. God is in control and sometimes what looks like it is bad for man, God means for good. The windshield is much larger than the rear view mirror. I have always been one who liked to look ahead with much more anticipation and excitement then to look at where I've been with regret. I had decided I was going to get out of coaching, at least for a while, and enjoy spending time with our three kids. Amy was nine, Andrew was six, and Ashlee was four, they needed a dad that was around and being a part of their lives. Diane had done a great job in my absence, but it was time for me to get more involved. In reflecting back on what had transpired over the last six years of my life, I could see that I had squeezed God out of my life in lieu of basketball and chasing a dream to be a Division I coach. We moved to Florida and I rededicated my life to Christ. I got more involved in church and refocused my priorities. In sports, there is a saying, "that you are what your record says you are," but that is a complete lie; it is never that black and white. In six years at Butler, we lost 14 more games then we won. But in my mind and to those who followed our program from the very beginning, I think we had come along way and were successful. In coaching, there are basically two types of coaches, those that build and those that sustain. I guess I'm one of those builders.

Welcome to My World

CHAPTER 10

Final Stop: The Sunshine State
(1985-present)

Diane and the kids still had to finish out the school year, so I had from March until May to think about what we were going to do. I was 100% sure of one thing I didn't want to coach basketball again for a while and maybe never. We had lived in cold climate parts of the country ever since we had been married: Michigan, Illinois, Iowa, Oklahoma and Kansas. Florida sounded pretty good to me. I had recruited Florida and spent some time in Florida, but always on the East Coast and in the Fort Lauderdale area. Obviously, in the winter when I was recruiting, the warm weather in Florida was great. However, I never really liked the Fort Lauderdale-Miami area. I thought it was too congested and a lot of the people who retired there were from the New York-New Jersey area, and the east coast. It was too fast and too pushy for a Midwesterner like me. Besides, God often goes ahead of us and prepares a way. Well, way back when Diane and I were living in Detroit and became friends with the Carlson's, we also met and became friends with the Tomkinson's. Tim and Diana had moved to

Clearwater, Florida, on the gulf coast a few years earlier. When I was looking for job opportunities and to relocate our family, I "just happen" to talk with Denny Carlson. He suggested that I get in touch with Tim about teaching jobs around Tampa Bay. I called Tim, who I hadn't spoken to for several years and told him I was looking for a job and we wanted to move to Florida. Tim was in the real estate business, so he had a pretty good handle on the demographics of the area. I was looking at our next move, as our last move.

According to the newspaper *USA Today*, thousands of people were moving out of the cold and to Florida every year. It just made sense to me that if Florida was growing that fast, there must be a big demand for teachers. Tim gave me some good advice about where I should look for a teaching position. He told me Clearwater and St. Petersburg were expensive places to live and had a heavy population of retirees. He thought that across the bay in the Tampa area, the demographics were of younger people, more cosmopolitan and the population was really growing. He didn't know anyone in the school system so he couldn't help me that way, but I was welcome to come and stay with them, and use his car to look for a job. A couple weeks later I was in Florida looking for a teaching position. I didn't know anyone in the school system; I got a school directory of Hillsborough County schools and just started at the top. The schools were listed in alphabetical order and the first school that I drove to that first morning was Armwood High School. I didn't have an appointment; I planned to stay in the Tampa area until I found a job. Armwood, was located in Brandon, a suburb of about 50,000 people just east of Tampa. In the 60s, Brandon was a small farming community of about 5000 people located on Highway 60 with a two lane road running through it, and one traffic light. Today, there are over 150,000 people and hundreds of traffic lights. I walked into Armwood that morning about 9 o'clock and asked the secretary if I could speak with someone about a teaching position. She asked me if I had filled out an application with the county school system, which I had. The Hillsborough school system requires a lot of paperwork, which goes downtown to the central office, when applying for a teaching position. However, the principals at the respective schools hire their own staffs. Armwood had opened the year before and was only the second high school in Brandon. The secretary informed me that Mr. Flagg, the principal, was not in the office, but the assistant principal Mrs. Hughes was in and she would see if she had time to talk to me. She not only had time to talk with me, but our "interview" went on for almost an hour. Needless to say- we hit it off pretty well. While she said she could not, at this time, offer me a job teaching (due to a hiring freeze on new teachers) she would get back to me within a few days. It was still only mid-morning so I had the rest of the day to continue looking at schools. I really wanted to teach in high school but I knew Buchanan junior high was looking for a physical education teacher. I drove up to North Tampa to speak with them about their opening. The principal was very nice and very interested in hiring me. I was surprised to discover that the school did not have a gymnasium, and all of my classes would be outside. I was excited to be moving to Florida and the beautiful weather, but I was not sure I wanted to spend six or seven hours every day in the Florida sun. I wasn't sure I wanted to teach 13 and 14 year olds all day either. I also discovered that North Tampa was very crowded and traffic was terrible. I drove to another high school: Gaither, in North Tampa and was told again about the freeze and I would have to make an appointment to come back. I liked Mrs. Hughes and already decided that I wanted to teach at Armwood and live in Brandon. That night while eating dinner at Tim's the phone rang and it was Mrs. Hughes, from Armwood. She was calling to tell me that she had talked with Mr. Flagg, the principal, and they were offering me a teaching position. Now there is no other way to explain how I got a job at the first school I visited in the area that I wanted to live (in less than an hour interview) except God. He had orchestrated it all! I was ready to get back to Kansas and start packing. We were headed for the sunshine state.

I was still getting a paycheck from Butler through the school year. Diane and the kids would be finishing school in May. We were planning on moving in June, or as soon as we could sell our house and find a new one. We also needed to find a job for Diane. Angie, our real estate agent, already had some people interested in buying our house. Again, just like in Salem, we did not even have to put our house on the market.

A couple weeks after I got back from Tampa, I arranged for Diane to come with me to Tampa to look for a job and a house. We stayed with Tim and enjoyed reliving our Detroit days. We had made an appointment with a realtor to help us find a house. We planned to go to a few elementary schools in Brandon to look for a job for Diane. I needed to stop by Armwood and see Mrs. Hughes about my health teaching position. I introduced Mrs. Hughes to Diane and mentioned that she was looking for a teaching position, too. Mrs. Hughes, immediately picked up the phone and called a friend of hers who was the principal at an elementary school in Plant City. Plant City is a town of about 20,000 people about 10 miles from Brandon. The principal at Cork Elementary school, Mrs. Gilbert, wanted Diane to come out that morning and interview for a position. Her interview went great. She wanted to hire Diane, but because of the teaching freeze she could not offer her a job right then. Mrs. Gilbert told Diane that she had a fourth grade teacher out on a maternity leave and she needed a substitute for the first three months of school. She told Diane that the school was growing and that if they opened up another fourth grade after school started that Diane would be in line for a permanent position. Again, just like two weeks earlier, we had sit down at Tim's for dinner after praying about a job for Diane, and the phone rang. It was Mrs. Gilbert who told Diane she could count on a job at Cork in the fall. We both had jobs now. Now, we needed to find a house. We had hired a sweet older lady as our real estate agent and had given her our price range. Because I was going to be at Armwood, which is in the north part of Brandon, and Diane was going to be driving out to Plant City, also north, we thought we should try to find a house in that part of town. Brenda, our agent, had arranged for us to see eight or 10 houses on the day before we were to fly back to Kansas. Brenda was really a hard worker and was really trying to help us find a house. We were having no luck, getting frustrated, and running out of time. Finally, in the middle of the afternoon, we asked her to show us some houses in South Brandon. The first house we looked at was a two-story house in a really nice area called Bloomingdale. The house had been on the market for over a year, and a bank had taken it over. It was really a nice home built in the early 80s, but it was out of our price range. Diane and I really liked the home and asked Brenda to make the bank an offer, a low ball offer. She didn't think they would take it but the house had been on the market for a while and we figured the bank might be motivated to sell it. We went back to Kansas not knowing whether we had a house or not, but we did have jobs. Brenda called a day after we got home to tell us that the bank had accepted our offer, we were getting a 175,000 dollar house for a whole lot less than that. The school year and the end of May rolled around pretty fast. We sold our house in El Dorado in the first three weeks that we had it on the market. Everything about our move to Florida was working out better than we even imagined, we both knew why.

We loaded up our rental truck and towed one of our cars, while Diane and the kids rode in our big blue Buick station wagon headed for Florida. It was a big thing for the kids to get to ride with me in the truck, so every couple hours we had to stop so we could change the "shotgun position." On the way, somewhere in central Mississippi on a Sunday morning, I blew out a tire on the trailer that was towing our car. We were out in the middle of nowhere with three kids on the side of the road. A man and his family came by on their way to church and stopped to see if they could help. The man went into town to a garage to get someone to come out with a new tire. His wife took Diane and the kids to their house and fed them lunch. They missed church that day, but they didn't miss Jesus. We were back on our way in a few hours in the hot August sun. Other than the flat tire our trip was rather uneventful. We ran into a huge thunderstorm going through Mobile, Alabama. Diane got a little freaked out about me leaving her and her getting lost. We made it into Florida where we started seeing these road signs about alligators so we "just had" to stop at a restaurant outside of Tallahassee where there were alligators. I think that was the first time the kids had ever seen a live gator in person.

We got moved into our new home in the Bloomingdale Estates community. We discovered that there were several kids our kids' ages on the same block. This was the biggest and nicest house we had ever lived in. Everyone had their own bedroom and bathroom. Diane and I had a nice big bedroom suite. Armwood, my new school, was about a 25 minute drive across town, and Diane had about a 35 minute drive to her school, Cork Elementary. We both really liked our schools. The teachers and staff made us feel welcome. Andrew and Amy rode with their mom to school at Cork. We found an outstanding daycare for Ashlee called Post Sunshine Ranch. I had a great teaching job at Armwood, team teaching health classes with the wrestling coach, Scot Tipton. Scot was from Ohio and had started teaching at Armwood the year before, the first year the school opened. He was a no nonsense disciplinarian and a very hard-working teacher. We met our classes in the auditorium, and even though we had 60 or more students, we had very few problems. Our class periods were 55 minutes, and we would take turns teaching, alternating each period. So we were actually each teaching three classes a day. If I was teaching, he would sit up in the back row behind the students to keep an eye on everyone and I would do the same when he was teaching. We had this great arrangement until he left Armwood to coach wrestling at the new high school in Bloomingdale. One of my best friends at Armwood was the basketball coach, Doug Woodard. We hung out together and talked a lot of basketball over lunch. Every year when the new school year started, he would try and talk me into helping him with the basketball program. And every year, I would tell him the same thing, which was I just wanted to "talk" basketball and not coach basketball. I was still tired and burnt out with basketball. Doug did a great job; his players loved him and played extremely hard for him. Several years later, when I began coaching at Bloomingdale where Andy played, he would give me a hard time about not helping him. Doug passed away in his 30s from cancer. I missed not seeing him on the bench coaching Armwood; it felt empty and strange.

I did start coaching again at Armwood but not basketball. The administration at Armwood could not find anyone to coach the boy's golf team, so I volunteered. I didn't know anything about coaching golf, but that didn't matter. They just basically needed a chaperon. The position paid $500, but it only lasted two months and gave me a chance to play a little golf myself. I decided that Armwood should have a girl's golf team also, so I advertised and promoted to try to get girls out to play. I only needed five girls, and in a school of over 2000 students, I thought that would be easy. I barely made it, five girls showed up at my meeting. I also got paid an extra $500 to coach the girls' team which I appreciated. Armwood was a good school, and our department head was a former retired Army Colonel who our principal Mr. Flagg really liked. We got whatever we needed for our program. The Col. believed that after working hard Monday through Thursday that Friday should be a film day and the day to relax.

Diane had only been teaching about a month when a permanent first grade teaching position opened. Mrs. Gilbert asked Diane if she was interested in moving from her tempo-rary fourth grade position to a permanent job teaching first grade. Diane had only taught fourth and fifth grades, so going down to first grade would be quite a change for her. She came home and told me that she had been offered a permanent job teaching first grade. I said "Great, you did tell her that you would take the first grade position didn't you?" She told Mrs. Gilbert she would have to think about it; she wasn't sure about teaching first-graders. I told her to go into Mrs. Gilbert's office first thing the next morning and tell her you will take the first grade position. I was not trying to be bossy or a male chauvinist; we needed the "guaranteed income" to make the mortgage payment and to pay the bills. Diane was not as con-fident in her ability to adjust and teach first-graders as I was. She was a good teacher, devoted, hard-working, and had 12 years of teaching experience. She would later tell me that she was really scared at first because "first-graders don't know an-ything." My response to that was "that is why they are first-graders!" After a few early struggles, she became a really good first grade teacher. Twenty-six years later, she retired from Cork as an outstanding first grade teacher.

Our whole family had adjusted to Florida, and we really liked Brandon. It was a rural, farm community that once had a lot of orange groves, but now had a lot of houses. Brandon was about a 15 minute drive east from Tampa and a very large military base called MacDill Air Force Base. Our church be-came a central focus for each of us. We joined a great church,

Bell Shoals Baptist, and met a lot of wonderful people. I got involved in the church after getting baptized, again. I began teaching a Bible study class and served on several different boards at the church, including a three-year term as a deacon. I taught a Sunday school class for 15 years and volunteered for other ministries at the church. We are still members at the church, 35 years after moving here. All three of our kids were raised at Bell Shoals and went through several of the youth ministry programs. Just like everything else in Brandon, the church has grown from about 500 members (in 1985 when we joined) to over 4000 today.

We also built some great relationships in our neighborhood. One of our neighbors, George and Lee Carapella, had a boy Andy's age and a girl about the same age as Ashlee. Damien, their oldest boy and Andy were always together. They played baseball together and would just hang out at each other's houses. George helped me coach their baseball team and was always willing to buy things for the team. He started a business selling diet products by mail order. After about a year, his business was really doing well. He asked me if I would be interested in coming to work for him. I had been at Armwood for five years and was making about $40,000 a year. George was going to pay me $1000 a week to handle all the advertisement for his products. I didn't know anything about placing ads in newspapers or magazines. He said I was a honest, hard worker and he could teach me. The business continued to do really well for the next year. I enjoyed what I was doing and soon caught on to placing the ads in major women's magazines and some of the largest newspapers in the country. We had some good products that had been successful in helping people lose weight. George liked to push the envelope about how much and how fast a person could lose weight using our products. Some of the claims caught the attention of the FDA, and instead of pulling back a little on the claims we continued to run the same advertisements. Our products really did work, but maybe not as fast as the ads claimed, at least not for everyone. We did offer a money back guarantee, but that did not satisfy the government. After I had been working for George for about six months and our sales were really doing well, I began to contact retail stores like Walgreens and GNC about putting our products in their stores. It was just a matter of time before we would be in a lot of retail stores and on our way to being a multi-million-dollar company. We could have been set for life. Instead, one day in August of 1991, it all ended when the FDA showed up at our offices and closed down our company. We were growing fast and could have been competition for several weight control products that were on the market. Perhaps one or more of our competitors had something to do with our sudden demise. During the period of time that I worked for George, we built a custom 3200 sq. ft. home with a pool in a very nice new subdivision. Now, I was out of a job and had a very large mortgage, at least, a large mortgage for two school teachers.

So the business gig lasted a little over a year, and I was back to the only other kind of job I had since college, teaching school. I could not get a job in a high school, and I knew I did not want to teach in junior high, so I took a grade school PE position. I actually was the itinerant PE teacher at three different elementary schools in the county. Fortunately, I worked with three different very good teachers who ran good programs. The good thing about being an itinerant is that I did not have to plan the activities, nor was I responsible for grades. I pretty much just showed up and did what I was told. The downside is that I had to travel to different schools each day so I really didn't develop any relationships or have a "home" school. I only did the itinerant job for one year before I got hired by Mr. Wheeler, principal at Yates Elementary school. Mr. Wheeler had been in the Hillsborough school system for over 40 years and had been the principal at Yates for about half that time. He was a little man in stature but ran a tight ship, and the teachers and students loved him. He was the only principal I ever worked for that would personally hand-deliver every teachers' paycheck every other Friday on payday. We got along great because we had an excellent physical education program, and I was always willing to do extra things around the school for him. My co-teacher that first year was a lady whose husband was a colonel in the Army. She was a disciplinarian and very organized; we made a good team. Our students performed a tumbling and gymnastics program for our parents at a PTA meeting. We also invited the parents to participate with our students at a country music "hoedown." It had been a long time since I had taught elementary school age kids, but I soon got back in the groove and enjoyed working at Yates. I had two more co-teachers during the 5 year period I was at Yates before leaving to return to high school. We were recognized around the county as having an outstanding PE program and I was proud to be a part of it.

In 1993, I began working as a volunteer basketball coach at Bloomingdale High School for Phil Zimmerman, the head coach. I never intended to coach basketball again when we moved to Florida. I had coached for 14 years, and my last six years at Butler had left me drained. But as Andrew got older and further along in school, he really became interested in playing basketball. He was small, but he had great hands, was smart, and began developing into a very good shooter. I could tell by the time he was in the seventh grade that he would be able to play in high school if he continued to work at it. He loved to play, but as a seventh grader he got cut from the middle school team. That actually worked out better for him because in the junior high programs in Hillsborough County they only played six games and the season lasts only two months. I signed him up to play in a recreation league where he played 12 games over a three-month period. He tried out again for the junior high team as an eighth grader and made it. I was working with him a lot at home and as he got stronger, he got better. The middle school that he was attending was a feeder school for Bloomingdale

High School. I was looking forward to him coming to Blooming-dale and getting into our program. I always thought that since I had coached hundreds of other dad's sons, it would be pretty cool if I could coach my own son one day.

CHAPTER 11

The Bloomingdale Bull Years: Volunteer to Head Basketball Coach (1993-2002)

D uring the basketball season of Andrew's eight grade year at Burns, we went to see a basketball game at Bloomingdale. I wasn't that interested, but he was, and in another year he would be going there to school so I was "all in" for him. There were about 100 people at the game, which I thought was embarrassing for a school with 2500 students. I learned later that was a pretty normal crowd for high school basketball games in the county. This was the first high school basketball game I had attended since we left Kansas, seven years earlier. Bloomingdale had over 10,000 people in the surrounding area and coming from my background in Illinois, I couldn't believe that there was no more interest in high school basketball than what I was seeing. I would find out during my years at Bloomingdale that Hillsborough County and Florida love football first and every other high school sport a distant "third." The Bulls, as they were called, were not very good and lost the game by a few points. They did have a few players that I thought had some potential, and with some discipline could be pretty good. Soon after the 1993 school year began, I made an appointment to go talk to Coach Phil Zimmerman at Bloomingdale about volunteering to help him with the basketball team. I didn't know Phil, but he was very open and receptive to me helping him. He was a really soft-spoken, laid-back individual who had been the basketball coach since the school opened in 1989. After visiting with him for an hour, he said I was too qualified to be his assistant. I was honest with him about my motivation for coaching and assured him I was not interested in being the head coach. I was interested in working with young men, but I really wanted to coach my son. He said that he understood and admired me for wanting to make that kind of commitment. Phil already had an assistant, Tim Sleyzak, who had been with him a couple years. Tim drove a truck at night delivering food to 7-Eleven stores. He loved basketball and loved being around the high school kids. Tim studied the game film and did all of the stats. Sometimes he would show up at practice having slept only a few hours and having to go back out on the road that night. It was hard to find good assistants in high school, especially when they don't get paid. Tim was a rare breed.

I was still teaching at Yates and because the elementary schools got out at 2:30, about 20 minutes before the high schools let out, I was able to get to Bloomingdale a few minutes before practice started. That worked out great since it gave Phil and I a few minutes to talk about what we needed to get done that day in practice. Coach Zimmerman knew the game of basketball and was "somewhat" organized. But I was "super" organized when it came to planning a practice, right down to the minute. I had always planned practices, even back in the days at ORU. I believed in keeping the players busy and on a tight schedule with no wasted time. I liked competitive practices, and I didn't like players standing around. I had been to hundreds of high school practices, and I could count on both my hands the coaches that were really organized and did not waste time in practice. At the beginning of every basketball season I would make out a monthly schedule, a weekly schedule, and a daily schedule. I did not like surprises; I wanted to make sure that I had covered everything and my players were prepared for any situation. After that first week of practices and "suggestions," Phil decided to let me organize the practices. He was always okay with what I thought we should get done that day. I appreciated that. Like with Coach Trickey at ORU, Phil allowed me to have a lot of input into the team.

The Bulls were coming off a 7-15 season the year before. Coach Zimmerman had several of those players back, and even though the leading scorer graduated, I thought the team would be better without him. The night Andrew and I saw him in the game they lost, I thought he hurt the team with his poor shot selection and his terrible defense. But it was his "soft" attitude that had infected some of the younger players that I was now coaching. That attitude surfaced about the second or third practice, and I needed to address it head on. One of our seniors, a guard and a good player, who had started as a junior, Matt Lavergehti, missed a three-point shot. Matt was the best outside shooter on the team, and was going to be one our captains. He was a smart kid and knew how to play the game. But after he missed the three point shot he began to pout and "jog" back down the court to play defense. I blew the whistle and everyone to stopped. I walked over to Matt, grabbed his jersey, and asked, "What the hell are you doing?" Everyone froze, including Matt. I lit into him pretty hard and loud. "I asked him if he thought he was going to make every shot?" "Regardless, whether you make it or miss it," I said, "it's over and you can't do anything about it so I want you to get your ass back down the court and play defense." I continued, "You are smart and supposed to be the leader, a leader doesn't act like that."

No one had ever talked to him like that before or addressed anyone else on the team like that. I certainly had the attention of the rest of the players on the team. That set the tone for the rest of the season. They realized there was a new sheriff in town and they were expected to play hard, play smart and play for each other. I competed and so would they. Matt ended up being a good captain for us that year. He led our team in scoring and made the All-Conference team. We also had a very good 6' 6" center on the team, Jeff Warbritten. Jeff also made All-Conference and received a four-year scholarship to play at a Division I school, Stetson University. In the back court with Matt was a junior point guard named Kevin

Perry. Kevin was one of the best high school point guards I ever coached. He was 6' 3", and could score inside or outside. Kevin was a competitor, and hated to lose. After going to a juco for two years, Kevin got a scholarship to play at Mercer University in Georgia. We had several other good players on that team. They knew their roles and played hard. One of those players was Jeremy Pope who was 6' 6". Jeremy was an outstanding defensive player, rebounder, and had a great attitude. The fifth starter was our small forward and one of the toughest competitors on a team made up of competitors, 6' 3" Charlie Cates.

These guys had won only seven games the year before, won 20 games, finished runner-up in the district, and were headed to regionals. The teams that were runner-up in their district had to play the first game of the regional tournament on the road against the teams that had won their district. We went to St. Petersburg to play a highly ranked Northeast Viking team. We beat them by two points in overtime. After that win, we went to Orlando to play Orlando Dr. Phillips, who was ranked among the top ten in the state. They were really athletic, very talented, and very well coached. We had developed into a really good team that was playing with a lot of confidence. We played a great game but lost to them by seven or eight points. My first year back in coaching after eight years was very rewarding. The team was fun to coach. They got better every game, and before the season was over, Bloomingdale was on the basketball map in the state of Florida. At the team banquet,

I told them that I appreciated the way they accepted me and accepted what I was trying to get them to "buy" into to be successful. I felt like the Wizard of Oz, I didn't make them into outstanding players, that was already in them. I just helped draw it out of them. The 1993-94 team started a run of winning basketball seasons that would go through the 2002 season; my last as coach of the Bloomingdale Bulls.

The 1993-94 school year was also very memorable in the Sutter household, because Amy graduated from Bloomingdale High School. She was supposed to graduate the following year, but she got all of her credits and with an outstanding GPA, she graduated in three years. Diane and I were not real happy with that, but she had decided that high school was not that exciting for her and she wanted to move on.

All three of our kids graduated from Bloomingdale High School with honors, earned academic scholarships, and then graduated from the University of Florida. Diane and I helped them all we could, but it was primarily through their own efforts that they got a college degree. Amy graduated from UF with a Master's Degree in education. Andrew graduated with a degree in nursing and later went on to get an MBA at Northern Florida University and a law degree from Florida Coastal in Jacksonville. Ashlee graduated from UF in three years with a Bachelor's Degree in business. Diane and I are so proud of them.

We have been so blessed with three great kids that are smart, hard-working, independent, and frugal. I think, to a great extent, their frugality is due to the struggles that we had when they were all young. Soon after George's business was shut down, we put our new house on the market. Our house was the second house built in the new subdivision, and even after two years the subdivision was only half full. Being the first house in a new subdivision had helped us get a good price when we built it. However, because the neighborhood was not fully developed, it was hurting our chances to sell it. Our dog, Spinner, loved not having neighbors. He could pretty much roam throughout the entire five-acre development. Andrew and I could take my shotgun down by the pond behind our house and shoot without anyone even knowing. We had our house on the market for four years before we finally sold it. We found out, up close and personal, what it was like to be "house poor." During those four years Diane and I worked every summer. She continued to teach summer school; she also got a retail job and worked some evenings and weekends. I worked for Florida Steel in their rebar steel plant. It was hard work but it paid well. We were busy putting out steel for construction projects all over the state. I worked 10 hour shifts, starting at 4 am and getting off at 2 pm. I appreciated the job, and we really needed the extra money, but going to bed at eight, before it was even dark, took some getting used to.

Our only vacation was our yearly trip to Illinois to visit our friends, the Whittington's. On more than one occasion, we would have to borrow from the kids' piggy banks to get enough money to buy some food essentials as we counted the days until payday. We vowed to never be "house poor" again, and in over 49 years of marriage, we haven't.

I continued to teach at Yates. Diane continued to teach first grade at Cork. Because she spoke and understood Spanish, she was offered the job of teaching English as a Second Language (ESOL) students. These were migrant students that did not speak English very well or not at all. Plant City is known all over the world for its strawberries and in October through March, there is a tremendous influx of Mexican and South American families that come to work in the strawberry industry. Diane would often start the school year with four or five students, but by Thanksgiving she would have 25 or 30 in her class. She loved working with the migrant kids. She ended up teaching ESOL students for over 20 years. She received several awards highlighting her as an outstanding teacher in Hillsborough County, including the Ida S. Baker Diversity Educator of the Year.

The 1994-95 season was going to be a reload season, we thought. We had graduated four of our five starters, but returned our outstanding point guard, Kevin Perry. He would be a key piece of the puzzle for any success we would have in the season. We also had three lettermen returning and a couple 6' 7" juniors coming up from the JV team. It was phenomenal that during my nine years at Bloomingdale, we always had several 6' 6" kids or bigger. One year, we had four players over 6' 6"; we were bigger than some college teams. My friend at Armwood, Doug Woodard, never had a player over 6' 3".

He was envious and told me it just wasn't "fair" that we always had such big kids. As we prepared for the 94-95 season, we were just hoping we could win half our games. That all changed when school started and John Hughes enrolled. John was a very talented 6' 7" center, who had moved in from North Carolina. John played two years for us, led us to a conference championship, and made All-Conference, and second team All-State. He also received a scholarship to Elon University in North Carolina. We truly hit the jackpot when he enrolled at Bloomingdale that fall.

We also had another transfer, Charles Griffin, a very athletic 6' 2" wing player, who enrolled at Bloomingdale as a senior. Charles had not played much organized basketball, but he sure did know how to play "street ball." He was a good kid, the fastest player on the team, and our best leaper, by far. He made us a lot more versatile and a little unpredictable. We had used three guards a lot the year before with Matt, Kevin, and a junior named Steve Parks so getting a "big man" like Hughes gave us a chance to be really good again. Stevie was a tough, hard-nosed 6' 2" guard who hated to lose. He only knew how to play one way, all out, pedal to the metal. I loved his mindset and his competitive nature. He was the consummate team player. He didn't care who got the credit or the headlines, he just wanted to win. I would actually have to throttle him back occasionally, like after a big win for us at Leto High School. They had a really good team. They had only lost a couple games when we played them. We were undefeated, so this was a big game for them.

They had a big banner hanging on the wall on one end of their gym saying they were going to "Rock Us!" It was a good game. We won by a couple points. Steve, in his exuberance, ran over and tore the sign off the wall. That didn't go over too well with their fans. I had to go get him and have him apologize to their coach. We still had a hard time getting out of there and on our bus. Actually, I thought it was pretty funny. It emphasized how important winning was to Steve. Stevie's dad was our team physician and a great asset to our program. Besides taking care of any injuries, he and his wife were always doing things for our team, like feeding them.

Soon after the season started we realized that this team was just as good as the 93-94 team. We were well on the way to another 20 win season. We finished second in our conference for a second straight year and runner-up in the district. We had created some excitement around school. We now had over three or four hundred students coming to our games. Our attendance went from about 100 to over 500. When we played our arch rival, Brandon High School, the gym was full. We even created enough excitement that we had four or five cheerleaders show up to lead cheers! I still had not gotten over the fact that the cheerleaders only cheered at the football games. The football team, which was terrible at the time, would have 20 cheerleaders and we could not get five to come to a basketball game. It all had to do with their "preparation" for cheerleader competition during the winter. It was the silliest thing I had ever seen. But we were getting a lot of support from our players' parents and that had not always happened. Bloomingdale High School was known as "Gucci high," meaning a lot of upper class kids went to school there. The student's parking lot had nicer, more expensive automobiles in it than the faculty parking lot. A lot of our parents were doctors, lawyers, and CEOs. Sometimes those types of parents think they know everything and try to dictate everything. After all, if you played a sport in high school, or even grade school, that qualifies you as an authority to some parents. That didn't happen at Bloomingdale very often in the nine years I coached there. Our 93-94 team had gotten us a lot of recognition around the state as a basketball powerhouse. The 94-95 team built on that reputation. We were getting invitations to play in the most prestigious tournaments in the state. Our kids were getting noticed by a lot of colleges, and several of our players received scholarships. Coach Sleyzak coached the team in a summer league and took them to camps at UF, FSU, and USF. Tim did a great job coaching them. One of the summer leagues we played in was in Lakeland about 25 miles from Brandon. There were 10 or 12 schools in the league, which provided us with some great competition outside of the county. One game was against a team from Auburndale that had a great 6' 9" player named Tracy McGrady. I wasn't at the game, but when Andrew came home, he told me about this phenomenal player that hardly warmed up before the game then scored 40 points against them. McGrady went to a prep school his senior year and then straight into the NBA.

This was also a good year for me and our PE program at Yates because we completed an all-purpose, air-conditioned building with room enough for us to have our PE classes inside when it rained or when it was too hot to be outside. We began the school year in August, which is the hottest month of the year, so we started out the school year teaching a unit in stunts and tumbling. The students loved it, but not as much as I did. It was a lot better than being outside in the Florida sun.

The 1995-96 season was special for several reasons, two in particular, to me. First, Andrew made it to the varsity as a junior, and I would finally get to coach him. He had overcome a lot of obstacles and worked hard to earn his spot on the varsity. He had been cut as a seventh grader and had only gotten to play sparingly on the Bloomingdale JV team. I was constantly encouraging him because I saw his potential and how much he loved to play. As a sophomore, playing on the JV, I was not very pleased with the way his coach was using him. He never started him and only played him when he needed an outside shooter against a zone defense or if he got way behind and needed some quick points. After a few games, I went to the coach and ask him to explain to me why if Andy was good enough to come into games when he needed outside shooting or when he was way behind, why would he never start him to avoid those situations in the first place? He had no answer because it didn't make any sense. I actually thought it was a case of discrimination because of my role on the varsity. He didn't want to give the appearance of being influenced by me. He continued to play Andy the same way, which actually made him more determined, and made him work harder to get better. There would be no doubt in anyone's mind that when he got to the varsity, he was good enough to play.

It was also a great year because the Bulls won their first district tournament in the six year history of the school. We had been knocking at the door the last two years and this year it would all come together. We returned two starters, including Hughes, and a really smart leader at point guard named Scott Odom. Scotty had played a lot the year before as a junior, splitting time with Kevin and Stevie. He was only 5' 7" but he was an excellent ball handler and passer. We had a 6' 7" backup center named Sean Paneranda, and a 6' 8" junior, Tom Buffington, who moved up from the JV team. Again, we had a front line that was as big as some college teams. In addition, we had another student transfer in John Gomillion. John was 6'2" a good athlete, very strong, and could play inside because of how well he could jump. We also had another transfer from out-of-state, a very good point guard named Zach Willingham. Zach was only a sophomore, but we knew he was going to be a really good player before he graduated. He was skinny, but already 6' 3", and really good offensively. Both of the Johns (Hughes and Gomillion) had outstanding years for us. They were both almost impossible to stop inside. Scotty, was excellent at running the team and getting everyone were they were supposed to be. Hughes was one of the best players in our conference and in our district. He led the team in scoring with a 20 point average and in rebounds with over 10 a game. We finished the season 19-5 and beat an excellent team from Sarasota to win Florida's 5A District championship. Andy would split playing time with another guard, but he was our best outside shooter and led the team in 3's.

Ashlee, our youngest, decided to become a Bloomingdale Bull that year, also. She had gone to Durant High School her freshman year, so she could play with her friends on the basketball and volleyball teams. We were not in Durant's school district. Diane would drop her off in the morning at her friend Natalie's house (whose stepdad taught at Durant), then pick her up after practice in the afternoon. I was happy when she decided to become a Bull and play volleyball for Bloomingdale. She proved to be quite the athlete too, making the top 10 list of kills and blocks within the district almost weekly during their season. She went on to make All Conference, and helped the Bulls win two district championships. She and her "posse" of Kendra, Suzanne, and Erin (or as I called her "Hank" after the great baseball player Hank Aaron) were very popular, and inseparable around school. They were all very involved in various high school activities. Ashlee was considered a fashionista even though she bought most of her clothes at Goodwill! She was pretty and personable so she could pull that off even at "Gucci high." She still remains close friends with that group of ladies.

Amy, who had started college the year before at Belmont University in Nashville, decided to change her major from music to education. She had qualified for a Bright Futures scholarship the year she graduated from Bloomingdale and decided to transfer to the University of Florida. Her mother and I were very happy that she would now only be two hours from home. As a parent, you always want what is best for your kids and want to see them happy. She thought going to Belmont was the right path for her so we supported that decision. I will always remember the day we went with her to Nashville to move her into the dorm. After lunch we left and started driving back to Brandon. We were both teary-eyed and neither Diane nor I said three words until we got to Atlanta, three hours from Nashville. We have had three children go away to college and I think it is harder to see the first one leave than the last one.

We moved in June of 1996 into a smaller house about 2 miles closer to Bloomingdale HS. We were so happy to sell the house and get rid of that big mortgage payment. We celebrated with a vacation to Chicago. We still took our annual trip to Benton, IL to see the Whittingtons, but we added 4 days in Chicago. We had a great time in Chicago, taking in a Cubs game at Wrigley, the museums, and a night boat tour through the city. Andy's number one objective at the baseball game was to get Harry Carry, the Cub's Hall of Fame announcer's autograph on a baseball. He waited outside the Cubs broadcast booth for an hour after the game for Harry to come out. As usual, Harry was "wasted" from all of the Budweisers, but he did sign a ball for Andy.

One of the many memories we made in Chicago happened the day we went to the museum downtown and couldn't find a parking place, so I just parked up on the curb in the grass. A few hours later when we came back, I had a $20 parking ticket, which I threw away. The kids were "shocked" that I was not going to pay the ticket. I said they should have provided more parking, and besides, I'm never coming back to Chicago. Probably not a good example for the kids, but they really should have provided enough parking for the museum! This was the first real vacation that our family had taken in four or five years. Diane did not have to teach summer school, and I did not have to work at the steel mill.

The most important event of 1996 was the wedding of our daughter, Amy. Amy was a junior at UF when she met this funny, smart, personable boy from Gainesville, Darrin Crosby. Darrin was a student at Santa Fe Community College studying to be a nurse in cardiology. They were both active in the Baptist Student Union on the campus at UF and had developed a friendship. Darrin's family was originally from Gainesville. He played football and tennis at Gainesville High School. While I liked Darrin, I was not totally "on board" with them getting married before they graduated from college. However, it worked out, they both got their degrees and both of them worked to pay their way through college. In May, they had a small, beautiful wedding at a local church that their friend's dad pastored, and a very unique reception at the museum in downtown Gainesville. Darrin went on to get his

Bachelor's Degree at the University of Central Florida. Amy graduated from UF with a Master's Degree in education, which has served her well in home schooling both her daughters. Abigail, our oldest grandchild, is 18 and in college. She is very independent, serious, and a hard-worker. She is like her mother. Anna Lee, their other daughter, is 15 years old and in the 10th grade. She plays tennis on the high school team, is funny, personable, and a creative thinker. She is like her father. Darrin and Amy have been married over 20 years now, which just goes to prove that maybe they did not need to wait to get married until after they graduated.

The 1996-97 team would accomplish something that our first three teams had not. We won over 60 games in the last three years, including a district championship, but we had never won our conference. We played in a conference with schools of enrollments over 2000 students. Bloomingdale High School had close to 3000 students, which meant we played in the largest class of schools in the state. Hillsborough County, as well as the state, was recognized around the country as producing great high school football players. Our conference, made up mostly of schools in the county, would send four or five basketball players every year to D1 schools. The 96-97 team returned two starters, Buffington and Gomillion, plus Andy, who had played a lot as a junior. Zach Willingham, had played limited minutes, as a sophomore. We knew he had the potential to be an outstanding point guard as he matured and gained experience. We had three or four kids move up from the JV team that had gone 15-5. One of those players was a 7 foot kid by the name of Nick Smith. Nick, would go on to be named the Gatorade Player of the Year in Florida, his senior year. He was recruited by practically every school in the SEC and over 30 other Division I schools. He ended up signing at the University of Illinois with a long time friend of mine, Lon Kruger. Again, as in the last three years, two kids moved in as juniors. Sam Gordon and Phil Hall, who were good basketball players and outstanding kids. We had one of the best basketball programs in the county so it is no surprise that good basketball players wanted to come to Bloomingdale. The school also had a reputation for having great academics. We never actively recruited a player, like with anything else, success begets success. We had a lineup of 7' 0", 6' 8", 6' 3", 6' 3" and Andy at 5' 10". We also had a 6' 8" player, Don Hines, who had only played one year of organized basketball. He became Coach Sleyzak's project and by the end of his senior year he was good enough to get a scholarship to a junior college. Andy, had an outstanding senior season, setting the school record for the most 3's in a game (9) and the most 3's in the season (69). Both of these records stood for over 10 years. Buffington struggled at times throughout the season with health issues. We discovered about halfway through the season that he was anemic. At 6' 8" he was still a force to be reckoned with. Zach, was a good player but there was way too much "coaching" going on at home, mostly with his older brother. Coach Zimmerman had to have a meeting with his dad about his attitude. This situation would escalate a year later when I took over as the head coach. Gomillion, had an outstanding senior season, leading our team in points. Even though he was only 6' 3" he could jump, and he was so strong that other teams had a difficult time matching up with him. Gaither and Chamberlain were two of the best basketball programs in the county for several years in a row. We finished second or third behind these two programs in `94 and `95. But this year we beat them both and won the Western Conference. We played in an outstanding tournament at Sarasota Riverview and lost by a couple points in the finals to the host school. We finished the season winning 20 games for the fourth straight year.

This was my last year at Yates Elementary. Phil decided to retire from coaching and just stay on at Bloomingdale to teach and continue as the P.E. department head. I was asked by several parents to apply and even though Andy was graduating I still was excited about coaching. We had some good players returning so that made the job even more appealing. Mr. Davis, our athletic director, knew that a lot of our success over the past three years was due to my coaching and working with the kids. Phil recommended me and thought it would be an easy and natural transition for me to become the head coach.

We celebrated Andy's high school graduation and my new job with a trip to Boston and Montreal. Everyone in our family but Amy, she was taking summer classes at UF trying to finish up her degree, went on a seven day vacation. We flew to Boston and rented a car. We drove up through New Hampshire, Vermont and on to Montreal. We spent five days in Boston and stayed lost most of the time. I am pretty good with directions and navigating new places, but Boston is a hard city for a tourist to get around in. This was in the days before cell phones and GPS. Some friends of ours at church who were from Boston recommended that we contact this older lady they knew who had a large house and stay with her. She was happy to have us and offered to let us stay for free. She was really sweet and hospitable. However, the house had no air conditioning, and the week we were there Boston had a heat wave. Even with the house open and a couple fans it was very difficult to sleep at night.

We had a great time touring Boston, going to Plymouth Rock, taking in the Freedom Trail, and catching a baseball game at Fenway Park. We spent a day at Martha's Vineyard and seeing many of the lighthouses. It was a beautiful drive up through New Hampshire and into Canada. I would have enjoyed the vacation more if I had not been sick with the flu and a terrible case of strep throat. I made it until we got to Montreal, but I was feeling so bad that I could hardly swallow. We got a recommendation from the hotel for a doctor who put me on antibiotics and recommended a day in the hotel room to rest. We did make it to a Montreal Expo's game, along with about 3,000 other fans. They played in the Olympic Stadium, which had a seating capacity of over 50,000, so it looked like there was no one there. Our final night in Montreal we decided to really splurge by going to dinner in a nice French restaurant. I could actually swallow again without pain. We ordered this French cuisine not really knowing what it was, besides expensive. I ordered a wild game entree which included ostrich, snails, and turtle. We didn't think it was that good, and except for the dessert, it was way over priced. We had a great time in Montreal, it is a beautiful city.

The 1997-98 school year rolled around very quickly. I saw several things that I wanted to change around the Bloomingdale program. Just like at Butler County when I first arrived, the basketball team did not have their own dressing room. The basketball coach did not have an office or a private place to talk with players, study video, or plan practices with the staff. The gym was typical public school "vanilla," and just like at Butler there was no game programs. The student involvement and attendance had gotten much better over the last four years, but we still didn't have cheerleaders at every one of our home games. Phil had tried to get the music department to supply a pep band; his request had fallen on deaf ears. I seemed to have a thing about getting into high schools where the music department is bigger than the athletic department. I had faced the same situation back in Salem, Illinois. Unlike at Salem, I never got a pep band at Bloomingdale.

I had established a solid working relationship with the athletic director, Mr. Davis, and with Mrs. Stelter, the principal. They respected my opinion about how to run a program and were willing to give me the freedom to do what I thought was best. They had over 20 applicants for the basketball position at Bloomingdale, which didn't surprise anyone who had followed our program. I got Mr. Davis permission to convert a storage room behind the PE dressing room that had not been used for years into a basketball dressing room. I also found a small room off of the gym that no one was using and converted that into my office. I must have spent a 100 hours that summer cleaning, painting, and making those areas into something that looked nice and were usable. After I had cleaned out the storage area and painted the room, I hired a man to come in and build individual, wooden lockers for the players. I ended up painting the new lockers, as well as the new stools I got for each player's locker. I had the dressing room and my office carpeted. Mr. Davis got us a nice, large, white dry erase board and a bulletin board for the dressing room. I went around to local businesses soliciting money to spend on our locker room, as well as a new scorer table. I raised and spent over $2000 on the dressing room. About two weeks before school started, I asked Mrs. Stelter to come down and see what I had been working on all summer. I will never forget the look on her face when I opened the door and she saw the dressing room. She said, "oh my, I had no idea you were doing all of this. We can't let the rest of the county know this, or they will think that all the basketball coaches have to have something this nice." It had really turned out nice. Our players took a lot of pride in having their own place to dress and hang out. I wanted them to feel special. A short time after school started, the volleyball coach went to

Mr. Davis and asked him if the girls could have a volleyball dressing room like the boy's basketball team. He told her if they could find another storage room and wanted to spend the time and "their" money to make it into a volleyball dressing room, they were welcome to do it. They were envious of what I had, but not interested in doing what I had done. I had also worked with Mr. Davis and the county to get our gym floor redone and some color added to it. I ended up doing a lot of the painting myself. I got our Bull mascot painted in the center of the court, and the out of bounds painted red to match our school colors.

Coach Sleyzak continued to coach the kids in the summer league just as he had done the previous three summers. It was at one of our summer games in Lakeland that I had my first and only "run in" with Zach's brother. Coach Zimmerman, had sat down with Zach's dad a year earlier about Zach's attitude and about his older son's "coaching" at home. Zach's brother, who played college football, thought that Tim was not using Zach the way he should be during the games. He had been critical and even had some harsh words with Tim on several occasions. I happened to be at the game and heard some of the criticism. After the game on the way out of the gym, he started again about how we should play Zach and how we were hurting Zach's chances at getting a college scholarship. Zach's brother was 23 or 24 years old and thought he knew a lot more than we did. I asked his dad to control his son and that neither Tim nor I was going to put up with his BS. His dad tried, but I could see who the boss in charge was, and it wasn't him. Finally outside the gym, I told him that he was putting his brother in a "can't win" situation. If he listened to him or his dad over us, he was not going to play. They were just screwing with Zach's head, and if they were telling him something at home different than what we were telling him at school, it was going to hurt Zach. I told Zach's brother that I decided who played and where they played. A few days later, his dad came to me and apologized and admitted Zach had to do what we asked him to do. Zach became an outstanding point guard for us but I always thought he was getting some "coaching" at home. He played at the community college level for a couple years then a season at Ball State in Indiana.

In Hillsborough County, there was one athletic director for all of the county high schools. The AD office made the schedule, assigned referees, scheduled the buses, and set the budget for all 20 high schools. The idea was that all schools would be treated equally, regardless of the socioeconomic environment. Unfortunately, what it really did was favor the lazy coaches and penalize those coaches who really wanted to work hard and excel. Any expense for out of county travel to play in Thanksgiving or Christmas tournaments had to be raised by the coach or the program. This "socialism mentality" even went so far as to make sure that every school had the same kind of uniform, warm-ups, balls, and every other kind of equipment. We had been taking our teams to nice Christmas Tournaments around the state for several years. We always had to raise the money to go, or the parents had to chip in with the extra money. I always needed money because I wanted a first-class program and I didn't want the parents paying all the time.

During that summer Robert Pazutti (the father of one of my players) told me about his insurance agent. Robert was one of our most enthusiastic and encouraging fans, not just cheering on his son Dan, but everyone associated with the team. He said his Nationwide Insurance agent was a big sports fan and was always looking for ways to help local sports programs. Bob's insurance agent, Bill Hoge, had built a remarkable insurance business. He was a true sports fan and wanted to support youth sports programs around the Brandon and Bloomingdale area. Bill was a single guy who worked hard, and was very generous. We were both from Illinois, and in spite of him being a Cub fan, we hit it off very well. Bill had given me some money during an initial visit when I went to his office and introduced myself as the new basketball coach at Bloomingdale High School. A couple months later when I went back to see him about helping with the expenses to play in a Christmas tournament, he asked me how much money I needed. I told him I needed to lease two seven passenger vans for five days and I needed enough money to put 15 players and coaches up in a hotel and feed them. He asked me what I thought it would take? I told him about $1500 because the host school was going to provide one meal a day and had gotten us special lodging rates. I was thinking if I could get half of that from him I would be able to come up with the rest from other boosters and parents. He wrote me a check for the entire $1500 right there on the spot. Boosters for high school programs like that are hard to find. Bill helped me all five years I was the coach at Bloomingdale. He also gave me my nickname, known only among our golf friends; Wiggler. The name comes from my business venture with my son, Drew, and son-in-law Darrin. Darrin's cousin had heard that there was money to be made in raising red worms. Supposedly they were used in dog food and in other products. We invested 2,000 dollars and got a shipment of worms that came by air into Orlando Airport where Darrin picked them up. He put them in totes and kept them in the garage until I could find a place to keep them in Brandon. Everything went well until someone in his family turned off the lights in the garage and hundreds of them got out and were all over the garage. Amy, our daughter, hates anything that is slimy and crawls but she was out in the garage with Darrin helping catch the worms to put them back in the totes. She said she just kept reminding herself that each worm was like ten or fifteen cents. I kept those worms in a barn outside of Brandon for several months before we discovered that they were not used for anything but fishing and we were part of a worm Ponzi scheme. We ended up taking about 3,000 red worms out in the pasture and dumping them. We lost about 2500 dollars on that business venture! My friends told me if that is all I ever lose on bad investments I should consider myself lucky. All of our friends say the same thing to me "I have never met another worm farmer".

Even today, all these years later, Bill and I talk practically every week. He is no longer a bachelor, but married with two kids. Strangely, his daughter, Rachel, and I share the same birthday, December 21st. We have played many rounds of golf together, and I have never beat him. My favorite "smack talk" when we were playing was on the rare occasions when I out drove him off the tee is to ask him if he thought he would be able to hit the ball that far when he got to be my age. He could hit the ball a long way off the tee, so outdriving him was rare. Bill has one of the brightest sports minds of anyone I've ever known, so hanging out with him is always interesting and fun.

After an incredibly busy but rewarding summer, it was time to get the 1997-98 season started. We had the nucleus for a really solid team with Smith back as our center and Willingham as our point guard. Gordon and Pazutti were both guards who had gotten some valuable experience the year before. Coach Sleyzak had done wonders developing 6' 8" Don Hines, who was starting only his 2nd year of organized basketball. He was a great kid who really wanted to get better. Tim had given him some valuable playing time during the summer camps and league. Moving up from the JV were two players that were athletic and outstanding young men, Phil Hall and Eric Green. Both of these players played much bigger then there 6' 2" height, both were very quick and could run the floor.

Phil was an outstanding track athlete, who ended up going to UF on a partial track scholarship. Eric started as a junior and senior. He also made the All-Conference team as a senior.

I had ratcheted up our schedule by getting us into a couple of really good tournaments. I wanted Smith and our program to get a lot of exposure around the state. I thought Smith would be our team leader, and with his skills, he could be a dominant player. I was wrong on both accounts. Nick, while very smart and talented did not compete like our past big man, Warbritten and Hughes. If he had played as hard as those two, he would've been a High School All-American. After coaching Nick for three years, I couldn't help wonder if he would have been 6' 0" and not 7' 0" would he even have played basketball? We finished the season with barely a winning record. I had over scheduled, and we were not nearly as competitive as I thought we would be. I was so frustrated with them that I brought them back to the gym after a horrible road game and had an hour practice. We hadn't showed up to play the game, so I thought maybe we could get better by practicing. It all boiled down to lack of leadership.

The season had even started off on a bad note when I felt like I had to dismiss the JV coach. Phil had hired a teacher to coach the JV team who did not know very much about basketball. It is really hard to find good, qualified coaches in high school to help you. If there is a teacher who has some interest and is not knowledgeable but is loyal and you can trust them to do what you ask them to do, you count yourself very fortunate. Mr. Dykes had been allowed to coach the JV team the way he saw fit. Phil and I both played a man-to-man defense 80% of the time. Mr. Dykes had the JV team playing a zone defense. I had a meeting with him soon after I was hired and explained to him what I expected. I told him that the number one objective for the JV players was to develop fundamentals and skills to play at the varsity level. He told me he understood and that the JV program would mirror the varsity program. I also had indicated to him that I wanted the JV team to play more up-tempo on offense. A week after our meeting, he was still running his practices the same way as before and playing a zone defense. . He was much more concerned about winning games and his ego than developing our young players to play on the varsity. I went to Mr. Davis and told him what had transpired and about my "talk" with Mr. Dykes. He understood and basically told me that it was my program, and my call to do what I thought I needed to do. I went to Mr. Dykes and told him that if he wasn't willing to teach and coach the players the way I wanted, then I had no choice but to replace him. I had no one at the time to coach the JV, but I needed someone who I could trust and someone who would do things the way I wanted them done. Looking back on my first year, I now see that even though I had been Coach Zimmerman's assistant for three years, it was a big transition year for the players. I was much more intense and demanding and we didn't have the same level of talent that we had the previous years.

We were coming off a rather disappointing 1997-98 season, but I was encouraged with the four seniors that we had coming back for the 98-99 season. I was hoping that one or more of our seniors would give us the kind of leadership that we had lacked the previous season. Green, Lewis Sheppard, Pazutti, and Hines were all seniors that had played a lot and were very capable of stepping up to provide some leadership on and off the court. We had two solid players and good students move up from the JV team, Ross Kirchman at 6' 5" and Lyle LaFountain 6' 3". Both were smart and scrappy players who would give us some size and depth. Smith was getting a lot of attention, and rightly so. He had great hands, a nice touch, and he was 7 foot tall. Nick was even capable of stepping out occasionally and shooting the ball from the three-point line. He broke all the school records in blocked shots and rebounds, and in spite of averaging a triple double, he barely scratched the surface of what he was capable of doing. We won 15 games during the `98-`99 season, with the biggest win coming against our cross-town rival Brandon High School. We had beaten Brandon on a pretty regular basis the last five years. The head coach retired and the assistant coach moved up as the head coach. He and a team dad who had twins on the team created an AAU team. The AAU team recruited players, and then funneled them into the basketball program at Brandon. There were several high school coaches in the area, including me, who knew they were recruiting. I confronted the head coach about asking one of his players to go to one of my player's house and talk to him about transfer-ring. The Brandon player told my player, who was only a freshman at the time, that Bloomingdale was not a "basketball school" and was never going to go anywhere in basketball. Of course, the coach at Brandon denied that he knew anything about it. I put their coach on notice that I knew what he was doing. They had three Division I players on their team. The twins (both 6'5") ended up going on to play at Oklahoma State University. We still managed to beat them in their gym that year. That was the only loss that they had to a county school in three years. We had a good year, but I thought if I would have had a floor leader we could have won several more games. Nick and Eric made the All-Conference team, and Don Hines had a remarkable season. He had improved so much in three years that he was offered a scholarship to Polk County Junior College, all of Coach Sleyzak's extra time and effort with him had paid off.

During this time, the Brandon and Bloomingdale area were growing so fast that the county could not build schools fast enough to keep up with the student population. Bloomingdale was an excellent academic school, so natu-rally, parents moving into this area wanted to be in the Bloomingdale school district. The school and facilities had been built to accommodate 2400 students, but our enroll-ment had grown to over 3000. The county made the deci-sion to put Bloomingdale on a "split schedule," which meant that grades 10-12 went to school in the morning and the over 800 freshman came to school in the afternoon. Because I was the basketball coach, I taught classes in the morning, from 6:50 until 12:00. I was up very early in the morning, but it also meant that on the weeks that we had first practice, our practice was over by 3:15 and I was home by 4 o'clock. The weeks that the girls' team had the gym first meant for a very long day. Our practices during those weeks would start at 3:30 and go to 6 o'clock. I would not get home until seven or later, a twelve hour day. I actually liked practicing after the girls because there were fewer distractions and we could go over our 2 hour allotted practice time, but it did make for long days.

I continued to build up the summer basketball camps, and raise money for the basketball program during the summer. We were getting 30-35 kids a week to come to our basketball camp. The job of getting money for the program got a lot easier after I met Bill. I had raised enough money to buy an electronic score table, which allowed us to rotate as many as six businesses on the front of the table. Each one of the businesses gave us 500 dollars a year to have their ads on the front of the table. The table cost over $5000. There wasn't another school in the county that had anything like it. I also put up record boards and advertisement boards put on the walls in the gym. We had a first class program and our players recognized that of the 20 schools in the county there was no one that had a better basketball program than Bloomingdale.

Andrew, our son, and me at one of my summer basketball camps.

The 1999-2000 season was Nick's last, and I was very optimistic. I should have tempered my expectations based on what had happened the year before. Nick was neither a leader nor a "hard nosed" competitor. He just never got out of "cruise control," or showed a sense of urgency. He had all of the tools in the world, but he never just took over a game. However, he was still one of the biggest recruits, figuratively and literally, in the state of Florida. We were invited to play in the best Christmas tournaments in the state because of the interest in Nick. Ocala had been hosting their tournament for over 50 years and some of the best teams from around state and country came to play in the tournament. Every game of the 16 team tournament was attended by 10 to 30 college coaches. We were not good enough to compete in the tournament, but I accepted the invitation strictly for Nick. We were matched up in the first game against a team from Fresno, California who had a 6' 6" player by the name of DeShawn Stevenson. Stevenson was one of the best high school players in the state of California and was being recruited by everyone. He ended up skipping college and going straight into the NBA. About a week before Christmas break, Nick's mother, not Nick, told me they were going to Illinois for Christmas. They would be driving to Illinois and not be back until December 26, the day we were to play our first game in the tournament. I couldn't believe what I was hearing; I was so upset. Our game was scheduled for 5 o'clock on the 26th, so I had planned to have a morning "shoot around" to get rid of some of the "Christmas hangover" and then drive the two hours to Ocala. Nick, obviously, would not be at the shoot around. The Smith's "thought" if they left Champaign, Illinois really early that morning they could be in Ocala for the game. The drive from his grandparents was about 13 hours, so I knew what kind of playing condition Nick was going to be in after riding in a car all day. There was really nothing I could do about it. If I had known earlier,

I would have gotten us out of the tournament, or I would have never accepted the invitation to play in the first place. I understood that family is very important and spending Christmas with family is very important. I asked if there was any way that they could leave Illinois late on Christmas day and drive back, at least halfway. Nick's mom told me that she didn't think that would be possible. They arrived in Ocala at the gym about an hour before the game started. We got destroyed, and Nick was terrible. Stevenson scored 30 points in the first half and we were down by over 20, it was embarrassing. Nick had sent a terrible message to the rest of the team about his priorities.

We had another so-so season, we beat the teams we should have and lost to the teams that were better than us. In one of those games against East Bay, a team that we were 20 points better than, we were ahead by only four points at halftime in our gym. I was not happy and lit into the team pretty hard during halftime. I was especially upset with Nick, who had seven or eight points and about that many rebounds. East Bay's tallest player was 6' 3", so Nick should have been dominating the game. After all of the halftime yelling, and on the way back to the gym from the locker room, I told Nick he should be embarrassed. Without any hesitation or an ounce of emotion, he said "we were winning and we could beat this team without him." He just never got it. We won 15 games again for the second straight year. Nick made All-Conference for the second time. He made All-State and was chosen the

Gatorade Player of the Year in the state of Florida. He was aggressively recruited by the University of South Florida, Florida State University, and the University of Illinois. Lon Kruger, who had left UF in 1996 to take the basketball job at Illinois, had been recruiting Nick for two years. Nick's grandparents lived in Champaign, and Nick's mother had attended the University of Illinois so there was a connection there. Ironically, Coach Kruger, left Illinois at the end of Nick's freshman season to take the job as the coach of the Atlanta Hawks in the NBA. That began a series of changes of coaches at the University of Illinois that affected Nick's basketball career in a very negative way. After Kruger, the University of Illinois hired Bill Self from University of Tulsa, but he would leave after three years to become the coach at Kansas University. Nick's senior season, he had to adjust to his third coach, Bruce Weber, who had been the coach at Southern Illinois University. I truly believe that had Coach Kruger, who originally recruited Nick or Coach Self, who also liked Nick, had he stayed at UI, Nick would have had a much better career. Coach Self called me after he got the Illinois job and asked me what I thought about Nick and his ability to play in the Big Ten Conference. Coach Self was trying to decide if he wanted to extend Nick's scholarship. Basically, I told him he had the natural ability, he was a smart kid and that I thought he could be a solid role player for him. He told me he wanted to come to Brandon and talk to Nick and his parents. Coach Self met us at the gym and asked me to put him through a series of drills, so he could watch him work out. Nick impressed Coach Self with his foot-work and his hands. I told Coach Self there was never any doubt about Nick's athletic ability; the only question was his desire. Nick's last year, 2005, Illinois went to the Final Four and finished the season 37-2, winning the Big Ten with a record of 15-1. Nick contributed to that team as a backup center, averaging about five minutes a game. Illinois beat Louisville in the semi finals. Nick scored five points and got two rebounds. Against North Carolina in the championship game, even though the Illinois center got into foul trouble early, Weber chose not to play Nick. Sean May, North Carolina's 6' 9" center, dominated Illinois inside but Nick never got in the game. I never understood Weber's coaching logic in that game; Nick could have given the Illini some inside presence and contributed. Nick graduated from the University of Illinois in four years with a Masters Degree. He was one of the best players to ever play at Bloomingdale High School, but I will always wonder what he could have done if he would have been a fierce competitor.

The 2000-01 season was my first in three years without Nick Smith. We were returning three starters from the team that won 15 games, and even without Nick, I thought we would be competitive. They were really good kids, hard-working and very coachable. For the first time in my six years of coaching at Bloomingdale, we did not have a player over 6' 3". We did have five players that were 6' 3" and for the first time in two years, we had a true point guard, we actually had two. Both guards came from military families and both were very competitive, smart, and very good. Jose Olivero had played as a sophomore on a good JV team and had demonstrated his leadership qualities. José only played for us one year, his junior year, before moving to Virginia. As a senior he helped lead his high school team in Virginia to the state tournament. José got a scholarship to Lehigh University and become an outstanding college player for them. Jean LaBraun was the other guard, who at 6' 3" was a really good two-guard. Jean started for two years and made All-Conference and all-state as a senior. With our entire front line of Kirchman, LaFountain, Brad Doss, and Daniel Pope returning, plus a transfer named Matt Mazur, we were not as big as in the past, but we did have a lot of depth.

After the struggles of the previous season, the 2000-01 season was a lot more enjoyable to coach. We didn't have all the drama that we had gone through the year before. One of the reasons for the success was the help and support that I received from several of the dads. Mr. Pope, whose older son Jeremy, had played for us in `93-`94 helped me in several different ways. Mr. Doss and his wife were great supporters and were always having the team over before or after games to eat. Mr. LaFountain was always willing to help us with whatever we needed done. We finished third in the conference and ended up 17-9. This was my eighth season at Bloomingdale, and I thought it was a good time to call it quits. We had a very good run and had established the Bulls basketball program as one of the best in Hillsborough County. Some of our teams over those eight years had been ranked in the state. Ten of our players had received college scholarships. The interest around the community and in the school had increased tremendously. Most importantly, for me, I had had an opportunity to coach my son Andrew. I submitted my letter of resignation to Mrs. Stelter at the end of the school year. She was surprised and asked me to reconsider, and to not make my decision public. She wanted me to "think over" my decision during the summer. At the time, I had no intention of coming back to Bloomingdale the next year as the basketball coach. Tim continued to run the summer program, but I was less involved than I had ever been. My heart wasn't into it and my body was tired. I didn't think I had the energy or excitement to continue. I received a call from Mrs. Stelter in July asking me if I had reconsidered and would I return for just one more year. I told her I would stay on as the coach for one more year. I should have followed my gut and quit.

The 2001-02 season, presented some unique struggles both on and off the court. With Jean the only returning starter and José leaving for Virginia, I knew we were going to struggle. I had some really good hard-working kids but not much athleticism. We were going to really miss Jose; he was such a solid leader. One of our low points came in a January game on the road. We were playing terrible and down at halftime to a team that we should have beaten. I was so disappointed and disgusted with our effort during the first half that during halftime

I said "we were playing like a f.... bunch of losers". I did not allow the players to use profanity and for the most part, in all my over 20 years of coaching, using profanity was not an issue. Well, at this particular game with a lot of built up frustration, it just came out. I apologized after the game to the players for the language but not for saying they were playing like losers. Every year that I coached, I tried to develop a bond with the players of trust and respect. That bond went between players, as well as to our staff. I thought it was always important for the players and staff to be able to feel free and uninhibited to say things in the locker room and know that it was going to stay in the locker room. No one, other than the team, knows all of the details and the ups and downs that transpire during the course of the season. The next day I got a call from the assistant principal, who wanted to talk to me about a phone call he received from a parent of one of my players. One of the ironic things about this whole situation was that Mr. Davis, the athletic director, did not call me in but the assistant principle for curriculum wanted an explanation. In nine years at Bloomingdale I had never had any conversations with him about basketball. A mom of one of the players on the team thought I should be replaced immediately. She said her son was offended by my language and for me calling him a "loser." Because we went to the same church, she had even called one of the pastors on the staff, a friend of mine, about the profanity. I don't know if I was more disgusted at her for calling the pastor, or at the pastor for calling me to discuss the matter. The pastor later apologized to me and told me he had no business getting into the situation; I agreed. I spent countless hours and a lot of energy before the situation was resolved. First, I didn't say they were losers. I said they were "playing like losers." Secondly, her son only played about two minutes in the first half. He was athletic, but he had a hard time remembering what he was supposed to do on the court. He really never got to play very much. This wasn't the first time I would have liked to mince my words, but it would be the last as a coach. Anyway, it was decided that I could finish the year as the coach. I was truly regretting that I had reversed my decision to get out of coaching. We struggled to win half of our games. There wasn't much joy in coaching for me. I was glad when the season was over.

My gratitude for being involved in the basketball program at Bloomingdale for nine years, four as a non-paid volunteer, was that I was informed less than a month after the season was over that my name was going into the county teacher pool for future assignment. That meant, that I no longer had a job at Bloomingdale teaching and that I would have to go to some other school for a job. I didn't even have a guarantee that I would be teaching health. I might not get a choice of where I was going; it could be a high school on the other side of the county or downtown. I could be teaching a totally different subject, depending on what the school needed. That told me what little appreciation the school administration had for my work over the past nine years. In Hillsborough County, it didn't matter how good a teacher you were if you taught PE, health, or driver's education, you are totally expendable because those positions were "saved" for coaches. The man who replaced me taught health, so I had to go.

There were over 20 applicants for the head basketball coaching job at Bloomingdale, which was a reflection on the job that we had done. We had won over 140 games, a district championship, a conference championship, and finished runner-up in the district twice in the nine years. We had competed in some of the best invitational tournaments in the state of Florida. I had worked tirelessly to make the Bloomingdale program a first class program. I wanted the players to feel special and to have pride in being a part of our program. Besides the success on the court, we had helped over 130 young men develop many different skills that would help them be successful in life. To me, the big picture was always to help take each one of the players further than they thought they were capable of going. I wanted my players to strive for that elusive goal of perfection, just as I tried to do. After 24 years of coaching, I was truly ready to hang up my whistle. I had so many great experiences and made so many great memories coaching basketball at ORU, ISU, Salem, BCCC, and Bloomingdale. Yes, and even way back in the day at Liberty Elementary School, teaching the fifth graders. I wouldn't trade any of it for anything in the world. I truly believe I made a difference in the lives of many young men. At least, I hope I did, because I certainly tried. I have been asked many times since I retired, if I miss coaching. My honest answer is no.

There are times when I miss the camaraderie and the building of relationships with the players. I miss working with the players and seeing them use what I taught them and to foster their success. I miss the excitement and competition of the game. But then I watch coaches yelling, sweating and getting upset, and I don't miss it so much. I always hated losing more than I enjoyed winning. I wish I was not made up that way.

CHAPTER 12

The Last Rodeo: Durant High School (2002-08)

Three weeks after school was out, there was still nothing of interested available through the county teacher pool. It looked like I could be teaching history at Gaither High School. Gaither was across the county, a 45 minute drive each way. I was not excited about the prospects, but I just kept telling myself that I only had another five years to go before retirement. I was checking in with the county placement office every week. During one of those weekly calls to the placement office I was asked if I would be interested in a health teaching position at Durant High School. Durant was a school that had been open about seven years and was located about 15 minutes from our home. Ashlee, our youngest, had gone there her freshman year. It was an outstanding school that had a reputation for having good teachers, solid academics, and was student-friendly. I immediately told them I wanted the job and would like to go interview with the principal, Joe Perez. I made arrangements to go to Durant the next day for my interview with Mr. Perez. The interview went well, and Mr. Perez offered me a job teaching Health. Mr. Perez had a reputation as an outstanding leader and a "hands on" principal. We got along great, and I enjoyed working for him for the three months that he was at the school. He was such a respected leader that he was offered a supervisory position downtown a couple months after school started. The new principal, Mrs. Bowden, had only been an assistant at Durant a couple years. Her family was from the Plant City area so she was very well connected in the community. I worked for her all seven years that I taught at Durant. I saw Joe at the fitness center a few months after he left, and whined to him about how he hired me, and then left me on my own. I will always be thankful to him for hiring me and allowing me to finish my teaching career in such a great environment.

Durant had great students with very few problems, and a very dedicated teaching staff. My co-teacher those first two years was a lady that was an outstanding teacher, who was working on completing all the requirements to become an administrator. Christie Rayburn was smart, and liked me, but most important of all, she was great on the computer. During my first year at Durant the school district was in the process of changing everything from paper to the computer. She set up everything for us to be able to record our grades, take attendance, record tardys, and put out emails to the parents of our students. Another lady who helped me with the transition to Durant was Peggy Peacock. Peggy and her husband Rick had been in my Bible study class for several years. Peggy was a secretary in the office and had been at the school since it opened. One of my good friends was the basketball coach, Jeff Shotwell. Jeff and I talked basketball on a regular basis. Just like Doug when I was at Armwood, Jeff asked me every year to help him coach, and just like with Doug, my answer was the same, no. There was no way I was getting back into the coaching business.

I enjoyed my time at Durant and could not have picked a better place to end my teaching career. I had my own class-room and a big office right off the classroom. Mrs. Bowden let us run our Health program, and made it easy for us to do our job. The highlight of my time at Durant was meeting my fu-ture son-in-law, Bryce Predmore. Bryce was an English teacher and the cross country coach at Durant. Bryce, an ex-Marine, was a big guy that had an independent disposition. He was a smart, no-nonsense teacher. Before he married Ash-lee and even after their marriage, I would refer to him as "Bradley" just to keep him honest and humble. He even claims to this day that I introduced him to a neighbor as Bradley; I didn't. There was one humorous experience that I had with Bryce at Durant. Soon after I met him I was assigned to help him administer the Florida Achievement standardized test that was given to all Florida students at the end of the year. The wrestling coach, Dennis Kitko, who was also a friend of mine, was also assigned to help Bryce. The first day we showed up in Bryce's classroom to help him, he practically ignored us. We broke for lunch and Dennis never came back. Later in the day I asked him what happened and where did he go? He said "Bryce is an ass and doesn't want any help. He acted like we are in his way, so I ain't coming back." Actually, there were about 24 students in his class and he really didn't need any help; however, we were getting paid and needed to be somewhere, doing something. If the principal wanted me to "hang out" in Bryce's classroom, that's what I was going to do. I thought it was funny and I wasn't offended at all. I was getting paid $32 an hour to hand out pencils that day.

Bryce grew up without a father being around so he had always kind of been on his own. He has done remarkably well and was very driven to be successful. Bryce became a member of our family three years later in 2009. I still like to remind my daughter that I knew her husband before she did. They have been married 11 years now and have a beautiful, redhead girl, named Shelby, who is eight years old. They also have the baby of the whole Sutter family, Benjamin, who is five years old. We are all anxious to see how big Ben gets, with a 6' 5" father and a 5' 9" mother, he has a chance to be a 6' 6" shooting guard; just saying! Bryce resigned in 2009 from teaching and took a job with Tampa Electric Company. He has worked his way up within TECO and is now a safety professional.

Ashlee, who is an outstanding teacher (like her mother), is the "torchbearer" for our family within public education. Although, teaching wasn't her initial plan out of college. Amy is also an exceptional piano teacher and does work on-line editing and advising college students on grammar and punctuation mistakes. Education is in the Sutter DNA.

I retired from teaching after 31 years, and I can honestly say that I enjoyed practically every one of those years. I originally got into teaching because I wanted to be a basketball coach. I had always enjoyed being around kids and seemed to be able to develop a good rapport with them. I always said that dogs and kids liked me! I discovered that just like teaching your own kids, if you are consistent, communicate and come across as a truly caring person, the rest comes easy. I consider it a privilege and honor to have been able to have some impact upon thousands of young people's lives.

My six years at Durant had also given me some insight into what life would be like during retirement. I was getting home from school every day by 3:15, so it seemed like I had half a day left to enjoy and do what I pleased. I wasn't used to getting home so early. When I was coaching, it was more like six or seven in the evening. I loved all of the free time and soon developed a routine of coming home and going back out for a run or a bicycle ride. I also started playing golf. I always stayed busy, and rarely was I bored.

Once I retired, at the top of my "to do" list was to become a "scratch" golfer. I had only been playing golf a few years, but I liked competing against myself. I was athletic, so in my mind, it would just be a matter of a few months, and I would have my golf score down in the low 80s. I began to work toward that goal. I was at the golf course across the street from where we lived about five days a week. I joined the country club and started hitting golf balls and playing. I took lessons from three or four different pros, and took the game very seriously, too seriously. I did improve from rounds in the high 90s to consistently shooting in the mid to upper 80s. I was practicing and playing a lot, and getting more and more frustrated because it seemed like I could never get those last few strokes off the scorecard. The game made no sense. In basketball, if you shoot 100 free throws every day for weeks you're going to get where you can make 90 or more out of 100. It just didn't seem to work that way in golf. No matter how much I practiced, I would still go out and shoot 40 on the front nine and 47 on the back or vice versa. I played basketball and baseball, but this was by far the hardest, most unpredictable game I had ever played. I spent a lot of hours and several dollars chasing a goal that I decided wasn't worth it. One day I was out playing golf with our son, Drew, and had a couple bad holes and was getting upset and frustrated. Drew said to me "dad, maybe golf is not your game." He was right. I do not have the right temperament for golf. I need more of a physical, competitive activity. I have played hundreds of rounds of golf, but there is one hole that stands out in my memory. The first round of golf I played after I retired was on a Saturday morning with my favorite foursome. I was playing with Drew, Darrin, and Bill, my good friend, at TPC golf course in Tampa. It is a very difficult course where they have played several professional tournaments. On the very first hole, a par four, I hit my second shot about 10 feet from the hole and made the putt for birdie. That's the way to start a retirement!

I don't know what I shot for the round, but I do remember that first hole. On the rare occasions now days when I do play, I have learned to just enjoy being outdoors, and the company and not take it too seriously.

Retirement is great and it seemed to grow on me. Maybe, at first, I felt a little guilty about not having a job to go to, but I realized I had worked all my life. I had gotten up at 6 o'clock in the morning, and worked five days a week for 30+ years. I started working at an early age and that work ethic has served me well. I often thought of my mom and how she worked all her life, and then passed away six months after she retired. I was never concerned about being bored or not having enough to keep me busy. Even on the days that I do not have anything "scheduled" I always find something to do to occupy the day. I think it is important to stay busy, and I enjoy having things to do. I have always been tasked oriented, a list maker. Unlike my friend, Tom Whittington, who retired six years before me and quit wearing a watch, I still maintain some uniformity in my life. I do want to know what time of the day it is.

One of the ways that I stay busy is with my memorabilia and sports cards "hobby" that became a business when I retired. I had collected sports cards when I was a kid, but it wasn't until Andrew was in his early teens that I got back interested in collecting. In 1985, when we moved to Florida, we started going to Spring Training games and other sporting events getting autographs. Drew and I had some of our best, most memorable father-son experiences collecting autographs of sports figures.

A couple of those experiences stick out in my mind, like getting up at 3 in the morning to get down to Sarasota to get Michael Jordan's autograph when he came into baseball camp for early batting practice. He would come in before 6 o'clock, so if you wanted an autograph you had to be in line by 4 o'clock. We had to go two mornings before we got him to stop and sign a basketball for each of us. Drew was relentless in his pursuit of autographs, like chasing Frank Robinson down the street only to be told he was not signing. Drew even offered to give him 20 dollars; he didn't think that was funny. He waited for over four hours to get Magic Johnson to sign a basketball only to be told "I don't have time." He did get to spend the day with George Brett and sit in the dugout during the game with him. He also just about got into a fight with a selfish, jerk because he would not step back after he had gotten Garth Brook's autograph. It's common courtesy and proper protocol to get one autograph and then get out of the way and let others have a chance. This day at the New York Mets Spring Training game this "knucklehead" had gotten Garth to sign a couple things but he wanted more. Drew asked him to move back and make room for others. He took offense to Drew's request and acted like he was going to physically attack Drew. I stepped in and told him he was being inconsiderate and he should get out of the way so other fans could also get an autograph. He did leave but Garth quit signing and Drew lost out on his autograph.

Since my retirement, I have taken it to a whole new level of selling and buying sports memorabilia. I do not go to the baseball Spring Training games like I once did, but now I spend a lot of time collecting NHL hockey team autographs. I have gotten hundreds of pucks signed by the Tampa Bay Lightning and other teams that come to Tampa to play. I usually go to a team's morning skate on the day they play the Lightning to try to get the players to sign pucks. I give some of the signed pucks to my two grandsons, some I keep, and some go on eBay to help defer my expenses and give me a couple extra bucks. I have a very nice sports memorabilia collection that I enjoy. Every piece that I have brings some nostalgia to mind, whether it is my childhood or my great times with my son. I do enjoy getting the autographs; it's like a form of competition. I will also enjoy giving all of it to my son, my two sons-in-law and two grandsons. I know they will appreciate and enjoy it.

Diane and I have been so blessed to be able to do a lot of traveling in our retirement days. Our whole family was able to go on one of our trips to Barcelona and Rome in 2001. Darrin and Amy had only been married a couple years, when we put together a 12 day cruise. That was our second trip to Rome, a city I love. Diane and I have made most of our trips with our good friends, Tom and Karen Ruggiero. Our travels have included: Alaska, Hawaii, a Balkan cruise which included Russia, a British Isles cruise that included Paris, back to Rome for a third time, and several places around the United States. We enjoy traveling together and enjoying God's creation. We have made hundreds of memories together. One memory that I get teased about happened during our Alaskan cruise when I mistook another lady on the ship for Diane. We were coming back aboard the ship from an excursion when I saw this lady, who obviously looked like Diane from the back. She was looking at pictures posted on the wall. I thought Diane had gone ahead of me and without thinking or paying any attention I walked up to this lady and gave her a "love pat" on the derriere. I don't know who was surprised more when she turned around and I realized it was not Diane. Diane, me, and the Ruggiero's were all apologizing and trying to convince the lady that it was a mistake. She was a good sport about it, and I didn't get slapped or thrown off the cruise. I liked to tell everyone that I saw that same lady several more times on the ship after that incident, and that she smiled at me every time. Diane has documented our travel memories with albums filled with pictures and memorabilia from all around the world.

On our trip to the British Isles I began having back problems. I had experienced some pain in my hip and lower back for several months and had tried all kinds of anti inflammatory, stretching exercises, and even a few visits to the chiropractor. Finally, my doctor recommended I go see a neurologist. He spotted the problem immediately. The MRI revealed a cyst on my spine that was causing pain on the nerve in my lower back. Dr. Le scheduled surgery for me right away. The surgery took less than an hour, and immediately my back was totally pain-free. I did give up running outside to avoid the pounding on my back from running on hard surfaces. Diane finally convinced me to join her in the air-conditioned fitness center where I now run my two miles on the much more comfortable elliptical.

In 2003, Andrew graduated from UF school of nursing. One of the students in his classes was a sweet, smart and personable young lady who was studying to be a physician assistant (PA). Colleen Kulik, her three sisters, and her mom and dad, have lived in Jacksonville almost her entire life. Her dad, David, was a CEO of a logistics company, whose headquarters was in Amsterdam. Her family is a very respected and recognized family in Jacksonville. Colleen was a Christian with great ethics, high morals, and a love for kids. I also knew that since Colleen's entire family lived in Jacksonville, there was a real good chance that that's where they would also live. It wasn't Brandon or Tampa, but it wasn't like Drew was marrying a girl from Montana. They wanted to have a big family, and Diane and I would get to enjoy our grand-kids. Drew, who used to go by "Andy" until he went away to college, had found a great life partner. There is an interesting story behind the name change. One day, when he was in the second grade, on the way home from school, he informed his mother that he wanted to be called "Andy." So we called him Andy. Strangely, Diane always wanted to call him Drew when he was growing up. But it wasn't until after he got to college he decided he was Drew. We always can tell when people in Drew's life remember him from by whether they call him Andy or Drew. He finished getting a degree in nursing and began working with orthopedic doctors in the OR at a Jacksonville hospital. He decided he wanted to get into the business side of running a hospital, so he enrolled in Northern Florida University to pursue an MBA Degree. Then he decided (even before finishing his MBA) that he was also going to get a law degree. He and Colleen were just married, they were both making good money and she was glad he was so ambitious. He was accepted to Florida Coastal School of Law and began working toward a law degree while still working at the hospital. His good grades and involvement in extracurricular activities at the school caught the attention of the staff who offered him a scholarship his final year in school. After graduation he was hired by the law firm of Holland and Knight. He began working with an attorney who did a lot of work with CSX Railroad Company. CSX was impressed with Drew's work so much that they offered him a job. He has been with the railroad company since 2011. Colleen was happy that he found his niche and finally finished going to school.

Drew and Colleen had a big beautiful wedding at a historic, large Catholic Church in downtown Jacksonville. Drew asked me to be the Best Man and I was very honored. I still have the handkerchief that says I was the Best Man, and I was so proud to be by his side that special day. While working on his law degree, they had their first child, Bridget. "B" is now 15 years old and a freshman in high school. She is very smart,

very competitive (now where did that come from) and independent. Seventeen years later, Drew and Coll, are happily
married with three more kids. Their second, Jack, my name-
sake, is a smart, athletic, 12-year-old. Caroline, who is sometimes called "Ruby," is a beautiful eight-year-old. Ruby was
my mom's name (Ruby Leilah) so when Colleen and the rest
of the family started calling her "Ruby," I loved it. Cecelia, or
"CC" is like her mother, a people person. CC is seven and is
referred to by the family as the "little mayor"; her mom is the
"real mayor" at the kids' school.

One final thought about the attorney gig. When our kids
were growing up we thought we'd have a lawyer in the family, just that it would be Amy. She was smart and very good
at presenting "her side" of the story. Diane would get so ex-
asperated with her some times that she would just resort to
the mom reply, "because I said so!" Diane would always tell
her that she should be a lawyer!

CHAPTER 13

Family and Retirement (2008-present)

When I retired in 2008, I made up my mind that I was not going to make any commitments with my time. I had been on a schedule and a regiment my entire life and now I wanted to be free to decide what and when I would do things. I volunteered for different ministries at the church, but only those that I could do when I wanted to, like the Busy Bee ministry (now called Hearts and Hammers). This ministry is designed for older or widow women who need a specific job done around their house that they are unable to do, like cleaning out their gutters or pressure washing their driveway. I had the freedom to go to their house, whenever I wanted to do the job. I am still involved with this ministry and get a great deal of satisfaction out of being able to help these women in need. I also got involved with the Meals on Wheels ministry, which takes food to those who are unable to get out or provide for themselves.

Diane continued to teach until 2010 when she was diagnosed with breast cancer. Our family had been so blessed that this was the first major illness of any one in our family. Fortunately, the cancer was caught before it had a chance to spread into the lymph system and other parts of her body. She had to have surgery and go through several months of chemotherapy and radiation treatment. She dealt with the situation exceptionally well, and even after being out of her classroom for a year, she decided to go back. The school system was undergoing some major changes with what was called Common Core curriculum. It was supposed to be a better, more standardized approach to education. It was supposed to bring all students up to a higher standard, but in fact it took away a lot of the teacher's creativity and individualism. The teachers were spending more time testing their students then teaching them. Core curriculum set education back several years and drove some excellent teachers out of the profession, including my wife. So even though Diane was only out of the classroom one year, so much changed that she felt lost when she returned. By October of 2011, she was so frustrated that she decided this would be her last year. After battling cancer and losing some of her stamina, we discussed whether she should finish the school year if it got to be too hard on her. There wasn't a rule that required a teacher to finish the school year. She was so relieved that she did not have to deal with all that was going on at school, and she could retire at the end of the first semester. Diane knew more about teaching and children than all those bureaucrats in Washington and Tallahassee put together. The county lost an excellent teacher, but she certainly put in her time making a difference along the way. I was glad that she would now be enjoying retirement with me.

In December 2012, I received some bad news about my friend Ken Trickey. Ken passed away after a short battle with dementia and cancer. I had spoken with him a few times in the last year and could tell that he was slipping: mentally and physically. We had not seen each other since the Final Four basketball tournament in St. Louis in 2004, Nick's senior year at Illinois. Ken had been my college coach at MTSU, my boss at ORU, and my friend for over 20 years. We had been through a lot together and had done a lot together. Four of the best years of my life had been spent at Oral Roberts University and with him. He was like a big brother to me. I still think of him and miss him.

An even greater loss to me happened four years later in July, 2016. My older sister, Judy, passed away at the age of 74. She always thought of herself as being my big sister even at the end when we were both in our 70s. Judy had a tough life; she was very young when she had a little girl, Lisa, out of wedlock. She also married a guy who was an alcoholic and abusive. She tried to make things work for her daughter's sake, but after 15 or 16 years, she got a divorce. After being a single mom for several years, she moved to a small town in northern Arizona named Springerville. She met and later married a man, Leon Baldonado, who treated her like a lady and made her feel significant. Judy opened her own beauty salon in Springerville and became very active in the community. She always loved kids and sports, so she became the president of the high school athletic booster club. She headed up the high school's major fundraiser each year by having a special weekend carnival. She was so "vocal" at the high school basketball games that one of the referees at a game one night presented her with her own stripped referee shirt to wear when she was sitting in the bleachers. She had been in failing health for several years, but she still was involved with the sports teams at the high school. Judy liked to give to others. Her charity and her legacy will live on in Springerville. She became a "big sis" to a lot of kids in that community.

My younger sister, Cherri, still lives in a small community near Oak Ridge, Tennessee. We both miss Judy very much. We talk and text often about the "good ole days" in Galatia. She has a son and a daughter and eight grand kids. She is now enjoying her much deserved retirement as well.

I have always thought that next to a person's faith, the most important thing in this world is your family. I grew up in a great family and was surrounded with people that I knew loved me and encouraged me to "shoot for the stars." Diane and I have been so blessed with three great kids and eight grand kids. You have heard it said that "if I would've known grand kids were so much fun, I would've had them first," that could apply to us. We do love spoiling our grand kids. Our family is not perfect but it is very close to it, and my favorite to be around. I look forward to seeing what our grand kids do with their lives. I know each one will be successful, and I hope and pray that they will each one grow up to love Jesus above all things. I look forward to being a part of their lives for years to come. Diane has not only been my "soul" mate but she has been my "sole" mate; she was and is the one and only. She has always been my number #1 fan. She is smart and independent, a perfect fit. I knew that back in 1971 on that first date when she went out with me and (unexpectedly) a basketball recruit to eat after an ORU basketball game. We made a perfect team, and since I have spent a very large part of my life putting teams together, I know a thing or two about teams. I think a person's legacy is in the hearts and minds of the people who knew them. I have thought for over a year now, since I started writing this memoir, how I would end it. (I actually wrote about the ORU basketball years over 10 years ago.) This might surprise those of you who read this, but I think you will understand. After all, you probably wouldn't be reading this if you didn't know me!

Paul Anka, wrote a song for Frank Sinatra called "My Way." A lot of people might not know that Anka got the idea for the song from an original French song 'Comme d'habitude'. Anka actually changed the words to fit what he thought that Sinatra would use. Anka might not use the words "me," "my," and "ate it up and spit it out" but Sinatra with his tough guy image and Rat Pack crew of guys would. It was no secret that Sinatra really did like the "mob guys" and the way they presented themselves. Ironically, even though this became Sinatra's signature song, his daughter, Tina, says her dad grew to hate the song.

He even hated to sing it, but every audience would request it. He always thought the song was self-serving and self-indulgent. So where am I going with all of this? I'm finishing my story! When I face the final curtain, I know what's on the other side because that was settled when Jesus was crucified. It's Jesus and heaven for me! I did live a life that was full; I traveled many a highway, and I enjoyed the ride as well as the destination. I know sometimes I did it "my way" whether it was right or wrong. But I always tried to get back to God's way, where you can never go wrong.

Regrets, I've had a few, but I wouldn't change any of them because each regret and failure made me stronger, and drew me closer to God's plan and purpose for my life. My biggest regret would be that I know I will not see all of my friends and loved ones in heaven. I planned my way, but God ordered my steps. Yes, I made mistakes for which I am sorry and have found forgiveness from a God who loves unconditionally. He does give a lot of "do overs." I faced a few "giants" along the way, and not by "my power or by my might" I was able to overcome. For what is a man, what has he got? This is the most important question in everyone's life. The answer is simple: what a man takes or sends to heaven when this life ends, that is truly all that endures. There are only two things worse than dying; to never have truly lived and to die without Jesus. I believe that everything good and positive in a person's life is from God. I truly believe He gave me a gift to seek perfection in my life, and to try and help others seek the best that is possible for them. My mom had a profound influence on my life. She really wanted to be a teacher and was not able to because of her family situation. I was honored to carry the torch for her.

Maybe there will be an addendum to this story, I am "only" 75 years old as I write this, but we are not promised tomorrow. In the meantime, *Welcome To My World.*

Our three children (from left to right): Amy, Andrew, and Ashlee

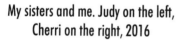
My sisters and me. Judy on the left, Cherri on the right, 2016

The family left to right Front: Shelby, Jack, Diane, Me, Cecilia, Caroline, Bridget Back Row: left to right Benjamin held by Ashlee, Bryce, Colleen, Andrew, Amy, Darrin, Anna, Abigail.

CPSIA information can be obtained
at www.ICGtesting.com
Printed in the USA
LVHW050154250621
691124LV00001B/50

9 780578 237336